BEST
MOM EVER!

Chicken Soup for the Soul: Best Mom Ever!
101 Stories of Gratitude, Love and Wisdom
Amy Newmark

Published by Chicken Soup for the Soul, LLC www.chickensoup.com
Copyright ©2017 by Chicken Soup for the Soul, LLC. All Rights Reserved.

Front cover photo courtesy of iStockphoto.com
Back cover photo courtesy of iStockphoto.com/bowdenimages (©bowdenimages)
Interior illustration courtesy of iStockphoto.com/exxorian (©exxorian)
Interior photo of Amy Newmark courtesy of Susan Morrow at SwickPix

Cover and Interior by Daniel Zaccari

Distributed to the booktrade by Simon & Schuster. SAN: 200-2442

Publisher's Cataloging-In-Publication Data
(Prepared by The Donohue Group, Inc.)

Names: Newmark, Amy, compiler.
Title: Chicken Soup for the Soul : best mom ever! : 101 stories of gratitude, love and wisdom / [compiled by] Amy Newmark.
Other Titles: Best mom ever! : 101 stories of gratitude, love and wisdom
Description: [Cos Cob, Connecticut] : Chicken Soup for the Soul, LLC [2017]
Identifiers: LCCN 2017931158 | ISBN 978-1-61159-954-1 (print) | ISBN 978-1-61159-265-8 (ebook)
Subjects: LCSH: Mothers--Literary collections. | Mothers--Anecdotes. | Mother and child--Literary collections. | Mother and child--Anecdotes. | LCGFT: Anecdotes.
Classification: LCC HQ759 .C453 2017 (print) | LCC HQ759 (ebook) | DDC 306.874/3--dc23

PRINTED IN THE UNITED STATES OF AMERICA
on acid∞free paper

25 24 23 22 21 20 19 18 17   01 02 03 04 05 06 07 08 09 10 11

BEST MOM EVER!

101 Stories of Gratitude, Love and Wisdom

Amy Newmark

Chicken Soup for the Soul, LLC
Cos Cob, CT

Changing lives one story at a time®
www.chickensoup.com

Table of Contents

3

~Wise Words~

4

~Always There for Me~

5

~The Strength of a Mother~

❻

~A Grandmother's Love~

❼

~My Role Model~

8

~By Heart, Not by Blood~

9

~Maternal Miracles~

10

~A Mother's Legacy~

Introduction

Moms. We love them whether we think they're perfect or not. Because we all know that the mom we have is *perfect* for us.

My mom was no exception. But here's the crazy/awful/weird thing. After working on this book for a year — coming up with the concept, collecting thousands of submissions, narrowing down the list to these 101 stories and making the chapters — on the very day that I was scheduled to start editing the book, December 28th, my mother was rushed to the hospital. She almost died and I burst into tears when I got home that night and found a thank-you note in the mail from her, telling us it had been the "best Christmas Eve ever." I think she somehow knew her days were numbered, because she and my father were the last to leave our house on Christmas Eve, unheard of for them. They had been the first to leave for the prior twenty years.

She was still alive as I sat by her hospital bed and edited the first couple of chapters over the next six days. And then she wasn't. We don't really know what happened, except that she had Type 2 diabetes and everything shut down at once. She may or may not have had cancer, too. She died right after the first diagnostic test — from the diabetes, not the possible cancer.

My mother's mother had lived well into her nineties, smoking cigarettes the whole way. So I had thought that my dynamic mother had lots of runway despite the fact that she thought the perfect diet was a couple of regular Cokes and a Snickers bar every day. In fact she demanded and received a Coke the last day she was alive, with only grudging consent from the doctors. I watched in amazement as her dangerously low blood oxygen level soared with that first sip of Coke. She smiled and whispered "Delicious" through her oxygen mask.

My mother only made it to eighty-five but she did it her way: traveling the globe right to the end; watching her beloved Mets and Red Sox; driving around with her ancient dog—who predeceased her by three days; and visiting her friends and relatives. She had already made her plans to go to Florida in March. She didn't feel the Mets could get off to a good start unless she attended spring training every year.

So I finished editing this collection while planning my mother's funeral, caring for my shocked eighty-seven-year-old father, and doing all the things that you do after your mother dies. I don't know if it was good or bad for me, but I do know that I loved these stories and laughed and cried my way through the editing process. Perhaps it accelerated my grieving and healing, or perhaps it was like rubbing salt in my wounds. But I'm a professional and this is what I do. I make my deadlines, or at least don't go more than a week past them!

So here it is. Our collection of 101 stories about everyone's "best mom ever," whether they're talking about their mothers, grandmothers, stepmothers, mothers-in-law, or anyone else who ever "mothered" them. We also hear from the spouses, talking about how much they admire their wives for the amazing job they do caring for their children.

What a wide variety of tales you are about to read! I'm sure you will love them as much as I did. Prepare to laugh out loud as you read our chapter about "Adventures with Mom," and you share Jan Bono's week stuck in a trailer home with her mother after a snowstorm and a collapsed carport block all their exits. You'll nod your head in recognition when you read about Sandra Plawski's mother in our "Wise Words" chapter. She told her children that wherever they were, when there was a full moon they should look at it and know that she was looking at it, too.

You'll think about how your mother comforted you, and you comforted your own children, when you read our chapter called "Always There for Me." I loved how Margie Williamson's mom waited for her every day after school with a pot of tea and a plate of cookies, so that she could support her daughter during her difficult freshman year. And I knew all our mothers would have done the same when I read Terri Rilea's story in our chapter called "Mom to the Rescue." Her mom ran to the mailbox during a terrible rainstorm, wrapped young Terri's *imaginary friend* in a towel, and ran back to the house with her.

I was so impressed by Pauline Koh-Banerjee's immigrant mother, who built a career in insurance sales after going through hard times with a mentally ill husband. She and many other heroes are honored in our chapter called "The Strength of a Mother." There's a great quote from Linda Wooten that says, "Being a mother is learning about strengths you didn't know you had, and dealing with fears you didn't know existed." That is so true. We have no idea how strong we are until we became those protective, fierce, dedicated warriors who watch out for our children.

Now, I'm not a grandmother yet, but I will be in a few months. So I loved reading about the strength of grandmothers as well, because they're the ones you turn to for all that unconditional love and acceptance when you need it. You'll read about those very understanding grandmothers in our chapter called "A Grandmother's Love" — grandmas who help their grandchildren through surprise pregnancies, family upheavals, difficult financial times, and other life changing events. You can always depend on a grandmother to come through for you. Here's my own mother at my kids' college graduation.

My mother was my role model in so many ways. Not only do I look like her, but I believe I inherited her intellectual curiosity, her love of travel to exotic places, and her can-do attitude. We just don't see the obstacles — it's like we're driving Humvees through life, getting where we want to go. So I loved editing our chapter called "My Role Model," in which we saw mothers overcoming challenges, quietly doing good deeds, and passing on all those wonderful life lessons by *accomplishing* things, not just talking about them. Prithwijit Das shares his own story about how he and his immigrant mom graduated with master's degrees in education on the same day from the same university, and what she overcame to get there.

Mothers routinely perform miracles. We learn that very early, and we see them making things happen throughout our lives. So I loved putting together our chapter called "Maternal Miracles," which starts off with a story by Tom Schwarz about how his mother always, and I mean *always*, knew when something bad was about to happen, and rescued her family from what would have been fatal accidents more than once.

And it's not just our mothers by blood who perform these miracles. In our chapter called "By Heart, Not by Blood" you'll meet the remarkable women who adopted or fostered the lucky children who were just plain *meant* to be theirs. A young man named Derek is one of them. He tells us that his mother revealed on his fourteenth birthday that she found him as a newborn in a shopping cart at CVS. And yet somehow he and his adoptive mom share remarkably consistent physical and medical characteristics, right down to having the same defective toe on the same foot.

I closed out the book with a chapter called "A Mother's Legacy" and that was the one that made me cry the most as I was editing. It kept reminding me of all the good things that my mother did and the lessons and characteristics that are her legacy to me. Every time I look in the mirror I see her, and I continue to obey her, even getting a haircut the day before the funeral. I could hear her saying, "Don't you think your hair is getting a little too long?" I was moved by Trudie Nash's story in this chapter. She was driving home after her mother's funeral, with no room in her car for a struggling young family she saw making their way through the pouring rain. Trudie grabbed her mother's umbrella from the pile of things she had taken from her house and handed it out the window to the young parents, who gratefully sheltered their two babies.

I guess that is symbolic of all our mothers — they are our shelters in whatever storms pass through our lives: our umbrellas, our cheerleaders, our chief advisers, and our role models for how to be the very best human beings that we can be.

~Amy Newmark
January 21, 2017

BEST MOM EVER!

Chapter 1

Mom to the Rescue

*She's always there for me when I need her; She's
my best friend; she's just my everything.
~Ashley Olsen*

Mom Goes to the Mountain

I may look quiet and reserved but if you mess with my
kids, I will show you seven different kinds of crazy.
~Author Unknown

My mother taught me a lot of things, not just the usual mother-daughter stuff like cooking and cleaning and how to dress. The major lesson I learned from her was this: When you have a problem, don't waste your time with middlemen. Go straight to the top, to the head honcho, to get the problem solved.

I watched my mother in action many times. One of my favorite incidents was when my brother. Ted was attending college in a little town in Vermont. The campus was lovely, situated on top of a steep mountain with spectacular views. There was a problem though. At the start of his sophomore year, Ted called home and told my parents, "They said I don't have a room on campus. They said they didn't get the deposit."

"Where are you staying?" my father asked.

"They have this house for visitors down at the foot of the mountain," Ted said. "It doesn't have any heat." Now, this was early fall and the weather is nice that time of year in Vermont. But winter comes pretty quickly to New England — cold, windy, and snowy. Ted didn't say what we all knew: It was also a long trek up that mountain to the campus. When winter came, he would have a hard time making it to class through all the snow.

My mother was angry. "They're crazy — I know I sent that room-deposit check," she said. "I'm going up there and straighten this out."

I thought that was a great idea. I knew Mom could handle the situation. She would get it resolved quickly. But what I didn't expect, and what I didn't think was a great idea, was that I was going with her. That past summer, Mom and I had taken a Greyhound bus trip from Kentucky to Nevada and back. We both had miles left on the bus ticket — enough for the round trip from New York to Vermont and back.

I tried to protest, saying I didn't want to miss school, but I soon found myself on a Greyhound bus with my mother, heading to Vermont. The father of one of Ted's college friends picked us up at the station and took us to the campus.

Mom marched right into the Student Life office, the canceled check in her hand and a determined glint in her eye. She spoke to the comptroller about the problem, reiterating that she and my father had indeed paid the room deposit. She wanted Ted back in the dorm. Now. The comptroller said the dorms were full and there was nothing he could do, ma'am, sorry.

My mother was short of stature, but when she was indignant, somehow she got taller. She stood up straight, looked the comptroller in the eye and said, "Where does the president of the college live?"

The comptroller probably thought Mom was bluffing. He had a little smirk on his face as he told us where the president lived. He didn't think my mother would go there. He didn't know my mother!

Mom beckoned to me. "Let's go." She was not bluffing. She was going to see the president of the college. In his house! She was not going to let her son freeze at the bottom of the mountain and trudge through mounds of snow to get to class. She had paid for Ted to live in the dorm and she was not leaving Vermont until he was in the dorm.

The next thing I knew, we were standing on the porch of the

president's house in the little town at the bottom of the mountain. I was mortified. I hadn't wanted to come here in the first place, and now I really wished I had stayed home. I was beginning to think Mom was going too far.

The president's wife came to the door and let us in. Mom introduced herself gently but pulled no punches. "I want to speak to the president," she said.

"He's busy right now," the woman said.

Mom smiled. "That's quite all right. We'll wait," she said. And we plunked down on a sofa in the living room. The president's wife was startled, but she recovered enough to offer us some tea. Soon the president himself came in. Mom explained the problem. The president realized right away she was not going to leave his house until he had done something—namely, found a room in the dorm for Ted. He promised to take care of the matter. He escorted us to the door, but Mom had the last word.

"I'll call you next week to make sure everything is all right," she said. By now, everyone on campus knew she would do exactly that. And if they didn't want her to come back, they had better get Ted a dorm room pronto.

The next night, after Mom and I returned home, Ted called. He played on the college's basketball team and hadn't been able to accompany Mom on her mission to get him back up the mountain, but he had heard what happened from a lot of people on campus. He thought it was pretty funny. And he was in a dorm.

That college did not soon forget the day Jane Tyler came to campus and shredded the red tape to get her son in the room that was rightfully his. My mother taught me some very valuable life lessons that day in Vermont: Never take "no" for an answer. Always stick up for what you know is right. And most important, don't be afraid to go straight to the top—of either the mountain or the chain of command. Go to the people who can make things happen. They will always remember you for it.

Years later, after graduating, Ted ran into the college's (now former) president at a function in Washington, D.C. After the usual greetings and handshakes, the president said, "And how is your mother?"

~Tanya J. Tyler

Unconditional Love

Mothers and their children are in a category all their
own. There's no bond so strong in the entire world.
No love so instantaneous and forgiving.
~Gail Tsukiyama, Dreaming Water

One day, in the spring of 1958, a woman gazed silently at a black and white photograph. The picture was of a little girl kneeling in the snow, her arm around a black dog.

"Her name is Tina," said the man who had handed her the picture. "She's seven years old. I love my daughter more than anything, but I can't keep her. My wife... she isn't Tina's mother, you know? She resents having a reminder around of my other marriage. I had to send Tina back to my ex-wife, to keep her safe."

The man twisted the hat in his hands as he continued, "But Tina's mother hasn't had Tina with her for years; she's remarried now with two kids and she... well, she's emotionally unable to deal with another one. You see?" He swallowed hard before adding, "My daughter needs a home."

The woman handed the photograph to her husband, who took it and studied it for several minutes before giving it back with a small smile. He said, "Well, honey, what do you think?"

The woman touched a finger to the image of the child smiling hopefully into the camera, and then looked into the eyes of the little girl's father. "Yes," she said. "We'll take her."

The little girl in the photograph was me. And the woman who agreed to open her heart and home to a child she'd never met was my new mother. My new father, of course, played an important, loving part in this decision, but it was my mother who was willing to take on the full-time, thankless, and often heartbreaking care of a previously abused child. Loving me would be a challenge for her from the very beginning.

In the first place, I didn't want to be there. I was heartsick at being taken away from my father, who I loved desperately despite his refusal to leave the woman who was abusing me. Moreover, I had a natural distrust of women. The two in my life so far had either abandoned me or beaten me. In my mind, why should this new one be any different?

My new father had a much easier time those turbulent first months, because he was gentle and quiet like my daddy. I bonded with him quickly. But when he went off to work every day, my mother was the one left to deal with a bitter, confused little girl.

I was in terrible shape when I arrived on my new parents' doorstep, not just emotionally, but physically as well. I was nearly twenty pounds underweight, had rickets, and suffered from constant ear infections and bouts of bronchitis. It was Mom who sat by my bed all those nights, who rubbed my chest with Vicks and gave me my doses of cough syrup and antibiotics. She made me chicken soup and hot strawberry Jell-O drinks. And yet, as I recovered, it was Dad's lap, not Mom's, where I sought comfort.

Like many abused children, I was a bedwetter. It embarrassed me and I tried very hard not to, but several times a night I drenched my bed. And several times a night, my mother would rouse from sleep to check on me. When she found that I had done it again, she would change my bedding, wipe me down with a warm, wet washcloth, and dress me in fresh pajamas. She would then kiss me and say, "It's okay, sweetheart. It's not your fault." I eventually outgrew this humiliating disorder, but in the meantime it cost my mother many hours of sleep. I don't think she ever heard a thank you from me for her patience, even though in the past I had been verbally and sometimes physically abused for my bedwetting by my previous mothers.

In the weeks and months to come, I tested my new mother's love again and again. When she asked me not to do something, I did it anyway. When given an order, I ignored it. When she attempted to discipline me, I would draw myself up to my full forty-six inches, look her in the eye, and say, "You can't tell me what to do. You're not my 'real' mother." Years later, Mom confessed those words had been like a knife in her heart. But she went on loving me anyway.

To help me make friends in my new school, she often arranged with my teacher to surprise my class with donuts. My new playmates would say, "Your mom is so cool!" I would glory in the attention, but I don't remember ever thanking her.

I look back on those early days and shake my head at the endless, loving patience my mother showed me. No matter how many times I hurt her feelings by refusing the affection she was so hungry to give, she never gave up. Night after night, she tucked me in and then sat beside me, stroking my head. "I love you, Tina," she told me, over and over. "Other parents have to settle for whatever children are born to them, but I chose you. And I'm going to keep on loving you, no matter what."

And one day, I finally believed her.

Mom's been gone now for more than thirty years and I miss her more than I can say. I wish I could have her here with me one more time to tell her how sorry I am for what I put her through in those early days, and to thank her for her unconditional love.

Was she the best mother ever? Well, if being willing to open her heart to a broken, homeless little girl is any measure, then yes, yes she was.

~Tina Wagner Mattern

The Gift

My mother is a walking miracle.
~Leonardo DiCaprio

When Hurricane Ike flooded our home in Seabrook, Texas, my family lost many possessions, but I was most saddened by the loss of my high school yearbooks. Other items could be replaced, but not the yearbooks signed by my friends, with best wishes for our future and 1970s phrases like "Love & Peace." These symbols of my youth were gone forever.

During the aftermath of that devastating hurricane, family, friends and co-workers came to our aid, helping out any way they could. My mother, however, went beyond the desire to help. She made it her quest to replace as many of our belongings as possible from her home in Rock Falls, Illinois.

When I sent her a copy of a story I'd written about the hurricane, which was later published in *Chicken Soup for the Soul: A Book of Miracles*, she learned of my sorrow over the loss of the yearbooks. That story sent her off on a seemingly impossible quest that resulted in an amazing gift of love. She vowed to find a copy of my 1973 senior yearbook.

Finding a thirty-seven-year-old yearbook was no small feat in itself, but she was also determined to find one without signatures. She quickly spread the word about her mission and managed to track down a few copies: one at a garage sale and one from a teacher, but the pages of both were filled with signatures. This simply wouldn't do, so her search continued.

One of my former teachers gave Mom the name of the current high school librarian. This was the lead she had been looking for. And, sure enough, the librarian had a blank copy of the 1973 yearbook.

"Do you want annuals from any other years?" the librarian asked.

Amazed at her luck, my mother exclaimed, "Sure, if you have 1970, 1971, and 1972 as well, that would be wonderful." When she asked how much she owed for the books, she was once again surprised.

"No charge for a fellow Rocket [the Rock Falls High School mascot]," came the reply.

It seemed that fate was in her favor thus far, but her mission was not complete. Next, she set out to get four of my closest friends from high school to sign each yearbook, even traveling out of state to get one of the signatures.

Since thirty-seven years had passed, writing an appropriate message took some serious thought on the part of my friends. The signers reviewed their own yearbooks to see what I had written to them and echoed those memories in their written passages to me.

My mother was thrilled beyond measure. Unable to deliver the books in person, she carefully wrapped her prized gifts and sent them off by mail.

Of course, I had no idea that any of this was happening. All I knew was that I received a mysterious message from my mother saying that I should expect a package. Then, she called my husband and asked that he take a photo of me opening the package, so she could see my surprise.

As you might imagine, I was not only elated, but also amazed at her accomplishment. Nothing could have prepared me for four signed yearbooks.

Every person involved with her endeavor was touched deeply by this gift of love from my mother. My friend Sue recalls, "After being on the phone with your mom, I always ended up with such a warm, fuzzy feeling because she just couldn't contain her excitement. Giving you this gift gave her such purpose and joy!"

Now, every time I look through the yearbooks, I feel my mother's delight — her joy in giving. They are no longer a symbol of my youth but are genuine icons of her love. This unique gift from the heart touched my soul as only a mother could.

~Dawn J. Storey

The Wind Beneath My Wings

We are each of us angels with only one wing, and
we can only fly by embracing one another.
~Luciano De Crescenzo

I sat in a giant hotel ballroom full of mothers and daughters. My arms were crossed and I was scowling. The Mother's Day brunch was as elegant as could be. Beautiful round tables were covered with white linen tablecloths, real silver utensils, and fancy china. There were beautiful floral centerpieces. All the mothers and daughters were dressed in their Sunday best. I was too, even though I would have much rather worn ripped jeans, a soft T-shirt, and a side ponytail.

Ugh, I thought, *why can't I be anywhere else but here?*

Some other mother's daughter started singing a beautiful song about her mother. She hadn't even made it through the first verse and my mom already had tears in her eyes.

Before the song, the girl had proclaimed that her mom was her confidante and comfort and the wind beneath her wings! That was nice for that girl, but I didn't need my mother's wind beneath my wings. I was thirteen years old, and I already had it all figured out. I was ready to fly… on my own.

And fly I did.

I spread my wings and sailed off to college in a different state.

I glided into a new job without ever looking down.

I swooped into a marriage with the man of my dreams.

I fluttered through my first pregnancy and flitted through the first few years of motherhood.

And then my second child was diagnosed with autism. The skies were no longer clear, and I came crashing down. My wings were broken, and I could not fix my little girl. My mom swept in and did all the right things.

She read the research and made her own version of CliffsNotes for each book. She took my older child out for special dates, so that he could continue to live a somewhat normal life. She came over to watch my kids when I needed a nap. She babysat for my daughter, who was a danger to herself and needed to be watched at all times.

She packed up and cleaned my house when we moved to a new district with a better special needs school for my daughter. She painted rooms in my house when we needed a change. She gave us money for therapy when we ran out. She came over when I called, and kept her distance when I needed space. She even babysat for several long weekends so I could keep my marriage intact.

That was when I realized it. My mom had always been there, huffing and puffing, blowing and fanning the wind below each of my life's events. Her wind was a gentle wind. So soft and so subtle that I never knew she was there... until I needed to know she was.

And now she is teaching me how to be the wind beneath my daughter's wings. My dream is no longer to fly alone. Now my dream is to do all the things my mother did for me for my daughter without her even knowing it. I will work and sweat, worry and pray, and take no credit when my daughter flies high in the sky. I will put myself second, always taking care of her needs before mine.

My daughter is thirteen now, and I think I will take her to that same Mother's Day brunch. I smile as I wonder if she will be thinking she would rather be anywhere else, wearing jeans and a side ponytail. I know that I'll have tears in my eyes, too, if someone sings a tribute to one of the other mothers. Because now I know the true joy of being a mother — being the quiet wind beneath my children's wings.

~Julie Hornok

The Last Easter Egg

When you are a mother, you are never really alone in
your thoughts. A mother always has to think twice,
once for herself and once for her child.
~Sophia Loren

M y parents and I were in Florida during my dad's spring break from teaching middle school. It was the first Easter we had ever spent away from home. As an anxious four-year-old, I had asked my mom several times if the Easter Bunny would be able to find us. She assured me there would be eggs — and that the Easter Bunny would fully understand why we didn't leave him any carrots.

On Easter morning, my parents and I discovered that the Easter Bunny had visited overnight and left eggs on the hotel's main lawn for all the kids. As we walked toward the group of adults and kids waiting for instructions, I began sizing up the competition. All of the kids were much bigger than me. It wasn't looking good.

"I will get an egg, right?" I asked my mom.

"Yes, of course," she replied, with a confident smile.

The resort staff member in charge of the hunt explained that when she yelled "Go" the hunt would begin, and all Easter eggs were fair game. I nervously clutched the handle of the plastic seashell bucket that was now serving as my Easter basket. My heart began racing as I watched some of the other kids crouch into a sprinter's pose in anticipation of the start.

"Get ready!" the staff member yelled. "We are starting in 3… 2… 1… GO!"

Kids darted across the lawn, running from palm tree to palm tree looking for the plastic Easter eggs filled with candy. I sprinted to the closest tree but did not find any eggs. My dad waved me on encouragingly as my mom walked behind me.

I ran to a nearby sandpit hoping there would be an egg hidden there. But there wasn't. I looked across the lawn and saw the other kids triumphantly holding up their plastic eggs and knew my chance of finding even one egg was diminishing by the second.

Just then my mom pointed out a palm tree across the lawn. "Look! There's one!"

A shiny blue plastic egg was resting on the ground against the base of the tree. I looked up at my mom in excitement. However, instead of grinning back at me, she was staring to the left, in the direction of another mom, whose son was plucking candy out of an egg. The two moms were alternating between looking at one another and at what appeared to be the *last* Easter egg.

I had never seen my very petite mom run before that day. She had been born with weak knees, due to an issue with her ligaments, and when she was in elementary school she had worn special shoes to correct a foot problem.

As the stare-down continued, I set down my plastic bucket and took off toward the Easter egg. And then my mom whooshed past me — running in her Easter dress and sandals toward the palm tree and the shiny blue egg.

"Go, Mom!" I yelled.

The other mom also sprinted toward the shiny blue egg.

In one last burst of speed, my mother reached the trunk of the tree, bent down, and scooped up the egg.

"Yay! I got an egg!" I squealed in excitement, jumping up and down in celebration.

My mom, beaming from her victory, walked back toward me and handed me the shiny blue egg. I held it up triumphantly, like the other kids had done.

I've forgotten what kind of candy was inside that plastic egg. And I can't remember what I did with that egg after our vacation ended. But I clearly remember my mom running as fast as she could toward that shiny blue egg. I remember the big smile on her face — a reflection of her love — as she handed me the last Easter egg.

~Anna Sofia Kendall

Hero's Cape

Heroes are ordinary people who
make themselves extraordinary.
~Gerard Way

It was one of those storms that turns day into night. I was pressed up against the door looking outside at the rain and wind.

I was crying and terrified, because my imaginary friend, whose name was Mary Okay, was caught outside. I saw her with my very own eyes. She was standing at the end of our driveway and clinging to our mailbox.

Mary Okay was screaming for my help! I knew I had to save her.

But how? I was just as terrified as she seemed to be. So, I did the only thing I could — I stood with my nose pressed against the screen and I wailed.

All of a sudden, my mother appeared. She was wearing white tennis shoes and she had a mint green bathrobe around her shoulders like a hero's cape. My mother the superhero flung the door wide open, leaped to the mailbox, opened her "cape" and wrapped Mary Okay safely inside it.

And then she ran back into the house, carrying Mary Okay, and we were saved.

I've never forgotten the bravery and all the things my mother displayed that day to a six-year-old and her imaginary friend. Mary

Okay may no longer be with me but as for my mother, she still wears the "cape."

~Terri Rilea

Spoiled Sweet

*Nobody can do for little children what grandparents
do. Grandparents sort of sprinkle stardust over
the lives of little children.*
~Alex Haley

My mom was a master when it came to spoiling her grandchildren, regularly doling out salty snacks, crunchy candy, and toys galore. Though I repeatedly asked Mom to dial back the spoiling, my pleas fell on deaf ears.

"I'm just so grateful that they're mine to spoil!" she would say.

Mom would take the boys grocery shopping for taco meat and shredded cheese but come home with ice cream and Cheez-Its. She introduced my sons to Diet Coke, cotton candy, and cap guns before they even started preschool. If she heard the kids wanted a toy, she'd go and get it immediately. Every time she visited she baked sugar cookies with my kids. Not only did my boys remain on a sugar high for a solid week following her stay but I would be stuck cleaning up spilled sprinkles and bits of dried dough for days.

The thing that bothered me most, however, was that my children preferred my mom to me. This was true mostly of my older son Kyler, probably because he and I lived with my parents for a stretch of time while I was going through my divorce.

We had moved in with Mom and Dad the November when Kyler was two. I had custody of Kyler for Christmas that year, and I eagerly anticipated Christmas morning with him. I envisioned him barreling into my room and jumping on my bed, squealing about Santa. Instead, I heard the pitter-patter of tiny feet scamper past my bedroom door at 7 a.m. and head into my parents' room. Then I heard him shouting, "Grandma! Let's go see what Santa brought!" My heart sank. It hurt playing second fiddle.

As he grew older, Kyler often chose to confide in his grandma instead of me. If he had questions about the birds and the bees, he called Mom. If he had a run-in with a bully, he talked it through with Mom. If he got in trouble at school, he spilled his guts to Mom.

I longed for my mom's glory to fade so that I could be more important in my child's life. But you know how the saying goes: "Be careful what you wish for."

Nearly four years ago, Mom died tragically and unexpectedly. Just like that, the spoiling stopped. The confiding stopped. The world stopped. I was angry with myself for having resented my mom for doting on her grandkids. I was ashamed for being jealous of her bond with my son. I should have been more thankful. I should have been more tolerant. I should have spoiled *her* more.

For months, I barely functioned as I processed my feelings of grief, grace, and gratitude. Then one day, about six months after Mom died, Kyler came down the stairs wearing pants that were too short and a shirt that was too tight.

I scratched my head.

What gives? I thought.

Then it hit me. My mom had always been the boys' primary shopper so I wasn't in the habit of buying them new clothes. It wasn't at all unusual for her to show up at my door with bags of clothes. "I was wandering through Macy's and found myself in the boys' department," she would say. "I just couldn't help myself!"

I chuckled at her shopping addiction and thanked her for the purchases, but I never fully appreciated how well she took care of my sons — or me. Her support for us was unparalleled and unconditional.

When I was a teenager, she helped me survive anorexia. When I was an adult, she helped me survive my divorce. When I was a mother, she helped me after I had hand surgery and was unable to unscrew a sippy cup lid, buckle my kid into his car seat, or even squeeze a shampoo bottle. Time after time, Mom came to my rescue.

And then there were those little things that meant so much. Every time she visited when my sons were infants, she offered to take the baby monitor so that I could sleep in. She would cheer me up by baking my favorite homemade honey wheat bread.

It's no wonder Kyler adored my mom. She told the best bedtime stories and gave the best back scratches. She offered the best hugs and baked the best goodies. She was the best listener and doled out the best advice. And while it's true that she never said "no" when the kids asked for cookies or candy, she also never turned down an invitation to crawl into a tent made of sheets and blankets despite her back pain. Her rule was that if it made the grandkids happy, she was in.

I always worried that Mom would spoil the children rotten, but the truth was that my boys came out kind, loving, and giving, just like their grandmother. So I guess you could say she spoiled them sweet. And she did the same for me. I learned how to parent by following her example, and that's why now, when my sons come to me with questions that span every topic — from sports to sex, school to scandals, Santa to Satan — I'm able to answer with truth, love, and good advice.

My younger son, Trevyn, was only two years old when Mom died, so I worried that he wouldn't have any memories of his grandma. He's six now and the other day I asked him if he remembers Grandma Heitger.

"Yes!" Trevyn exclaimed. "She made roll-out cookies with me!" Tears sprang to my eyes. The cookies. He remembered the cookies. I smiled as I recalled sweeping up those stray sprinkles and scraping bits of dried dough from my kitchen cabinets. It turns out it was worth the mess to make the memories.

"I have an idea," I said. "How would you boys like to help me bake some melt-in-your-mouth homemade honey wheat bread?"

"I dunno," Kyler hesitated, recognizing that this food wouldn't result in a sugar high.

"It's Grandma's recipe," I said.

His eyes lit up. "Oh?"

"I'll need help stirring the dough and rolling it out," I said.

"You mean, like cookies?" Trevyn asked.

"Yeah, kind of," I said. "But you also have to punch the dough and really put some muscle into it."

Trevyn grinned. I could tell what he was thinking: "What could be better than punching food?"

"I'll do it!" he said, then added, "Wait. Will there be sprinkles?"

"Sure, why not?"

If we were going to celebrate the spirit of a woman who knew how to deliciously spoil people, festive sprinkles atop a loaf of bread seemed fitting.

"I'm so glad you're my mom," Trevyn said, as he reached for the measuring cups.

"Me, too," Kyler added. "We have the best mom in the world."

I knew how they felt. I had the best mom, too.

~Christy Heitger-Ewing

Show, Don't Tell

Call your mother. Tell her you love her. Remember,
you're the only person who knows what her
heart sounds like from the inside.
~Rachel Wolchin

During my first pregnancy, my mother couldn't wait to meet her new grandchild and help me while I adjusted to motherhood. But to her great disappointment, I told her I wanted time to bond with the baby before she flew down to help.

Always the headstrong and independent daughter, I wanted to do things my way, and I asked her to wait a couple of weeks before she visited. She graciously honored that request, and after her two-week ban, Mom arrived with her suitcase brimming with baby gifts and handmade blankets. She oohed and aahed over baby Emily and held her as much as possible, even jumping up to respond when she cried in the middle of the night. I almost felt like I was in a competition to get to Emily first.

Mom also did the laundry, put fresh sheets on my bed, and cooked dinner every night. I appreciated all her help, but I was already feeling pretty competent at mothering. After a weeklong visit, I was happy to pack her off to the airport and have my baby to myself again.

A month later, it was a different story. My "easy" newborn had developed colic and cried for hours on end. I no longer felt like a competent mother. In fact, I was overwhelmed. I made a tearful call to my mother to see if she would come back to help. She immediately booked a flight and came to my rescue.

Now I was overjoyed to have someone jump up in response to my crying baby — there was plenty of crying baby to go around. Mom bundled up Emily in the stroller and walked her around the block so that I could have quiet breaks. She walked the floors with Emily while my husband and I went out for a quick bite to eat. She accompanied me to the pediatrician and helped me implement the bland diet he recommended for me so that my breast milk would irritate the baby less. Just having my mother there helped me stay calm and not feel crazy or inept.

In other words, Mom was a lifesaver. This time when she left, I was a lot more reluctant to see her go. But she assured me that she'd come back if I needed her. Luckily, like a textbook case, the colic disappeared at three months, and I had my easy baby again.

Although we lived 500 miles apart, Mom and I visited as often as we could to make sure Emily would grow up knowing her grandmother. And my mother continued to help me, filling in occasionally as overnight babysitter so that my husband and I could have a weekend away. While it would have been nice to have Mom right down the street, we made do, and I appreciated all of her selfless support and love.

Two years later, when I was pregnant with my second baby, Mom again planned to come to help. When I called her from the hospital to let her know that she had a new grandson, she was thrilled, but when I asked her when she would arrive, she said she would have to check her calendar. She had a couple of appointments that week.

Apparently, Mom hadn't anticipated the 180-degree change in my attitude about needing her help. After a surprised pause, I said, "Mom, I don't think you understand. I have a newborn in my arms and a toddler at home. I'm not leaving this hospital until you get here!" She was on a flight the next day.

While I had resisted my mom's help, wanting to be a mother in my own way, the reality was that she was there for me in whatever way I needed, whenever I needed it. She let me have my space and independence when that's what I wanted, and she came to my rescue when that's what I needed. She did it all graciously, too, with love and selflessness. Mom didn't *tell* me how to be a good mother; she simply *showed* me how.

~Marjorie Woodall

That Long Ride Home

*[A] mother is one to whom you hurry
when you are troubled.*
~Emily Dickinson

An icy silence chilled the crisp autumn air even more as my mom drove me home. I had only been away at college for two months and already I'd been written up several times by the dormitory resident advisors for partying. I'd also been experimenting with multiple types of dangerous drugs. And then I passed out, high, after a residence hall judicial board meeting, only to wake up the next day in the hospital having a spinal tap. My mom was praying hard on that drive home while we decided on my future.

I had never been a hard-core partier or drug user, but all of the freedoms of university life had sent me over the edge. It was my own fault, but despite that, as I look back I can clearly see one amazing thing: The ever-present, caring image of my mom.

After I had passed out, an even worse thing had happened. I had fallen backward onto an unforgiving marble floor. Not only was I knocked unconscious, but I had two grand mal seizures that night.

When I woke up in the hospital after a spinal tap, I looked across the room and saw my mom, with her arms folded, her brow furrowed, and her foot tapping. I felt bad for the mess I had made of things. She asked me about the pot pipe that she found when the staff gave her my clothes, and I said it was someone else's.

The spinal tap showed no risk of paralysis, but weeks later I would learn that I lost my sense of smell forever from the accident. Also, when I did get the green light to leave the hospital, I was in no condition to return to university life. I was still in a daze when I began that long car ride home with my mom.

My mother was a drug and alcohol counselor and was probably in shock that her own son might be a substance abuser or even an addict. I didn't say anything on the drive. I just stared out the window as the miles of highway went by. Then my mom asked one simple question that changed everything.

"Jonathan, were you using drugs?" she asked, while knowing full well the ugly truth.

"No," I replied. But lying to her broke my heart. It was the first time I lied to an adult who was so important to me, who was a leader for me.

I remembered that lie, and later I dedicated my life to being honest and living the right way. That day, sitting in the front seat of the car next to my mother, was when my life began to change. I had been so close to disaster — to a lifestyle of dishonesty, addiction, disgrace, and ruin.

My mom nurtured me and I went back to college. The amazing residence director at my dorm gave me a second chance. She allowed me to stay in housing as long as I regularly saw a university counselor.

That counselor helped me quit using drugs and alcohol, and in fact, I became a model student. In my second year I even led a Bible study after a spiritual conversion topped off my first year of college. Then, in my last two years, I persevered and made the Dean's list twice.

One day while walking across campus, my own process of recovery became crystal clear. I saw two students who were clearly using drugs. My heart went out to them because I remembered my own past. Looking into their eyes, I said seven words that would chart the direction of my future forever. And I only hoped it could help them in their future too.

"There's no greater high than being straight," I told them. And as those words came out I realized full well their truth for my own life.

Since then, I have finished college and added a few degrees, even a Ph.D. and a fellowship in education. I've given back wherever I could and counseled addicts and other troubled young people.

The message of life and hope that I learned from my mom on that long ride home has never left me. As she gave me the room to learn life's most important lesson, and supported me along the way, I realized the heights to which I could soar.

Thus, I learned I could overcome anything that came my way. My mom's love during my college years has always stuck with me. It was what opened the door toward my destiny.

~Jonathan Doll

Best Teacher Ever

There is no school equal to a decent home and no
teacher equal to a virtuous parent.
~Mahatma Gandhi

Dad was an English teacher who taught high school students by day and college students by night. Mom stayed home and homeschooled their four children until the high school years. I was the oldest; my sister Catherine was second. The other three of us had no trouble learning to read, but Catherine still could not read by fifth grade, and worse still, did not even know the alphabet.

My mother did some research and decided that Catherine had some sort of learning disability. She enrolled Catherine at a public school in order to obtain access to state resources. Catherine made many friends at school and amazed everyone with her gift for telling creative stories in class at a moment's notice, but she still couldn't master reading. After all the testing was done, the school had my parents come in. They were told they should just take Catherine home. Based on the test results, the school did not understand how she was as high functioning as she was.

Tears of grief streamed down my dad's cheeks, but my mom's jaw was set in quiet determination. As they walked back to the car, she turned to him and said, "I know she's not stupid."

Soon thereafter, my mom stumbled upon a learning system that focused heavily on lesson repetition and building slowly on the previous exercises. She worked with Catherine for four hours every morning while the rest of us studied on our own. It was frustrating for both of them, but she often told a weeping Catherine, "Failure is not an option. You're going to learn to read, or we'll both die trying! You *have* to learn to read! You *will* learn to read."

In time, Catherine got it. By the time she graduated from eighth grade, she was reading almost at grade level. She continued improving and was reading above grade level when she graduated from a public high school.

Catherine came to love reading and writing and even corresponded online with her future husband while attending junior college. All of this because of a wonderfully devoted mother who was absolutely the best teacher ever — for all four of us.

~Emily Dupree

BEST MOM EVER!

Chapter 2

Adventures with Mom

*Twenty years from now you will be more
disappointed by the things that you didn't
do than by the ones you did do.*
~Mark Twain

11

Hostage Situation

She raised us with humor, and she raised us to
understand that not everything was going to
be great — but how to laugh through it.
~Liza Minnelli (on mom Judy Garland)

I love my mother. Really, I do. But if Mom had died under mysterious circumstances during a wicked winter snowstorm a few years ago, not a jury in the land would have convicted me. Especially not a jury of my peers.

I had headed north on Tuesday, Christmas Eve. "The five-day forecast calls for highs in the upper 40s and lower 50s with a slight chance of precipitation toward the end of the week," proclaimed the radio weatherperson.

Great, I thought. *I can come home late Thursday or early Friday and not have to worry about ice on the roads.*

But by Thursday afternoon, ice on the roads was the least of my worries.

I'd lived in western Washington my entire life. I'd seen snow before. And freezing rain. And floods. But what I saw in the week between Christmas and New Year's was a sight heretofore unimagined.

Fast and furious, fat furry flakes quickly made driving impossible. By Friday morning, a full sixteen inches of snow turned my car into a giant sloping igloo. I looked at Mom. She looked at me. "I guess I'm going to be here a while," I said, and poured a little Bailey's Irish Cream into my coffee.

On Saturday morning another seven or eight inches of the white stuff obliterated the trail to the mailbox. Freezing rain was predicted. I sat transfixed before the television, which now aired only news and weather.

The rain started late Saturday evening. "Melt," I prayed. But it didn't melt. The combined weight of snow and frozen water became the hot news topic. Store rooftops succumbed to the pressure. Marinas caved in on hundreds of yachts. A quarter million people in the Puget Sound region lost their electricity as falling trees wiped out power lines.

"We could be worse off," I told Mother that Sunday morning. "We have heat and lights and plenty of food left from Thursday's gathering."

And then the carport collapsed.

It sounded like a bomb. Twisted metal and a mountain of snow slammed into the side of Mom's mobile home. Luckily, no windows were broken, but the wreckage trapped us inside, blocking the front door. Although I had cleared snow away from the back door the day before, the snow that had drifted during the night was blocking that exit, too.

I looked at Mom. She looked at me. I poured a little more Bailey's into my coffee.

"I don't mean to be critical," she said a short time later, "but isn't that the same outfit you wore yesterday?"

I pulled my bathrobe snugly around me and replied, "Do you see any real point in my getting dressed?"

I set the coffee cup on top of the television and flipped through the channels. Mom picked up my mug and wiped the nonexistent water rings under it.

I opened several containers of holiday goodies and set a hearty meal of fudge and cookies and nut clusters on a plate in front of the television. Before I could return to the kitchen, Mom had put the lids back on the canisters and the milk back in the fridge.

"How big is this mobile home?" I asked her.

"Fourteen by seventy, but that includes the hitch."

"So we're talking approximately 980 square feet of living space, right?"

"More like 900," said Mom. "Not counting the walls, the cupboards, the counters, the appliances, the furniture…"

I looked at Mom. She looked at me. "Where's this water coming from?" she asked, running a sponge across the counter where I had assembled my breakfast.

Traced to its source, the water was coming from damage done to the roof edge when the carport gave way.

"Got any duct tape?" I asked. I stood, perched precariously, on the kitchen counter top. "Got any plastic food wrap?"

Mom handed both items up to me and I constructed a makeshift drainpipe, funneling the water from the leak directly into the sink.

"How'd you figure that out?" asked Mom.

"I watch *MacGyver*."

My window of opportunity came the next day. My brother helped me wade through the knee-deep slush between the back entrance and the street where my car was parked. "How'd it feel to be sequestered with Mom for a week?" he asked. "I'm surprised you two didn't kill each other."

I smiled as I hugged him goodbye. "Not guilty," I replied. "She's all yours now."

Slowly pulling away from the curb, I looked back at my mother, standing in the window, waving both hands. It could have been worse, I thought, waving back. I could have been stranded with someone I didn't love…

~Jan Bono

12

The Kroger Queen

The quickest way to get to know a woman
is to go shopping with her.
~Marcelene Cox

I admit it; I'm not a normal girl. I absolutely hate shopping. Who wants to battle thick traffic on confusing roads just to end up in a huge building packed with humanity and sensory overload? No, thank you.

My mom, however, is an expert shopper.

I did not fully appreciate shopping as a skill until the summer Mom had a fall and was banned by doctor's orders from driving for a while. This did not stop the shopper from doing her thing.

"Could you maybe take me to Kroger since I can't drive?" Mom asked one day.

I really didn't want to go, so I suggested, "Well, if you're too dizzy to drive, you definitely shouldn't be going to a store, right? I mean, what if you would, I don't know, crash into something and cause a scene?"

But nothing could separate Mom from Kroger. Not even a concussion. Kroger is like a second home to her. "I think I'll be fine," she said. "I just need a few items."

Uh-oh. I had heard that line before.

I found myself setting off for terrifying territory the next day. I thought we could leave right away in the morning, to get it over with, but Mom wanted to get all her coupons ready first. She sat at the table, cutting coupons out of newspapers and ticking things off her grocery list. Around noon she was ready. She added a very large stack of coupons to her already bulging "coupon wallet." There must have been seventy coupons in there!

If I thought Mom's shopping strategy ended with the coupons, I was wrong. As I pulled into the parking lot, Mom said, "Take the road to the right. If you go left, you have to stop for pedestrians."

I turned into a parking space, pulling forward into the empty space in front of us. "Why are you doing that?" Mom asked.

"That's so I can drive forward instead of backing out," I replied smugly. "I do have a strategy too, you know."

"But we need to park with the trunk facing out," Mom protested. "If the trunk faces toward the other vehicles, it's hard to put the groceries in."

Defeated, I re-parked, losing the thirteen seconds I had gained by taking the road to the right. We got out and I looked in the direction of the carts. "Oh, no, we can get those inside," Mom said.

Inside, I got a cart and was heading for the grocery section when Mom said, "Stop! I always wipe the handlebar. You never know what germs are on there."

I had walked right by that little canister of sanitary wipes and never noticed them. If I had noticed them, it would never have occurred to me to use them on the cart. I was ready to crown Mom "Queen of Kroger" right then, but the shopping hadn't even begun. Mom took the cart from me, muttering something about lack of control, and gave me a list of things to find.

There were three things on that list, all roughly in the same category. In fact, they were all in the same aisle. I wandered that store for almost half an hour, looking for the first item, and had quite a bit of trouble finding the other two, which may or may not have been right next to the first one. At one point, I considered hiring one of the Kroger staff as a personal shopper. I finally found the things I was assigned and tracked down Mom. She, of course, had already gotten most of the other things on her list.

Once the initial shock wore off, I noticed a strange thing. The Kroger shoppers could be neatly divided into two categories: 10% were painfully out of place, like me, and 90% were avid shoppers like Mom. I even recognized the same look in their eyes. They were mostly moms, and all of them were dead set on getting that twenty-cent discount on their toothpaste and eggs. I even began to understand why Mom liked going to Kroger. These were her people!

After detouring to make sure there was nothing she wanted on the sale rack, Mom headed to the checkout. I watched in amazement as the subtotals and totals appeared on the screen. All that work clipping coupons paid off, because Mom saved about thirty dollars. I started plotting how to get Mom to do my shopping for me for the rest of my life.

~Hannah Yoder

Melba Faces Assisted Living

A good laugh is sunshine in the house.
~William Thackeray

I was very proud of myself for having persuaded my eighty-two-year-old mother to tour an assisted living facility. I had even found one that was near the home in which she had lived on her own following my father's death ten years earlier.

My mother was tough. She was the descendant of hearty pioneer stock that had braved the elements before settling in Salt Lake City. And she was the ninth and last child of a polygamous dad and, as such, had been forced to fend for herself in order to get her fair share of the family's limited resources.

Yes, my mother Melba was a toughie for sure — a terror on the road, and aggressively independent. She didn't cook anymore, but subsisted largely on McDonald's Filet-O-Fish sandwiches. She didn't need to clean the kitchen that way, and, in fact, she found the racks in her automatic dishwasher were ideal for filing and sorting her mail.

Nevertheless, it was time for her to move out of her house and into a facility where she could have some assistance as she continued to age. I thought that she was accepting my decision, too, because she handled the tour of the facility so well. She was the essence of grace, nodding politely to those I hoped would be her new "neighbors" and complimenting the tour guide on the cleanliness of the public areas and private rooms. She didn't even grill the guide on how frequently fish sandwiches were served in the dining room.

Everything was going beautifully and according to my plan. But then, as we stood outside the business office, Melba gently took my hand and asked, "So, Gordon, do you think you're going to be happy here?"

~Gordon Osmond

Old Yeller

Families are like fudge — mostly
sweet, with a few nuts.
~Les Dawson

Like many kids who grew up in the 1960s and 1970s, I had a mother who could be classified as a "yeller." Back then mothers yelled. They'd yell at the umps at their kids' baseball games. They'd yell "Hello!" to neighbors across the yard as they hung damp laundry on the line. They'd yell their kids' names into the air when it was time for dinner, and they would yell again if they weren't in the house within five minutes after the streetlights went on.

My mother was a mighty yeller. If there were such a thing as competitive yelling, without a doubt she'd be in the winner's circle. She'd yell to her kids up two flights of stairs, causing the doorbell chimes to buzz from the vibration of her voice. She'd yell at my father — a lot. And when she was mad, that particular type of yelling would often be peppered with colorful language.

One afternoon in spring 1968 was exceptionally notable. One of my little friends playing at my house after school ran into our living room with a smile that showed her obvious delight. "Your mother just told your father to [expletive] in his hat!" she gushed.

I know everybody thinks their mother is special, but how many people can pinpoint the moment they came to that realization? How lucky was I?

I really was lucky. For as far back as I could remember, my mother would hug me until I could barely breathe and tell me I was "so beautiful" and "so smart." That said, one day when I was trying to understand the wonders of nature, I asked her, "Is the air blowing the trees around, or are the trees moving and that's what makes it windy?" She gave me an incredulous look and yelled, "WHAT THE HELL KIND OF STUPID QUESTION IS THAT?"

How many people can pinpoint the moment when they realized they might not be that smart after all?

Often my mother yelled at the television. "DON'T TAKE HIM BACK, YOU FOOL," she'd shout to characters with poor judgment and low self-esteem on *As the World Turns*. One time I saw her yell at nobody at all: My father and I watched her bolt from the couch to answer a phone that was ringing on the television. "Helloooo" she said sweetly, before barking select curse words when she only heard dial tone and then slamming down the receiver.

For a good part of my life, there was no escaping my mother's yelling. She was a stay-at-home mom, and I mean that literally. Over the course of many years, my mother suffered from agoraphobia, an irrational fear of being in public places. Having five children over a fourteen-year span, Mom developed a home-based lifestyle that became increasingly comfortable, to the point where she became fearful of leaving.

To ease the anxiety, Mom was often doped up on "nerve pills," which kept her sacked out on the couch for most of the day. It seemed that she'd wake up for only two things: *Jeopardy!* and the weather forecast during the six o'clock news. Considering she never left the house, the obsession with the weather seemed a bit peculiar. Perhaps she was only wondering, *Will I need the heavy afghan over me tomorrow or just a light cotton blanket?*

I do stand-up comedy and often joke about my mother's agoraphobia, on stage. I can joke only because Mom was able to overcome it. After many years of being a prisoner in her own home, she joined a support group for people with agoraphobia and other types of fears. Together they would practice everyday things that most of us would find quite unremarkable: walking through a mall, riding an elevator, driving over a bridge.

Her next step was to get a driver's license and soon after, her own car. More accomplishments followed; she enrolled in a continuing education class at the local high school, and then got a part-time job as a bookkeeper (her first job since she was a teenager). She and my father divorced and Mom began working full-time. Secure in her independence, she bought a house and, realizing that twenty years of *Jeopardy!* was no substitute for a formal education, enrolled in classes at the local community college.

At age fifty-eight, she was awarded an associate's degree in accounting and at sixty-six, she went on her first business trip — to midtown Manhattan of all places. Imagine my mother walking through Times Square, when she was once afraid to step off the front porch!

In her early seventies Mom remarried and moved from New York to Idaho. Her new husband was sweet, kind, and as luck would have it, very hard of hearing. Mom was able to continue her yelling. They had a beautiful life together, racking up many miles of travel. After Jim died last year, Mom moved to Florida to live with her two sisters. One is all but deaf and the other has a hearing aid, so now Mom can use her yelling for good purposes.

We now live on opposite sides of the country, but I travel to Florida when I can, and Mom, who's eighty-two, visits me in Las Vegas. She flies by herself. Of course, the first thing she says at baggage claim is, "What time is *Jeopardy!* on here?" To this day she still yells answers — I mean, "questions" — to hesitant contestants: "WHAT IS THE BYZANTINE EMPIRE?"

When she's able to come to my stand-up shows, she laughs heartily as I perform the material she inspired. I do a bit about how my sister and I would run outside when we were in trouble: She'd be standing at the door yelling, "GET BACK IN THIS HOUSE!" and from the sidewalk we'd calmly reply, "Come on out and get us." We weren't stupid — to her, fresh air was like kryptonite.

I proudly point to Mom during the shows and tell the audience that if they're lucky enough to still have their mother, they should treat her like the Queen Mum. Afterward people typically mill around, eager to chat with Mom and tell her what a good sport she is to be the butt of my jokes. I hear her voice, not yelling this time, but distinctly above the others.

"That's my daughter!" she says.

~Linda Lou

A Nice Christian Boy

Love as powerful as your mother's for you leaves its
own mark... to have been loved so deeply... will
give us some protection forever.
~J.K. Rowling

A nice Christian boy... my mother's dearest wish for me, her only child. I can only imagine her distress as I reached my thirtieth year with no prospects, Christian or otherwise. Mom didn't pressure me, only occasionally inquiring, "Have you met anyone yet?" When I did date someone, she suppressed her curiosity, asking only a few questions: Where was he from? What did he do? How did we meet? I think that's why the one time my mother tried to fix me up is etched so clearly in my mind.

July heat filled the air as we drove to church. The sun warmed my neck as we walked down the sidewalk, up the steps to the tall, red double doors. The steeple jutted into the blue sky and the bell echoed through town, calling all to God. Growing up, I'd driven by this little church on the corner many times, but I'd never been inside.

A committed member of the Christian church in Wallowa for decades, Mom had recently changed her affiliation and joined the Presbyterian church in Lostine, nine miles up the road. Her decision surprised me, and we talked often about how much she liked her new community and the new minister, a young man with literary interests and a modern approach to the gospel. She accepted an appointment to Deacon, taking on a new leadership role. Having lost interest in church in my teens, I didn't usually attend when I came to visit. On this trip, however, I wanted to support Mom's enthusiasm for her new church so I accepted her invitation.

Passing through the doors, I received a program from a smiling, older woman who greeted me by name. She looked familiar, but I had been away and couldn't recall her name. Goosebumps prickled my arms as we entered the cool sanctuary. I immediately regretted the thin fabric of my flowered dress. I envied the sweaters and shawls of the congregants scattered in small groups throughout the pews. Elderly ladies whispered to each other, looking over their shoulders to smile and wave. I wondered if everyone returning home experienced this same enthusiastic curiosity.

We joined my Aunt Ruth and cousin Linda in a center pew near the back. They had joined her in this new congregation. Linda hugged me tightly as I passed her. Ruth clasped my hand firmly as I slipped onto the cool wood between her and Mom. I jumped as the pianist and organist joined forces in the prelude, their music echoing from floor to ceiling, bouncing off the wooden pews.

With a swoosh of black robes and a gleaming white smile, David, the minister, ascended the pulpit, and I figured out my mother's plot. Snippets of conversation filled my head… "very handsome"… "quite intelligent"… "single"… "hope we can keep him here." The smiles. The waves. The whispering. They were all in on it. I sat, trapped like a rat, directly in eyesight of the altar, feeling like I had a target painted on my forehead.

In a strong, clear voice, David welcomed everyone, made a few opening announcements and asked for introductions and prayer requests. Cheeks flaming, I smiled tightly as my mother stood to introduce me. More smiles and waves from the crowd. Apparently oblivious to his role in the unfolding drama, David nodded in my direction, smiling warmly. A little disarmed, I realized Mom had not exaggerated his good looks… dark hair, high cheekbones, and angular features. Wishing for magical powers of invisibility, I dropped my gaze to the floor, memorizing the speckles on the carpet as my toes gripped my sandals, digging into the soft surface.

I breathed a sigh of relief as we dropped our heads in prayer. I didn't realize that the trouble had just begun.

It started a few lines in, during the general request for relief for the sick and the tired, comfort for the poor, and food for the hungry. As David earnestly prayed for the downtrodden, he uttered the word "hungry," and my mother's stomach growled like a grizzly bear just waking from hibernation. I sucked in my breath, squeezed my eyes shut, and formed a prayer of my own: "Please, don't laugh." God deserted me in that moment. My mother too, as she clamped her hand over her mouth and started to snicker. Burying my head in my lap, hands covering my face, I tried in vain to stifle the sound. David continued to pray, although who the prayers were for now escaped me.

Aunt Ruth chuckled briefly and regained her composure. Mother quieted. Taking deep breaths, I swallowed my laughter and sat up. Maybe no one heard us? Suddenly the back of the pew began to shake, vibrating with the rhythm of a powerful laugh. Linda! The dam burst. Snickers became full-blown, belly-splitting laughter. My mother flew from her seat, escaping through a side door. Aunt Ruth's elbow dug into my ribs in a vain attempt to silence me. Tears stung my eyes. No amount of humiliation could stop the contagion of giggling. Only the end of the prayer and the chords of the first hymn could soothe us with enough sound to cover our sin. With the singing, my mother snuck quietly back to her seat. Mortified, I looked at my family, red-eyed and tear-streaked in our complicity. David never missed a beat.

The service continued without event, but the doxology brought the knot back to my stomach. David descended the stairs, taking his place at the door to thank everyone as they left. From each corner of the room they came. Groups of gray-haired ladies in pastel sweaters, polyester suits, and flowered cotton. Patting my back, grasping my elbows, they swept me forward in a sea of good intentions. I glanced back at my mother, in my eyes a desperate plea for help. She smiled and shrugged her shoulders.

They deposited me in front of him, and David began to grasp the situation. As we stood face-to-face, surrounded by hopeful busybodies, his cheeks reddened. Relieved to no longer be alone in my suffering, I smiled. The sincerity of my apology for our hysteria during the prayer eased the tension, and David clasped my hand. His smile reached all the way to his eyes. We shared a laugh at our mutual embarrassment.

Mom rescued us, coming to stand by my side, thanking David for his sermon and apologizing, again, for our outburst. As they talked, I could feel the fondness and respect between them, and warmth filled my heart. Mom slipped her hand in mine as we turned to leave.

David resigned a couple of years later. I never met him again, but felt Mom's disappointment when he left. I don't remember his last name or know where his journey took him, but I often wonder how his path unfolded. I wonder if anyone contacted him when my mother died. I imagine he would have felt her loss deeply. Although our acquaintance was brief, he lingers in my memory as a truly nice Christian boy.

~Amelia Zahm

Our Best Laugh

What the daughter does, the mother did.
~Jewish Proverb

I am the eldest of four daughters. When I turned sixty-five and became eligible for Medicare, the government employee who was registering me asked how I felt about this significant birthday. I told her that I loved my sixties and was very comfortable with this new milestone. I explained that the person who was having a difficult time was my mother. That her first-born had turned sixty-five was almost too much for her to believe.

My mother and I are twenty years apart. When I reached my seventieth birthday, my mother reached her ninetieth. My mom is still a vibrant, sharp and active woman in this new decade of her life. As for *my* new decade, I am grateful to have made it in good health, but the number itself is almost ridiculous to me. If pushed for a number, I would answer that I feel like I am in my fifties.

When I celebrated my seventy-first birthday, I made myself a promise. I had begun to notice that I was missing the audio in movies. I could not quite discern the words in the dialogue. I vowed to have my hearing tested, only sharing my plan with my husband.

I had watched my mother go through the process of getting hearing aids a few years earlier. She did not like wearing the devices. She insisted that she could hear perfectly without them. This was debatable.

I made an appointment and was tested. A week later I walked out of the hearing lab wearing hearing aids. I did not allow my new secret

to in any way impede the bounce in my step as I walked down the street. People smiled at me and I smiled back. No one knew, I thought, that I was a woman who wore hearing aids. Symbolically, this was a reality that aged me. I would not allow it to make me feel older. What I had forgotten was that the bag I was swinging, filled with batteries and the contract I had signed, had the name of the hearing aids in bold red letters printed on both sides!

When I got home, I called my mother and shared my news.

"Mom, your seventy-one-year-old daughter and her ninety-one-year-old mother are on the phone at this moment talking about our hearing aids. Can you believe this?"

My mother and I started to laugh. We were laughing from our souls. We had shared so many intimate moments in our lifetime together, but nothing represented the passage of time to us like this reality. My mom's ears had listened to me from the day I had learned how to speak. She was my confidante. She was my friend. And now, mother and daughter were speaking as peers, as two women who could not really comprehend that the other had reached this time and this need in her life.

The more we tried to talk about it, the harder we laughed. I had not remembered enjoying a laugh like this with my mom in a very long time. Although she had tried her hardest to age gracefully, being ninety offered many challenges. Hearing aids had been one of them. Our twenty-year age difference never seemed so unimportant. I was delighted that my new acquisition brought us shared laughter and established another life bond.

~Elynne Chaplik-Aleskow

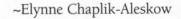

The Best Day Ever

*We laugh, we cry. We make time fly. We
are best friends, my mother and I.*
~Author Unknown

It was a warm Saturday afternoon in early spring 1961. Mom and I had spent a long, fruitless day shopping in the city for my wedding gown.

I was exhausted, and my feet were killing me. We'd begun shopping early that morning, trudging from one department store to the next with little success. To my dismay, every dress I loved significantly exceeded our budget. Each was more beautiful than the last, the fit flawless. My heart broke as I was forced to walk away because of the numbers on the price tags.

We decided to abandon our search for the gown and concentrate instead on finding material for the bridesmaid dresses. We eventually selected a beautiful brown chiffon fabric with large pink polka dots, only to be disappointed yet again. We needed enough material for six attendants, and the bolt was two yards short of the amount specified by the pattern. Although there were other lovely fabrics, I had my heart set on pink and brown as my wedding colors, and no amount of coaxing by Mom could change my mind.

Our luck didn't get much better as the day wore on. My excitement at finding the gorgeous wide-brimmed hats that would be the perfect complement to my attendants' dresses was short-lived. We needed six, and no matter how many times I counted, there were only five in stock. My shoulders slumped. I could not imagine my bridal party wearing any other hat.

The despair must have shown on my face because Mom insisted, "Let's take a break and get something to eat. I'm starving!"

I don't know if Mom was actually hungry, or if she thought food and a break might cheer me up, but I agreed that it was a good idea.

We headed over to Newberry's lunch counter, sat down, and ordered our usual shared triple-decker club sandwich with fries, a cherry Coke for me, and black coffee for Mom.

Halfway through the meal, I reached for a napkin and managed to tip over my soda. It drenched the entire counter, pouring onto both our dresses like a cascading waterfall. That was the last straw! I burst into tears.

The gentleman sitting next to me quickly grabbed a handful of napkins and helped us clean the mess while attempting to avoid getting any of it on his own clothing. Mom remained calm, moving the plates aside to mop up the remainder before the waitress came over with a damp cloth to give the counter a final wipe. I sat there helpless, useless and dejected, alternately dabbing at my tears and my saturated dress.

I managed to compose myself enough to apologize to the other customers sitting near us and to the sympathetic waitress. She quickly refilled my drink without asking. After finishing our soggy sandwich, we decided it would be wise to head home and make dinner for my father and two brothers rather than chance another misfortune. Mom slipped her arm through mine and gave me an understanding smile as we headed for the closest bus stop.

Although relieved to be heading home, I was equally disappointed in what I considered the waste of a valuable weekend day.

As we sat at the back of the bus, each absorbed in our own thoughts, a giggle bubbled from Mom's lips. I looked at her, and without saying a word, began to giggle, too. Before we knew it, we were laughing until tears rolled down our cheeks. Every time we tried to speak we were unable to get the words out. I swear we laughed uncontrollably for at least twenty minutes, doubled over and completely oblivious to anyone around us.

When I glanced out the window, I saw that we had almost missed our stop. I reached up and quickly pulled the plastic-coated bell cord to signal the driver. As the bus slowed to a stop, we stood and held on to the sturdy metal pole, waiting for the back door to open. It didn't! I reached over and pulled the cord again. The door still remained shut!

We finally looked toward the driver to see if he was aware of the problem, and he motioned for us to come to the front of the bus. To our surprise, when we got there, he declared, "Ladies, there was no way I was going to let you off this bus without finding out what was so funny! I have never in my life seen anyone laugh as heartily as the two of you!"

Mom was quick to respond with, "We just had the best day ever!" Then she began to laugh again. I was too dumbfounded to speak, and quickly stepped down to exit the door.

"Mom!" I exclaimed after getting off the bus, "Why would you tell him we just had the best day ever? Nothing went right! It was an awful day!"

"Honey," she replied, "Any day I get to spend with you and laugh as hard as we just did, is the best day ever!"

I reflected on Mom's words as we walked the remaining five blocks to our home. She had to be much more tired than I was, yet she hadn't uttered one word of complaint. Instead she insisted she'd had a great day because she got the chance to spend it laughing with me.

I realized she was right. It *was* a great day filled with love and laughter! No matter what the situation, the two of us being together always made everything better. I smiled as I looked at her and said, "Thanks, Mom."

The decades have flown by. Mom and I have shared so much since that day in 1961 — from the births of my five children to the deaths of my father, brother and husband. We have continued to support each other through it all.

Ten years ago, Mom suffered a rather severe stroke and needed full-time care. Without hesitation I left my home in the capable hands of my youngest son and moved in with her.

Despite everything she has endured, my mother has never once complained. I feel privileged to spend every day with this courageous, optimistic woman.

There are times when I get tired and discouraged, but Mom's positive outlook and beautiful smile always get me through the difficult days and long nights. It is during these trying moments that I remember that bus ride home, and how Mom turned a disastrous experience into a beautiful, precious memory.

Thank you, Mom, for always showing me that the love and laughter we share as mother and daughter can triumph over even the worst of times. I promise you that we will continue to laugh for many years to come, because any day I get to spend with you *is* the best day ever!

~Connie Kaseweter Pullen

Mom's Texas-Sized Sacrifice

Grown don't mean nothing to a mother. A child
is a child. They get bigger, older, but grown?
What's that suppose to mean? In my
heart it don't mean a thing.
~Toni Morrison, Beloved

Sunday evenings are quite busy in my home. I am usually consumed with preparing meals, ironing clothes for the week, and reading bedtime stories, but one item on my to-do list is special. That is my weekly chat with Mom. We always talk church, family, and work. This particular Sunday's talk, however, was different.

"You know, I've been thinking a lot lately about how much I'm missing out on the boys' lives—milestones, school functions, and sporting events. In a few years, they will be graduating and moving on. What do you think about me moving to Texas?" Mom asked in an apprehensive tone.

To be honest, I couldn't believe it. Of course, we all would be elated if Mom moved closer, but could she just leave the only life she has ever known? How does one just pack up sixty-plus years in a matter of months and not look back? All of these questions swirled around in my mind while I attempted to process her question.

"That is a wonderful idea," I replied. "We all would be so excited to have you here!"

Mom put her home on the market and played the waiting game. Week after week, for three months, potential buyers viewed the three-bedroom, ranch-style home nestled between soaring oaks. Within a few months, the home sold. There were hiccups along the way, but Mom persevered, determined to be with her family.

Whether it was working the same job for thirty years, supporting my brother and me through school and extracurricular activities like dance recitals and tennis matches, basketball games, and bowling tournaments, or driving four hours to pick me up from college when I was sick with the flu, Mom has always been there. Whenever her children, grandchildren, siblings, or friends need her, she's always ready to assist.

The closing of one chapter breathes fresh, new life into another. Making the decision to leave behind a familiar home and life proves the great lengths Mom will go to for those she loves. Today, she is having the time of her life, for she is right where she longed to be... with family!

Never in a million years did I imagine my mother leaving her home to relocate to a new home, a new community, a new church, and a new way of life, but I wouldn't expect anything less from a mother whose heart is as big as the state she now calls home. As the saying goes, "Everything is bigger in Texas..." including Mom's love.

~Karla B. James

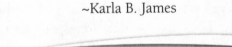

It's Never Too Late

It's never too late to be what you might have been.
~George Eliot

My mom sprinkles joy wherever she goes. Right now she is probably writing an encouraging note to a friend, complimenting someone she has encountered in the hallway, or reading the newspaper to an ailing resident in her retirement community. Or maybe she's planning the next show by the Prime Life Follies, an entertainment group she started ten years ago for assisted living complexes and nursing homes.

Growing up, my mom thought about becoming a dancer, but she didn't have the opportunity until after retirement. Then she joined her first group, The Hot Flashes. Once she donned the tap shoes, "Dancin' Grammy" was born.

There seems to be no end to her energy as she tap-dances her way into people's hearts, bringing smiles to sad places. But this is nothing new for my mom.

A lifetime educator, she was recognized in the 1980's as her school district's Teacher of the Year. I remember the evening phone calls to students' homes when she took a break from grading papers. They were not the typical bad-news calls many parents would expect. Usually she was calling about something positive. She recognized students who made small steps forward and helped even the unruly ones reach their full potential, revealing gifts they often did not see.

I was the youngest of seven children and life wasn't easy for my mother. I remember sitting on the back of her bike as she took me to a daycare center for low-income families on her way to Rosary College, where she was pursuing an education degree. At home she was tough because she had to be. It was not an easy childhood, but we learned from watching her. Her work ethic and determination trickled down to all of us.

I could write a book about my mom, and maybe I will someday. Better yet, we may write one together, as her dream to be a writer has not yet been fulfilled. But she got one step closer by attending the Erma Bombeck Writers' Workshop in Dayton, Ohio. We were a mother-daughter pair of newbies. Actually, we were known as virgins, officially "Erma Virgins." My mom was a lifelong Erma fan and for years she had talked about writing a book, so I knew attending this workshop would be a perfect Christmas gift. The three-day conference was jam-packed with information and helped launch our writing careers.

Day one started with our decision to "divide and conquer," a strategy designed to soak up more knowledge from concurrent sessions. But by the end of the day we had conquered not a thing except finding bathrooms and snack tables.

By day two we focused on companionship and together attended a workshop on the use of social media tools to build a digital brand. I peered over at Mom's notes, knowing she had no idea what Facebook Live was on "The Facebook," as she called it. Next, we found our way to lunch as the program began with the announcement of the conference king and queen. As the master of ceremonies spoke of a mother-daughter team she had met the previous day, I realized she was talking about us. I was overcome with emotion when we heard, "Will our new queen, Lori Mansell, please come forward with her daughter Julie?"

On the stage, the keynote speaker placed a bejeweled plastic crown on Mom's head, and the new queen was offered a moment at the microphone. "I've always wanted to be a writer, and you've all inspired me," she began. "This is a new beginning. I'm going to write a book. It's never too late!"

With that, the Erma Virgin had become the Erma Queen, inspiring more than 350 attendees from all over the country. Throughout the afternoon, fellow writers greeted her with bows and hand kisses. Selfies with the royal family became commonplace. The queen perfected her regal wave.

And just before we departed for our Indianapolis castle—home—we had a divine hallway encounter with the Bombeck family. After a photo shoot with Erma's children, we made our way to the car, and the Queen was on a cloud the entire drive home. The next day she sat down at her computer to draft her first story, "Queen for a Day," typing away with the crown still proudly secured on her head.

From mother of seven to grandmother of eighteen, Dancin' Grammy, now better known as the Erma Queen, continues to inspire everyone she meets. She has many titles, but my favorite is Mom. She has been a symbol of sacrifice, encouragement, perseverance, selflessness, and joy—all wrapped in bountiful, unconditional love.

May my mom's zest for living create a ripple effect, serving as an empowering example of kindness and encouragement to all who cross her path as she continues to tap-dance her way through life. No doubt her book will one day become a bestseller. There's nothing she can't do—even now at the ripe young age of eighty-eight.

Indeed, it's never too late!

~Julie Osborne

Mom's Macaroni Money

Candy is childhood, the best and bright moments
you wish could have lasted forever.
~Dylan Lauren

We didn't have a lot of money while I was growing up, but one would never have guessed. Mom and Dad tended a large garden that yielded wonderful crops of vegetables. They nurtured a flock of chickens that provided us with fresh eggs. Mom learned to sew, and made our clothes. She honed her cooking and baking skills by watching my grandmother, who lived next door, and soon rivaled her teacher in pie baking.

As the four of us — one boy and three girls — got older, Mom yearned to give us an allowance. After reading one of the hand-me-down women's magazines from Grandma, Mom found a way to do it.

She instituted a unique system of paying an allowance to each of us without actually using money. I was eleven, my brother Terry was nine, and our two little sisters were five and three. Each of us was capable of doing something to help Mom. She couldn't wait to try this innovative reward system on her children.

Each time we completed our assigned chores, helped her around the house, or gave a hand to a younger sibling, Mom wrote in a notebook she carried in her apron pocket. Four empty canning jars labeled with our names sat on the kitchen counter. Payment came in the form of elbow macaroni, each piece of pasta equivalent to a nickel. Mom recorded the macaroni transactions in her little notebook.

Once a week, Mom called us together and, as we danced around her, she placed the macaroni we had earned in our hands. We had the pleasure of depositing the little noodles in our jars. The younger girls, Judy and Gail, had to be reminded not to eat their allowance, as they both had a fondness for uncooked pasta.

At the end of the week, we got to spend a portion of our allowance by shopping at Mom's candy store. On our payday, Mom set up her little candy store on top of the clothes dryer in the laundry room. She took pride in displaying little wax bottles of flavored liquid sugar, wax candy lips, Tootsie Rolls, and packs of candy cigarettes. With our macaroni allowance, we could even buy full-sized candy bars. We nearly lost our minds with excitement.

On special occasions, some of our accumulated macaroni allowance could even be redeemed for cash. Mom taught us how to save for something special, and to this day, we value that lesson.

One day, Dad invited Terry and me to run errands with him. It was a big deal to be asked to go to town with our father. When Dad was done, Terry and I thought we'd head for home, but Dad parked in front of the corner drugstore instead. "Come on, let's get a treat," he said. We followed him to a bank of cushioned, shiny stools in front of the soda fountain.

Dad motioned for us to climb up on the stools. We twirled back and forth, grinning at our reflections in the mirror across from the long marbled counter.

Dad turned to us and said, "Whaddya want?"

Dumbfounded at having a choice, we stopped twirling and asked him what he was getting.

He said, "My favorite, a root beer float."

Terry and I ordered the same. If Dad liked it, we'd like it too.

When the frosted mugs were placed on the counter in front of us, we learned about instant gratification. We sipped and slurped the cold root beer until we had to spoon the ice cream out of the glass.

In subsequent days, we got in trouble for arguing over who was going to do chores for Mom. We annoyed her by asking over and over what we could do to earn more macaroni. Every so often, Terry and I asked for some of our elbows to be converted to cash instead of candy. We were then allowed to walk the quarter of a mile to the drugstore and that glitzy soda fountain. We always ordered root beer floats.

A few months after this wonderful allowance system was put in place, all four of us had dentist appointments for cleaning and check-ups. The dentist had gone to high school with Dad and felt quite free to express his alarm at the condition of our teeth. We all had cavities.

"What on earth has been going on, Mary?" he asked my mother.

She blushed and, without going into detail, admitted, "I guess I've been more lenient in allowing them to eat sweets."

And that, as I remember, was the end of Mom's macaroni allowance candy store, but the lessons we learned about earning, saving, and dental hygiene are still with each of us today.

~Nancy Emmick Panko

Snow Day

Be thankful for what you have;
you'll end up having more.
~Oprah Winfrey

The playground teemed with kids doing spins, flips, and daring feats of all kinds, including my own upside-down antics on the monkey bars. But then a familiar voice interrupted my act.

"Barbara, time for supper," called my mother from the edge of the play area.

"Okay," I replied, as I flung my knees over my head and prepared for an impressive dismount.

As Mom returned to our campsite and my tennies hit the soft sand, a new freckle-faced friend ventured to guess, "Is that your grandma?"

The carefree mood of the afternoon suddenly turned heavy. No matter how often I heard that question, I couldn't help but wince. Through a quick, quiet mumble, I admitted, "No, she's my mom," and ran to our camper.

Mom was thirty-six years old when she had me. When I grew up in the 1970s, thirty-six was on the older side for mothers. I felt different—sometimes even cheated—because of my "unique" circumstance.

There was Jody's mom, a savvy shopper the same age as my idol Olivia Newton John. There was Karen's mom, a bouncy city type who sported a colorful collection of jersey-knit miniskirts and other hip fashions. She even roller-skated on the weekends.

Then there was *my* mom. In comparison, she seemed unexciting, drab, and so out of touch with matters of "importance." I often chided her about everything that made her unlike my friends' mothers.

There were Mom's practical polyester pants: "Can we please buy you some jeans?" There were her weekly trips to Lorna's Beauty Shop for a set and comb out: "Can we please buy you a curling iron?" And there was her preference for Andy Williams over Andy Gibb: "Can we please listen to something else?"

But one blustery winter morning changed all that. That was when I saw my mom in a whole new light.

As a Minnesota fifth grader, my schoolmates and I lived for snow days. And, on this particular Tuesday, there seemed a direct correlation between the level of our antsiness and the growing mounds of snowflakes collecting on the metal frames of the classroom windows.

As spitballs flew across the room and ponytails were pulled by even the most reserved students, a "knock, knock, knock" sounded from the back of the room. I turned to see our formidable principal and was surprised to see my mom standing next to him in her parka.

"I've come for Barbara," Mom announced to my teacher.

My stomach lurched. Who was sick? Who was dead? There could be no other reason for her visit. As I put away my books and wriggled into my coat and boots, the curious stares of my classmates followed me to the exit.

When the door closed behind us, and all of the other kids were out of earshot, we paused as I donned my hat and mittens. I prepared myself for the bad news.

"The radio says that school will be closing at one o'clock," she revealed. "But I'd like you to come home with me now. Sound okay?"

"Sure," I replied, with the best nonchalance I could muster. Getting out of school before everyone else! I was the luckiest kid alive!

We threw open the school doors and trudged through shin-deep drifts to our car. I plopped down into the passenger seat. I thought we would head home, but despite the unplowed streets and swirling snow, my mom turned the car toward town.

"We have a couple of stops to make," she said.

She spotted a parking space outside the local five and dime. Her mission?

"First, some new puzzle books for our afternoon at home together."

Once inside, I had my pick of the magazine rack full of crosswords, jumbo word-finds, and *Archie* comics.

Kitty corner from the dime store was the grocer.

"I think we need some special snacks, too," said Mom.

Some chips. Some pop. A candybar. All of my favorites made their way into the cart.

Upon arriving home, Mom and I snuggled under quilts. We spent the afternoon watching game shows and cartoons.

It couldn't have been a better day.

It turned out that I was the only kid in town with a mom who allowed me to "skip" school and who treated me to my favorite things. I was the only kid with a mom this cool.

More than thirty years later, I became a mother myself at a very ripe forty-two years old, a whole six years older than my mom when she had me. Undoubtedly, there will be times when my daughter will be embarrassed by my existence, will wish she had a different mother than me — someone younger, prettier, smarter, richer, and cooler. But I was raised by a great role model. My mother was true to herself, and on snowy days and other days, she was always eager to make me feel special. These are the qualities that made my mom stand out from the rest. I pray I'll make a similar mark on my own little girl's heart.

~Barbara Farland

BEST MOM EVER!

Chapter 3

Wise Words

When your mother asks, "Do you want a piece of advice?" it's a mere formality. It doesn't matter if you answer yes or no. You're going to get it anyway.
~Erma Bombeck

The Full Moon

We are always together even though we are apart.
Though distance may be between us, we are
never separate in heart.
~Ethel GG Kent

I had just fallen asleep when the phone rang. I looked at the clock on the nightstand; it was 2:30 in the morning. The past three days had been intense, emotional, and heartwrenching. My mother was very ill and we were told she could pass away at any time. Her doctor had suggested we call in hospice to help us through the final days.

I struggled to wake up as I answered the phone. "Hello?"

The voice on the other end said, "Hello, may I speak to Sandy?"

"This is Sandy." I could feel the tears starting to build up and my heart beat faster.

"Sandy, this is Kim from the nursing home. You should come as soon as you can. Time is growing near for your mother."

"Alright, thank you Kim. I will be there as soon as possible."

"I already called your sister; she is on her way," Kim added before I hung up.

"What's going on, honey?" my husband asked as he turned on the lamp by the side of the bed. I struggled to keep my voice from sounding shaky. "That was Kim. It's time, so I'm going to get dressed and head out for the nursing home."

"I'm going with you," he said, and started to get up.

"No, that's okay. I'll go by myself. You have to go to work in the morning. I'll be fine. I'm going to call Gabriella. She'll go with me and I'll call you as soon as I get there. Go back to sleep." I went to his side of the bed and hugged him.

I knew my husband really wasn't prepared to deal with my mom's passing. He had a hard enough time dealing with what Alzheimer's had done to her. I got dressed in a hurry and called my niece Gabriella. She lived down the road so I would pick her up on the way to the nursing home, which was twelve miles away.

I noticed I was shaking as I put the keys in the ignition. I sat for a moment and told myself to calm down and think about what she was like before Alzheimer's. It was then that I noticed there was a full moon. It was big and bright, and as I pulled out of the driveway on to the road I remembered something from years before.

I was a senior in high school and graduation was just a few days away. I had just come home from a friend's house and I wanted to say goodnight to my mom if she was still awake. I tried not to make any noise as I walked down the hallway to her bedroom, and I caught her unaware that I was there, sitting on the edge of her bed looking out the window. There was a full moon and its light was so intense I could see her face clearly.

I stood in the doorway for a few seconds watching her. She was looking up longingly as though she was watching for someone or something. Then she looked over at me and motioned for me to sit next to her.

I sat down and put my arm around her, because for some reason I felt the need to comfort her. In a quiet, loving voice she said, "Isn't it beautiful?"

I nodded my head in agreement, for I had always loved a full moon, and then I asked, "Is everything okay, Mom? You look a little sad."

She smiled and hugged me and said, "Yes, I'm fine. I was just sitting here thinking about your brothers and sisters. I always do that when the moon is full. I hope that they are looking at it too, and it gives me a sense of connection. I started doing this when your oldest sister got married and moved away, and I have been doing it as each of my children has left home."

I could see tears in her eyes and for the first time I was aware of how much she missed her children. I hadn't realized how lonely she was and how much she needed that connection as each of us grew up and moved away. She placed my hands between her two work-worn hands and rubbed them lovingly. I always loved how warm and comforting her hands felt. They were strong, hard-working hands that made meals, did laundry, and soothed me when I was sick. I felt a lump starting to form in my throat and I knew this would be a moment I would remember for the rest of my life.

We sat there together enjoying the moon, and I wondered if any of my siblings knew about our mother's moonlight connection. After a while Mom broke the silence. She looked into my eyes and said, "You'll be leaving for Hawaii in a few days to help your sister after her surgery. I'm glad I could share this moment with you. You are my last baby to leave home, and I want you to remember I will always be sitting here by this window when the moon is full. And I hope no matter where you live you will watch the moon, knowing that I'm here doing the same thing. It will be a connection that we'll always share." Her face was expressing all the love she had in her heart for me.

That intense love has given me strength so many times over the years when life has gotten difficult. It helped me then in the car as I drove to the nursing home to say my final goodbyes.

By the time my niece and I arrived, my mother had already passed away. I walked into her room and one look at her told me she was finally at peace, free from the ravages of the disease that had taken so much of her away from us already. My sister and nephew had been with her and they confirmed she went peacefully in her sleep. I bent down to kiss her cheek one last time and whispered to her, "Mom, there is a full moon tonight. Don't forget to watch it from wherever you are. I'll be doing the same." As I walked out of the nursing home that morning, I looked up at the moon and knew she was watching and thinking of all her children.

To this day, each time the moon is full, I sit and admire it, sometimes for hours, and I always remember that night sitting with my mom and being surrounded by her love.

~Sandra Plawski

The Noisy Nest

The present moment is filled with joy and happiness.
If you are attentive, you will see it.
~Thich Nhat Hanh

The baby howled as I made my way down the two flights of wooden back steps. They were wet with snow and slippery. I gripped the rough gray railing with one hand and held my squirming daughter Kelly with the other. Her tiny face was scrunched with fury and her wails were so insistent that I felt frightened. My heart pounded as I made my way through the back alley and into the yard next door. I knew everything would be okay if I could just locate my mother.

She must have heard us coming because she stood still, broom in hand. She'd been sweeping snow from the walkway. Her cheeks were pink from the cold wind. Instead of a smile, she greeted me with concern. I knew she had read my face as I'd approached, just as she had all my life. "What's wrong?" she asked.

I held the baby out in surrender. The blanket flapped as my daughter flailed. "I can't take care of this baby," I said simply. My mother didn't take the bundle from my arms as I expected. She smiled slightly. She looked me in the eyes. And then she replied firmly, "You *have* to take care of that baby."

I stood, shivering and pondering. This was not the response I wanted. Couldn't she hear the baby crying? Couldn't she see that I was no good at this? I was waving the white flag. I wanted her to fix this problem, just as she had so many times before when I needed her. Instead, she shook the snow off the broom and took off her gloves.

"Come on in the house. I'll make some coffee," she said. I must have relaxed at that small offer of support, for at that moment the baby stopped crying... finally.

Mom held Kelly while I gripped the coffee mug tightly. "She cries if I hold her, and cries if I don't," I explained.

"Does she cry *all* day?" Mom inquired.

"Well, no," I admitted.

Mom continued: "She sleeps, drinks her bottle, snuggles up to you?" I wiggled in my chair, just as I had during childhood inquisitions. I glanced over at Kelly, content in my mother's arms. Her tiny blue eyes were fixed on me, as if to ask, "What's the problem here, Mama?"

I set the mug on the table and stood to reclaim my baby. Her sweet, familiar scent evaporated the stress in the air. Her tiny fist gripped my shirt, reassuring me that our bond still existed. I looked at my mother, feeling both foolish and relieved. She stood and placed an arm around my shoulders. "You were my seventh child," she reminded me. "By the time you came along, I was confident and experienced. But with my first child, you can bet that I often felt overwhelmed."

She ran her hand over Kelly's downy hair. The baby showed no signs of our afternoon struggle, while my own hair remained damp and disheveled from sweat and worry. "Crying is the only way babies have to communicate. Try to listen to her cries and hear them as language. She's not crying to annoy you; she's trying to convey a message with the only voice she has."

I looked down at my tiny infant and knew that I could never quit on her. Besides, my mom had made it clear that there was no backing out now. We would get through this newborn stage. My mother had gotten through it seven times! I thanked mom for her help. Once again, her gentle guidance had steered me through a storm and back into clear skies. As I headed back to my own home, Mom reminded me, "It won't always be so hard. Children grow fast. Before you know it, you'll have an empty nest and you'll miss her."

Kelly and I survived those early months. As Mom predicted, she grew quickly and soon mastered language. Her babbles turned to words, and then sentences. She chattered and sang and her soft voice filled my heart with warmth and love. We took long walks, hand in hand. My toddler became a girl, a teen, and then a woman as I watched in wonder.

One day, as I walked alone on the path we used to share, I heard a frantic commotion in a nearby tree. Three baby birds were wildly calling out, their necks stretched high. Their cries filled the air, sounding an urgent alarm towards the sky. With a whoosh, the mother bird swept in, rapidly filling the open beaks. She flew off quickly, and the babies resumed their loud and relentless pleas. Again, the mother reappeared, silencing them for a moment. I looked at her with empathy as she tried to smooth her ruffled feathers.

"It won't always be so hard, Mama Bird," I whispered to her. "They grow fast. Before you know it, you'll have an empty nest, and you'll miss them…"

~Marianne Fosnow

Deploying Intuition

One of the most important relationships we have
is the relationship we have with our mother.
~Iyanla Vanzant

I was fidgeting and nervous before entering the restaurant to celebrate my twenty-fourth birthday. My family would be meeting my new boyfriend.

Dinner went smoothly and at the end my boyfriend surprised us when the bill arrived. "I hope it's okay with everyone, but seeing as I won't be able to take Sarah out or buy her dinner for a long time, I would like to pick up the check tonight."

Randal was leaving the next day to finish his one-year deployment in Afghanistan.

I had always told my parents that I would never fall in love with a soldier. I didn't think I was strong enough to survive that kind of relationship, with all that time apart and so much danger.

We went back to my parents' house after dinner and my mother managed to steal Randal away from the group for a few minutes. I watched them share a private conversation and a hug.

The next day I watched the man I loved walk toward the plane that would take him thousands of miles away from me for eight months.

I knew that I wanted to be with him. To me, he was worth the wait and the pain that I would endure while he was away.

My mom comforted me. "That boy is so in love with you," she said. "I could tell from the first moment I saw him."

"Really?" I asked, giddy but unsure.

"Oh, yeah. Without a doubt. Don't be surprised if things progress quicker than you think."

"What do you mean?" I said.

"I can see him wanting to marry you. He told me last night how much you mean to him and I can tell you feel the same way."

I trusted my mother's judgment more than anyone else's and hearing her words gave me the reassurance I needed to go into this deployment confidently.

My mom was right! Randal and I fell deeper in love from opposite sides of the world. With nothing but a telephone and letters between us, we embarked on an adventure neither one of us was prepared for. Weeks later, Randal shocked me by proposing.

I needed the opinion of the person I knew would always be honest with me. "Mom, Randal asked me to marry him. Be honest; do you think it's too soon?"

"Sarah, love doesn't have a rule book," she told me.

Months later, after our wedding, my dad reminded me that I had once declared that I would never marry a soldier. It was my mother who helped me see the truth. She has always known what is best for me.

~S.L. Blake

The Red Jumper

The most important trip you may take
in life is meeting people halfway.
~Henry Boyle

I was four years old, standing with my arms crossed, my lips pressed into a thin line, and my brown eyes ablaze with indignation. There was no way Mom was getting me to wear that red corduroy jumper.

A good friend of Mom's had passed down the jumper to me when her daughter outgrew it. She probably assumed I would be thrilled. I was far from it.

"It's too red!" I shouted, as I stormed off to my room, trying to unbuckle one of the straps. My little fingers were not yet coordinated enough to unhook the metal from around the button.

My poor mother dropped her head. My tantrum was making us late for a family outing. She could not understand why I hated the jumper so much. The fabric felt stiff and weird on my skin, but my young brain was unable to express that at the time.

My mom, ever so innovative and smart when it came to dealing with my brother and me, came up with a plan.

"It's so cute. I just don't understand," she said. "Tell you what. Just try wearing it for today, and I'll never ask you to wear it again."

That worked. I wore it that one day, and never again.

Almost twenty-five years later, my four-year-old daughter sat on the floor wailing in a corner of my bedroom. Her big, brown eyes dripped tears that soaked her face. Her hair stuck to her cheeks.

She was enraged by my attempt to dress her in the flowery blouse she had picked out herself for preschool graduation. Five minutes before it was time to go, she changed her mind, and decided to put on an old, stained, and ill-fitting T-shirt that belonged to her older sister.

If we were headed to the park, a friend's house, or to the grocery store, I would not have cared. In that moment, however, all I could think about were the pictures we would take. This was her first graduation and she would care about those photos when she got older.

The rest of the family, including my mom, waited patiently in the living room for the clothing feud to end. We were at a standoff. I declared we were not going if she did not change. I stretched the flowery blouse out on the bed and told her she had five minutes to decide. Then I left the room.

"I'm so frustrated," I whispered as I walked into the living room. "I don't get it. I just don't understand."

I felt like I was not handling the situation well. I looked up to see my mom eyeing me from across the room.

"Hmm," she said. "I seem to remember a young girl throwing a tantrum over a red jumper. Maybe she gets it from her mother?"

I stood dumbfounded at how correct she was. Our lives had come full circle. I also remembered how she had calmly dealt with that outburst.

I turned and went back into the bedroom. My daughter stood wearing the new blouse, but looked very unhappy.

"Do you like the way this shirt feels on your skin?" I asked.

"No," she sniffed.

"I'd like some nice photos of you today while you graduate and get awards. I'm so proud of you that I want to take your picture. Is that okay?" I asked.

"Yeah," she said.

"I can help you pick out something else nice if you are not comfortable in this, or you can try out this new shirt and wear it to your graduation and then never wear it again," I said.

She thought for a moment, and then answered. "I'll wear this to graduation, but then can I give it away?"

"Absolutely," I said. My mom was right, as usual.

Even though I am a mother, a college graduate, and a business owner, it's clear there is still so much I have to learn from my mom. I am grateful I can pass her wisdom on to my children. Maybe in twenty-five years my daughter will turn to me when she's a mom, and I'll know just what to do to help her.

~Mary Anglin-Coulter

26

Silver Linings

If you change the way you look at things,
the things you look at change.
~Dr. Wayne Dyer

The summer I turned sixteen, I had surgery on both of my feet. It was my first surgery, my first experience with anesthesia, and the first time I would lose my mobility. I would be in casts for two and a half months.

Mom, however, could always be relied on for optimism. "Find the silver lining," she'd say. "There's always a silver lining somewhere, no matter how bad the situation gets."

After about a week of that motto I finally snapped and asked her what, exactly, the silver lining of my situation was. Mom didn't even have to hesitate before she said, "Once your feet heal, you'll be able to walk better. You'll learn new hobbies this summer that you wouldn't be able to do if you were out riding your bike."

Mom had to help me with the most mundane tasks for the first few weeks after the surgery. Movement exhausted me. Mom helped me brush my hair, go up and down the stairs, get to the bathroom, and even bathe. "Where's the silver lining?" I asked her. "I can't even brush my hair by myself!"

"I'm here to do this for you, and I don't mind," she replied calmly. "The silver lining is that you have a mother who loves to help you."

I grew restless inside the house and Mom offered to take me on walks in the wheelchair. We enjoyed going out after dinner to watch the sunset. As we watched the sky turn from blue to pink to purple, Mom would smile and say, "This is a silver lining: I get to spend this time with you."

When the casts came off but the pain didn't go away, and I couldn't walk any better than I had before, we learned that I had complex regional pain syndrome. The full impact of the situation didn't hit us until a while later, and that was the first time I remember seeing Mom hesitate. She remained steadfast, though. "There's a silver lining," she promised me. "We just haven't found it yet."

As my walking grew worse and I became more reliant on Mom to help me go to the grocery store, the bank, or the post office, she used to say, "I'm so glad that I'm able to help you with this. Remember; this is a silver lining."

This went on for several years.

Eventually, I had to give up my career as a chef because I couldn't handle the physical demands of the job. "What's the silver lining now, Mom?" I asked. "I don't know what to do."

"Now you'll get to choose a different career, and start fresh," Mom replied. "There's always a silver lining."

When I became an editor and told her I was going to write a book about invisible disabilities, Mom was ready, as always, to be optimistic.

"See?" she said with a smile. "There's your silver lining."

It took a long time, but eventually I learned that there was a common denominator in all of Mom's silver linings. She was right — they were always there. But she was the one who always found them, because so many of them had to do with her very presence. Now, thanks to her, I can find them myself most of the time. And I know that the biggest silver lining of all, no matter what happens, is her — my mom.

~Amy Anderson

27

Approved

A true soul mate is a mirror, the person who shows you
everything that is holding you back, the person
who brings you to your own attention so
you can change your life.
~Elizabeth Gilbert

My mother's illness had started about five years after my father died, the doctor pronouncing that she was in "no immediate danger." I allowed this statement to comfort me, which wasn't difficult, because my mother continued to produce marvelous textile designs, go out with friends, phone relatives, and have her hair colored.

Over time, though, her rare blood disease caught up to her. In our weekly phone calls, she confessed she had to stay in bed most of the time.

As my mother got sicker, my life was improving. I'd gotten a divorce after twenty years of marriage, but during my mother's final days, I met the man I knew was absolutely right.

By the time my relationship blossomed, my mother had been moved to the hospital. She refused to see friends and relatives, but I insisted on visiting. I tried not to look at the thin white hair she was no longer coloring. She always exclaimed how good I looked with my shiny bob haircut and trendy outfits.

At every visit, I adjusted her pillows, filled her water pitcher, and pulled up the chair beside her bed. She brushed away my questions about her health or the latest procedures and asked about me. We joked about my life A.D. — After Divorce. She saw my glow beneath the make-up, and, before I told her anything, asked who my new man was.

I gushed about Matt's dark good looks, sense of humor, fiery positive attitude and poetic gentleness, and especially his encouragement of my lifelong writing aspirations. She nodded, and I beamed, blushed, and kept talking.

It felt like high school. Most mothers and daughters coexist in frosty tolerance or outright war during adolescent angst, but we'd been like girlfriends. I'd admit my latest crushes, describe friends' constant re-pairings, and report the teacher gossip.

During those years, despite all the demands on my mother — family, household, and textile design assignments — she'd always made room for our talks. With a platter of her superb brownies before us, we'd suspend all diet resolutions and groan, giggle, and analyze everything.

In college, when I'd just met Franklin, the man I'd marry, I told her everything, and we planned my wedding down to the smallest detail.

Many years later, with trepidation, I announced my decision to divorce Franklin. She didn't gasp, lecture, or try to dissuade me. Instead, over a batch of fresh brownies, she supported me.

Now, as I told her about Matt, she was just as keenly interested, although emaciated and weak. Always the mother, she was putting others first. Surely she'd be justified in talking about her condition. Yet she dismissed my concerned questions with a casual wave of her hand and asked more about Matt.

Then, one day, I took her home, armed with instructions and medication. Later that week, she reported proudly that she didn't need to sleep as much and even went out a few times with her friends.

A month later, Matt asked me to go away for the weekend to a picturesque country inn. Thrilled and nervous, I immediately phoned my mother. We squealed, laughed, and started planning my wardrobe. The next day, I left a card on her kitchen table with the inn's phone number and ordered her to call day or night.

The weekend was glorious. When Matt and I had a little fight, we resolved it quickly, unlike the long icy sulks of my former days with Franklin. Instead, I apologized first, Matt hugged me, and we went for ice cream.

As we packed late Sunday night, my mother's call came through the inn phone. She said she'd fallen and blacked out.

"When did this happen?" I asked.

"Yesterday morning."

"What! Why didn't you call then?"

She said, "I didn't want to spoil your weekend."

I shouted, "I'm coming right over."

Matt drove me directly to her apartment. I helped her dress and took her back to the hospital. In the cab, even as she gasped in pain, she asked about my weekend.

The doctor stabilized her and then motioned me out in the hall. When he shook his head, I couldn't bring myself to ask how long she had.

I knew that now she had to meet Matt. She'd always put it off, likely believing she might embarrass me by her looks.

This time she agreed, and two days later, Matt came with me to the hospital. She was lying on four pillows, her hair combed. He leaned over the bed, put his hand gently on her arm, and kissed her cheek. I could see her eyes brighten as he talked.

I tiptoed out to the visitors' lounge across the hall. Fifteen minutes later, he came in and said my mother was asking for me.

I sat down beside her. Her eyes were glowing and tearing at once. "Yes, darling," she sighed. "He's the one." Exhausted, she fell asleep.

I kissed her on the forehead and tucked the covers tighter, trying not to let sorrow engulf me. Then I went to Matt in the lounge. We left the hospital, and I knew he could feel my joy at their finally meeting and the grief I couldn't stem. He steered me to a nearby café.

"I felt a chemistry," he said. "Her eyes were clear and she spoke distinctly. She seemed to have an urgency to get out what she wanted to say."

I nodded, my throat constricting.

"She looked square at me, right into me."

I'd confided a lot about Matt, but I had no doubt she had seen even more than I had told her.

He took my hand. "She looked so happy and then whispered — I'll never forget — 'Take care of her, Matt. Love her as I was never loved. I want to die knowing she has this.'"

I couldn't stop the tears.

A week later, at my daily visit, she looked even thinner, and her skin had a translucent glow. The pillows were stacked on the floor, and she lay flat in the bed.

Breathing with difficulty, she spoke quickly. "Your father and I were never really happy. I thought my love could cure his frustrations with his life. I did my best, acting like the silent good wife and suppressing my art, but it was a constant trial." She tried to sit up, and I calmed her back down.

She insisted, leaning on one arm. "Franklin was a fine man, but he didn't want you to be who you could be and grow in your writing. Matt — he's not afraid. I see how much he loves you. You deserve a real relationship, sweetheart."

She fell back. I kissed her and smoothed her hair. Three days later she died.

Now, married to Matt for many years, I discover daily his ever-deepening love. I wish my mother could know this man who believes in me, rejoices in my publications, and loves me despite a few more pounds and not so random acts of selfishness. I see her often in my mind, finding the strength to raise herself up in the hospital bed as she delivered her prophetic, precious legacy: "Matt's the one. Yes, darling, you deserve him."

~Noelle Sterne

28

Princess Sissy

Every girl deserves to be treated like a princess.
~Heidi Montag

I was on the playground one day, and some kids were making fun of the hair on my arms. Evidently it was thicker than the hair on their arms, so they were relentless and made me cry. "Oh, gross! Look at the hair on her arms. She's gross. Get away from her; she'll grab you with her hairy arms. Run!"

Needless to say, it was a bad day. I got home and snuck into the bathroom and shut the door. I took out my dad's double edge razor and started to shave the hair off my arm when suddenly my mom opened the door and grabbed the razor from my hand.

"Sissy, what do you think you're doing? You could cut your arm off!" Mom put the razor on the shelf and turned me around to face her.

"The kids were laughing at me because I have all this hair on my arms. They kept laughing and saying bad stuff about me."

"Do any of the other girls have hair on their arms like you?" Mom asked.

"No! Just ugly old me!"

"Do you know why the other girls don't have hair on their arms like yours, Sissy?" Mom said lovingly.

"Because they're prettier than me?" I said, sobbing.

"No, Sissy, it's because you're going to be a princess. How many princesses do you know?"

"Cinderella and... Sleeping Beauty and... I can't think of any more."

"Do you know why you can't think of any more?"

"No."

"It's because not every little girl gets to be a princess. Having a lot of hair on your arms is a sign that you will grow up to be a beautiful princess. Those other girls will just be normal women. You are special."

"I am? Did you have lots of hair on your arms when you were little, Mom?" I asked as I wiped my nose and eyes.

"No, Sissy. I'm just a woman with a very special little girl who will grow up to be the most beautiful princess ever. Now you know the secret of being a princess."

The next day I went to school with my little secret. One of the girls came up to me and made a comment about the hair on my arms. I smiled at her and said, "That's because I am going to be a princess. Look at your arms; you have hardly any hair. You're just a regular girl. I'm special. Only special girls get to be a princess."

All the girls were looking at the hair on their arms that day. Mom was right. Not every girl can be a princess. I was the only one in Mrs. Turney's second grade class.

~Bev Walters

29

My Mother Warned Me

Most mothers are instinctive philosophers.
~Harriet Beecher Stowe

Several months ago, I fell while walking my dogs down a country road. A passerby called 911, and three fire department vehicles responded. One of the paramedics peeled me off the asphalt and rushed me to the emergency room. My right eye was swollen shut; the left was masked by hair stuck to the grime on my face. Blood covered my T-shirt, and several gauze bandages did little to stop the flow. There was a steady pounding in my ears as I strained to answer the paramedic's questions. I lay there, trying to focus on a happy thought, concentrating on my Lamaze breathing, feeling almost tranquil, when a sudden fear shocked me.

I was wearing ratty underwear.

Throughout my childhood and teens, my mother told me to wear clean underwear, warning me, "If you ever have an accident..." The idea that emergency personnel would be more concerned about the condition of a patient's undergarments than injuries never occurred to me until I was an adult. Nevertheless, those and other words of wisdom stayed with me.

Over the years, my mother cautioned me against other dangers lurking in otherwise harmless situations.

Any trip to the beach or a swimming pool included a stern reminder not to enter the water right after eating food. As a child, I was too excited to bodysurf the waves to eat anything, but a mere glance at food was enough for her to make me sit on a blanket for a full twenty minutes. It didn't matter that I rarely ventured more than a foot into the water. If I'd had so much as a piece of chewing gum, I risked doubling over with stomach cramps that would render me helpless as the waves pulled me out to sea. Although experts no longer support that theory, I'm not ready to discount my mother's expertise.

When I was a teenager, "big hair" was in style. My mother made a few unflattering comments about my hairdo, none of which affected me. However, her tale of the girl whose hair was so teased that a spider nested in it and gave birth to baby spiders, which then bit her all over the head, had its effect. I didn't give up the look, but I was careful to do a daily spider check.

There were other cautions, most of which have been disproved; nevertheless there's something about a mother's admonitions that carries more weight than a hundred scientific surveys. I still don't read without full light for fear of going blind. I chew my nails and risk a build-up of clippings in my stomach. I know if I swallow watermelon seeds, a vine might grow inside me. And I know that if I crack my knuckles I might wind up with joints the size of golf balls.

I know that chicken noodle soup cures almost anything, leaving a scrap of food on a plate is wrong (because of the starving children in China), blasting music leads to deafness, too much television dulls the brain, and going outside in the cold with wet hair invites a virus.

Over the years, I must confess, there have been a few times I tossed caution to the wind and challenged my mother's advice. Although expert studies, common sense, and Dr. Phil have disputed much of my mother's reasoning, each time I ignore her logic, a slight sense of danger nips at me. No matter what the experts say, I know that somehow my mother is still right.

~Alison Shelton

Last Gift

*I cannot say goodbye to those whom I have grown to
love, for the memories we have made will last
a lifetime, and will never know a goodbye.*
~Author Unknown

"Your mom wants to see you right away. She said to bring paper and a pen," the aide relayed to my sister as she walked into the nursing facility.

"Mom, what is it you want?"

"Write down all that I am saying and read it at my funeral service and not one day before," my mom instructed.

For the next few weeks Mom shared her thoughts.

I had reservations about Mom's wishes to have her last words, mostly for her seven children, read at her funeral. I didn't want to hear something so personal for the first time in a room full of people I didn't know. But I knew it was what Mom wanted, so I kept silent.

In her final days she was under the care of hospice. The chaplain came to visit. We told him of the incredible legacy she left in her role as a mother, teacher, and friend. We shared how she cared for and was loved by so many. He asked if he could pray with us. Mom had woken up for a few minutes, and he asked, "Is there anything you would like me to pray for?"

Mom pointed to us, her children, and whispered, "All of them."

A few days later she passed into eternity. Her children, one of her former students, and one of her former co-teachers spoke at her service. We all told stories that inspired the audio/visual person to say to me, "I never knew your mom, but I wish I had. This is the best service that has been held here."

The last thing on the program was the reading of her final words:

To my friends and students: No greater blessing a woman could have than to have loving, faithful friends and caring students at the end of my life. You all gave me comfort.

To my children: I had the most wonderful kids in the world. I always tried to be a good mom and to make things special for each of you.

Remember walking together to church several miles on Sunday morning? Every night when you were little we said our prayers together. Though times were hard and we were dirt poor, we had laughter and fun. On Easter we would dye eggs with coffee and color them with crayons. One Christmas you kids went out into the fields and picked a tumbleweed for a Christmas tree. We decorated it with silver bells and angels made of cardboard and foil.

There was laughter at the dinner table, especially when I burned the biscuits. I remember you kids riding on my sack when we picked cotton. Your dad would always make sure each of you had a bologna sandwich, a soda, and a cookie to eat. We would earn enough money to go to the fair. Remember the good, forget the bad, and always have love for each other.

To Penny, my oldest daughter: God blessed me with a beautiful brown-eyed angel for my first-born. You were exactly what I ordered. Do you remember me telling you not to buy cheap perfume and not to read True Love magazines? I don't think you ever did. You were always a pleasant and sweet child and grew up to be a hard worker. I am very proud you have been a good wife and mom. Your dad and I loved it when you came to Redding to see us after we moved. It was like having a party. I could always depend on you. I was always grateful that you could show strength and courage in the middle of a storm.

To Marsha, my second daughter: Your name means war-like. You would come to live up to that name. You were my beautiful blond daughter that would break little boys' hearts. How were we to know you would grow up to be our protector in our last years of life? At times you had to overcome huge obstacles and yet you endured. Through your weakness you found strength. I hope that you will always be happy that God allowed you to be here, near your mama in her last days.

To Samuel, my first son: Sam was my true warrior. He faced difficult roads and endured until the end with faith and courage in the one who created him. [Sam had died years earlier from cancer.]

To Stephen, my second son: Thank you for treating me like a Great Lady. I always felt special when every Mother's Day you would bring me a corsage. Through your eyes I could see how much you loved and treasured me. No mother could have a greater blessing.

To Bruce, my number three son: When Bruce was born, he was sweet and special. When he came into the room he would always snuggle up to me and say, "I love you Mom." Bruce was my gentle giant. [Bruce died tragically at a young age.]

To Philip, my fourth son: You are my most patriotic child. I always believed you could be President one day. During your life I saw your strength and courage grow and watched you use your talents to overcome many difficult situations in life. You became a Godly husband and father. You were a true blessing to your dad and me and to all who are blessed enough to know you.

To Stanley, my youngest: You are my quiet and peace-loving child.

A true fisherman. I am happy to be your mother. I am so proud of the man you have become — patient, kind and soft-spoken. As we talked I found you, my son, expressing words of wisdom. I am so proud of you.

My Children, I am honored that God allowed me to be your mom. God was good to me because you all chose to follow Him. You have given your dad and me some beautiful and talented grandchildren, great-grandchildren and great-great grandchildren and wonderful sons- and daughters-in-law. Always remember to put your concerns and any problems in God's hands, He is capable of handling them.

Do not cry for me. I am happy in Heaven with Dad and Sam and Bruce. I will see you all when you get here.

Love,
Mom

Mother's last words confirmed what I already knew. In her eyes each of her children was special and unique. In her eyes each was her favorite — a child she could not have lived without. With her last words, she released her children to be free and happy. I will tuck away in my heart her last gift to me and the memories of my extraordinary mom.

~Penelope Childers

What Mothers Learn

The only source of knowledge is experience.
~Albert Einstein

MATERNITY CLOTHES
1st Baby: You begin wearing maternity clothes as soon as your OB/GYN confirms your pregnancy.
2nd Baby: You wear your regular clothes for as long as possible.
3rd Baby: Your maternity clothes ARE your regular clothes.

PREPARING FOR THE BIRTH
1st Baby: You practice your breathing religiously.
2nd Baby: You don't bother because you remember that last time breathing didn't do a thing.
3rd Baby: You ask for an epidural in your eighth month.

THE LAYETTE
1st Baby: You pre-wash newborn's clothes, color-coordinate them, and fold them neatly in the baby's little bureau.
2nd Baby: You check to make sure that the clothes are clean and discard only the ones with the darkest stains.
3rd Baby: Boys can wear pink, can't they?

WORRIES
1st Baby: At the first sign of distress — a whimper, a frown — you pick up the baby.

2nd Baby: You pick the baby up when her wails threaten to wake your firstborn.
3rd Baby: You teach your three-year-old how to rewind the mechanical swing.

PACIFIER
1st Baby: If the pacifier falls on the floor, you put it away until you can get home to wash and boil it.
2nd Baby: When the pacifier falls on the floor, you squirt it off with some juice from the baby's bottle.
3rd Baby: You wipe it off on your shirt, pop it back in, and compliment yourself on building your child's immune system.

DIAPERING
1st Baby: You change your baby's diapers every hour, whether the child needs it or not.
2nd Baby: You change the diaper every two to three hours, but only if needed.
3rd Baby: You try to change the diaper before others start to complain about the smell or it is visibly sagging.

ACTIVITIES
1st Baby: You take your infant to Baby Gymnastics, Baby Swing, Baby Zoo, Baby Puppet Show, and Baby Story Hour.
2nd Baby: You take your infant to Baby Gymnastics.
3rd Baby: You take your infant to the supermarket and the dry cleaner.

GOING OUT
1st Baby: The first time you leave your baby with a sitter, you call home five times.
2nd Baby: Just before you walk out the door, you remember to leave a number where you can be reached.
3rd Baby: You tell the sitter not to call unless there is bleeding.

AT HOME
1st Baby: You spend a good bit of every day just gazing at the baby.
2nd Baby: You spend a bit of every day watching to be sure your older child isn't squeezing, poking, or hitting the baby.
3rd Baby: You spend a bit of every day hiding from your children.

SWALLOWING COINS:
1st Child: When first child swallows a coin, you rush the child to the hospital and demand X-rays.
2nd Child: When second child swallows a coin, you carefully watch for the coin to pass.
3rd Child: When third child swallows a coin, you deduct it from his allowance.

FAMILY PHOTOS
1st Baby: You snap a shot of every new milestone: first burp, first smile, first sitting up, first tooth, first banana, first step, first birthday party...
2nd Baby: You take photos of the two kids together.
3rd Baby: "Mommy, how come there are no pictures of me?"

~Chava Dumas

BEST MOM EVER!

Chapter 4

Always There for Me

Parental love is the only love that is truly
selfless, unconditional and forgiving.
~Dr T.P.Chia

A Pot of Tea

Each person's life is lived as a series of conversations.
~Deborah Tannen

I got off the bus and slowly walked up the driveway to our house. It had been my first day of high school... an exciting, confusing, scary day. I had gotten lost moving between classes a couple of times, ending up in the wrong halls. I didn't know most of the kids and I felt overwhelmed by all the new people I was meeting.

I walked into our house physically and emotionally exhausted. My mom took one look at my face and put the water on to boil. Within minutes, we were sitting at the kitchen table with cups of heavily sweetened tea and homemade cookies. My sisters weren't back yet from their schools, so I had my mom's full attention.

This was a treat because Mom was usually so busy, caring for my grandmother who lived with us and my two younger sisters, who seemed to need her attention more than I did. I had begun to feel like my voice couldn't be heard over all the other noise in the household.

Mom and I sat at the table talking for more than an hour. She asked me questions about how things had gone, and by the time the hour was over, I had begun to share my fears, concerns, hopes, and plans.

The next afternoon I slowly walked up our long driveway again... still tired, still anxious, still questioning if I was going to survive high school. When I opened the door to the kitchen, I saw my mom sitting at the table waiting for me. The pot of tea was already made. The cookies were on the plate. The two cups were set out.

As I walked through that door that day, and every day for the rest of that year and the next, my mom waited for me at the table with a pot of tea and a plate of cookies. And an hour to explore what I was experiencing, who I had met, how my classes were going. There was no limit to what I could share with my mom. And there was nothing on my mind that she didn't care about.

Mom and I kept that daily appointment until she went back to work, bringing in the income that would enable me to go to college. When our afternoon tea days ended, I felt a great loss. Yet, I was confident there was nothing I couldn't share with her.

I have my own daughter now and she has a daughter. I make sure to spend focused time with each of them as well. There's nothing like a regular heart-to-heart talk to build a relationship and create a wave of confidence to carry our children forward.

~Margie Williamson

My Cheerleader

A daughter-in-law cannot be perfect by herself. A
beautiful mother-in-law helps her be one.
~Author Unknown

Before I met the man who would become my husband, I worried. First I worried whether I would ever meet him at all. Then I worried about whether he would take my career seriously — I am a writer, and I know that it's easy for someone to say he supports and values your work, but harder to share all the rejection and uncertainty without ever so much as implying that maybe you should get "a real job."

Finally, I worried about his mother.

I do possess qualities that mothers tend to appreciate. I am calm and a good listener. I'm relatively tidy, do not drink or smoke, and love to bake. However, my career is not a stable one. The mother of the man I almost married years ago had wrinkled her nose every time my writing came up in conversation. She had talked about all the young women she knew who were making "good, honest money" in traditional office careers, with paid vacation time and Monday to Friday workweeks.

When I received a prestigious writing fellowship to move to California and work on a book, it came as no surprise that she didn't see why I would ever take it — and, it quickly became apparent, neither did her son. When we broke up, I vowed to myself that I would not settle for anything less than a partner who truly appreciated and valued my writing career. However, it seemed like too much to hope for a mother-in-law who would do the same.

I met Allyn, the man who became my husband, on a rainy February night at an ice cream shop, when no one in her right mind would be craving ice cream. It felt like a scene from a movie: the fogged-up windows, the cozy warmth of our conversation, the ice cream melting in our small paper cups as we talked and talked. It was immediately obvious how close Allyn is to his family — as I am to my family — a trait I very much admire. But it made me even more nervous to meet his mother.

Indeed, it wasn't long before Allyn invited me to lunch with his mom, Barbara. We picked her up at her house — a gorgeous, stately home on a shady tree-lined street. Barbara came out to the patio to greet us, a lovely woman with a genuine smile and a warm hug. I loved her instantly.

"I'm so happy to meet you!" she exclaimed. "Allyn's told me so much about you. I hear you are… a writer?"

And there it was: out in the open.

"Yes, I am," I said hesitantly, trying to gauge her expression. "I moved here for a writing fellowship, actually. I'm working on a novel."

"A novel? Oh, how amazing! I would love to read it sometime."

I realized a curious thing about Barbara that day, and in the days and weeks to come. She was not showing interest in my writing to be polite, or to make conversation. She was being sincere.

"I'm not a writer myself," Barbara confessed to me later that first afternoon, as we drank iced tea and flipped through an album of Allyn's baby photos. "But I have always loved to read and I admire writers so much. The way you are able to weave magic out of words."

With every photo Barbara turned to, she had a new story to share — detailed, funny, intricate. She made me feel like I was part of the events she described. And I suddenly realized why I felt such an immediate connection with her: while she may not call herself a writer, she is surely a master storyteller.

For her birthday that year, Barbara insisted there was only one thing she wanted from me: a manuscript copy of my novel, newly finished.

Nervous but excited that she wanted to read it, I printed out all 300 pages and spiral-bound it into a book. When Barbara unwrapped the gift, she began to weep. Tears sprang to my own eyes. Never before had someone treated my work with such reverent joy.

Like my own parents and brother, who have always been my biggest fans, Barbara reads everything I publish — stories, essays, book reviews, blog posts. She curates a growing stack of books and literary journals and spiral-bound manuscripts I have given her, which she shows off to guests as her "Dallas Shrine." Any time I thank her for believing in me and showering me with so much support, she shakes her head like I'm being ridiculous. "Honey, writing is your gift. It's what you were born to do. No belief necessary — it's a fact!"

Her words buoy me up and keep me going. When I receive yet another rejection letter from a publisher, when I face the blank page of writer's block, when yet another promising market or contest yields only disappointment, and it feels like I might never reach that place I am so diligently and earnestly striving for — I think of Barbara, my new mother-in-law, waving her pom-poms for me proudly from the reader's chair. She makes me feel a little more sure of myself, a little more hopeful, and a lot more loved than I did before she came into my life.

~Dallas Woodburn

A Phone Call Away

No mother and daughter ever live apart, no
matter what the distance between them.
~Christie Watson

It was moving-in day. I was exhilarated as we set up my dorm room. But as I stood on the lawn with my mother, watching the other kids happily wave goodbye to their parents, it hit me — I was going to be alone. I started to cry and I held onto my mother as though she would disappear from my life without a trace once she got in the car.

While I had been away from home without her before, those trips were always short. This time we'd be separated for most of the year. I was not ready for this.

My mother was crying, too. But through her tears, she tried to reassure me. "I will call you tonight," she said. "You can call any time, even at three in the morning; I will always answer. And we'll see each other soon. Thanksgiving is not that far off. You'll see."

Those words and the phone calls helped me immensely those first few months.

I called her constantly, but I still missed her and phone calls could only do so much.

I made one quick visit home in October for my mother's birthday, but I mostly focused on my schoolwork. Math class was particularly challenging, so when I got an A on a project, I was thrilled. But when I called my mother to tell her, I broke down in tears.

By the time she answered the phone I was already sobbing. I didn't like the fact that I had to *call* her to share my good news. I wanted to *be* with her, to tell her in person. I told her that I was done and I wanted to come home.

My mother made shushing noises, and when I was finally quiet, she said in a soft reassuring voice, "Listen to me, you *can* do this. I know you have worked hard and will work harder to make me proud, like you always do. Just because we are miles apart does not mean that I'm not with you. You are stronger and smarter than me. You are capable of more than you think. I'm always only a phone call away, day or night."

That conversation lasted another three hours.

I have never forgotten her words. Nor have I forgotten the numerous conversations after that. My mother always made time for me.

Sometimes I find myself being critical of my mother's choices. And while I admire her fierce personality, I sometimes wish she would remember we are different people. I'm a bit of a hermit. She's not. That is frustrating for her, but she never judges. After all, she's the one who spent hours upon hours on the phone with me my freshman year. I know I can rely on her, whenever, wherever, however. I hope that I will be the same kind of mother one day.

~Leila Feliciano

She Did It with Dresses

A mother is the truest friend we have.
~Washington Irving

I got dumped the spring I was nineteen. There was no official goodbye. He just announced he was spending the summer with friends three thousand miles away.

My parents had liked him, but they didn't react when I shared my news. They were stoic New England people, children of the Depression. They kept their emotions hidden. I did, however, notice a sideways glance and eyebrow language pass between them.

The following weekend, my mother casually commented that it would be nice to pick up a few new summer dresses. She didn't say anything about my ex, but clearly she was taking me for some retail therapy.

I picked out a swingy violet sundress, a teal pin-tucked rayon, and a black knit sheath. I felt much better, and while I was thanking my mother I said, "We should enjoy breakups more often."

I never saw that boy again and I wore the violet dress from that curative day to my rehearsal dinner several years later. It seemed like a fitting way to celebrate my new life, with the right guy.

My mother's love was quiet and intuitive. She knew just what I needed, and she did it gracefully, without lengthy laments, sunny sermons, or positive pep talks. She knew that I needed to feel bright and pretty again.

   She did it with dresses.

~Allison Howell

She Was There

*Happy is the son whose faith in his
mother remains unchallenged.*
~Louisa May Alcott

Mama had my brother when she was twenty. I came along two years later. My dad was a juvenile diabetic and lost his eyesight at the age of twenty-nine. They divorced shortly thereafter, and he moved an hour away. We saw him every other weekend and for a few weeks each summer until he died a few years later.

My mother was thirty-one, raising two headstrong boys by herself with very little money. She didn't have time for housework and she didn't attend PTA meetings. She wasn't ever going to be crowned Mother of the Year, but that didn't matter. She wasn't a hugger, but we knew she loved us. She disciplined us when necessary and ensured we were in church every Sunday morning.

Mama worked full-time at a factory. I think her pay peaked at seven dollars an hour while my brother and I still lived under her roof. She wound up working there a total of thirty-seven years. It would've been longer, but the plant shut down. In the eighteen years I lived with her, I recall her missing only one day of work. She set a great example for her two boys.

It wasn't easy for her and it wasn't always pretty. The house was a mess, and I don't mean just a little clutter here and there. It was filthy. The house was infested with roaches and there was no air-conditioning, so the house was always warm and muggy.

We didn't have the best of anything, but we always had something, which is more than some can say. We had a roof over our heads, although at one point the ceiling literally fell in. There were times the utilities were disconnected. We had a couple of cars repossessed. Sometimes we had mayonnaise sandwiches for dinner, but at least we didn't go to bed hungry. My mother did the best she could, and I'm grateful for that.

Somehow, she managed to take us on a vacation every year — to Florida, the Smoky Mountains, and Washington, D.C. Sometimes she had to borrow the money to fund these trips. Perhaps she could've spent that money on other things, but I'm grateful she showed us a life outside of poverty. It gave us something to strive for.

My mother wasn't a strict disciplinarian but she could mete it out when necessary. I remember when I got caught playing hooky from second grade for a whole week. Mama only became aware of my truancy when she received a call from the school secretary. She raced home in her old car, with sparks flying up from the undercarriage when it crested the driveway. When she got through with me, I couldn't sit down for a week. That was how things were done back then. It worked for me.

She was a devoted fan, too. My brother played football, and she was there for every practice and every game. I wasn't much of an athlete, but she was there when I was in the fifth grade spelling bee. I came in second and she was proud.

In high school, she let me drive her to work in our one old working car, so that I could drive to school instead of taking the bus. We didn't have much, but driving my own car to school seemed pretty special.

Shortly after high school, I moved out of the house. I just needed to spread my wings. Since the house was literally falling in, mama moved in with her longtime boyfriend, who she later married. Just a few months later, my wings were clipped, and I thought I had nowhere to go, but I did, of course. They welcomed me in, no questions asked. When I needed her, she was always there.

She was there at midnight when my car broke down on the

Interstate when I was going for my Army physical. She was there when I graduated basic training at Fort Leonard Wood, Missouri. She was there when I received my bachelor's degree from Auburn University at Montgomery. She was there at Fort Benning to pin on my rank when I was commissioned as a Second Lieutenant in the United States Army. She was there at the armory when I returned from my third tour in Iraq. She was there the first time I worked with comedian Jeff Foxworthy. She was there when I got married, and she was there when I went through my divorce. She was always there.

As my comedy, speaking and writing career continues to grow, I find myself doing some pretty cool things. Recently, I was flown to Tampa on a private plane for an event. My sixty-six-year-old mother had never flown and had vowed to never do so. On a whim, I jokingly asked her if she wanted to go. She did. It was one of the best days we've ever had, and the show was one of the highlights of my career, mostly because she was there. As always.

~Jody Fuller

Hidden Treasure

*All I am I owe to my mother. I attribute all my success
in life to the moral, intellectual and physical
education I received from her.*
~George Washington

Mom was selfless. She would stay up late into the night typing my term paper or hemming a new dress I wanted to wear. Then she'd fix me Cream of Wheat in a glass to drink as I got ready the next morning so I wouldn't leave for high school on an empty stomach. We lived in the country, but Mom cheerfully drove me and my five siblings all over town.

She enrolled in college after she finished raising us, earning a master's degree in special education. Then she continued pouring love, healing, and individualized instruction into a new generation of children.

Later in life, Mom developed Alzheimer's disease. About that time, I published my first chapter book for kids. Excited, Mom pulled out a manuscript she'd written years before and asked if I would help her get it published. She had submitted it to publishers way back when, but she wasn't willing to make the changes they suggested. Now she was ready.

We read the manuscript together — a mystery titled *Hidden Treasure* set in the foothills of the Ozark Mountains during the Great Depression. I laughed at her talking animals, but marveled at the descriptions of the settings. I felt like I was there. The plot was captivating and realistic. My mom was an incredible author!

She had to explain so many things to me… farm life in general, the Dustbowl, tramps roaming the countryside, one-room schoolhouses. She drew a map so I could picture the locations of the farm, the school, the cave, and the underground river.

Aside from a few visits, we worked long distance. I lived in Texas and she lived in Indiana. We would talk for hours on the phone as I drove to work and back. Like Mom, I was a teacher.

Mom's world gradually darkened. She was no longer able to live on her own. Diabetes, crippling arthritis, and COPD added to her physical difficulties. She became depressed and slept most of her days away.

At times, when I called, she couldn't even remember what she'd eaten for lunch. But when I brought up her book, she came alive.

I would read an edited scene to her, and she would argue that I had messed it up. One particular time, as we talked about an incident where the young girl in the story fell at school and hurt herself, Mom said, "You mentioned the wrong side. The bump was on the left side of my head."

Ah. My first awareness that much of Mom's story was true. No wonder she enjoyed reliving those scenes. No wonder she recalled vivid details of the setting and the clothing the characters wore. No wonder she was adamant about the dog being named Hector. We're talking major ownership here!

In the end, complications from COPD took my mom's life before Alzheimer's completely stole her memory. I am thankful for that.

As I sat by her bed in her dying hours, we talked about her finished book. I promised her I would get it published someday and dedicate it to her grandchildren.

Day by day, she faded in and out. Her lucid moments grew less frequent. But she could pull it together when necessary. At one point, my eight-year-old nephew came to visit Mom. I was amazed when she opened her eyes wide and asked to be propped up in bed. She then carried on a complete conversation with him about school and how much she loved him. He didn't stay long, and Mom immediately went back to sleep when he left.

When I saw how she was with my nephew, I yearned for the same kind of contact. I wanted to be young again — to run into my mother's arms and hear her say she loved me. I sat on the edge of her bed and rested my head next to hers on the pillow. My eyes filled with tears as I shut them and tried to drink in the sound of Mom's breathing and feel the heat of her body next to mine.

Then she touched my cheek and gently wiped away my tears. I opened my eyes to find hers filled with tears as well. "I love you," she whispered weakly. "I love you so much."

I crumbled and stretched myself across her body. And Mom, who hadn't the strength to even lift her arms ten minutes earlier, wrapped her arms around my body and kissed my face.

She was Mom again. The mom I knew growing up. The mom I needed and depended on and had taken for granted. Selfless. Caring. Loving. "I love you," I whispered, so grateful for the privilege of calling my hidden treasure "Mom."

~Barbara E. Haley

Making It Work

What do girls do who haven't any mothers
to help them through their troubles?
~Louisa May Alcott

I thought the dress would be perfect for my first high school formal dance. "Look what I bought today!" I exclaimed to my mom.

"Wow!" my mom said. "It's beautiful."

Then she looked at the v-shaped neckline. I could feel her hesitation begin to brew the way you can feel a storm that's about to roll in.

"The neckline seems a little low," she said. My fourteen-year-old eyes rolled so far back in my head I could have seen the kitchen sink behind me.

This wasn't the first time my mother had reacted to my necklines. I'd worn tank tops that she stared at intensely, as if she could will the fabric to grow and turn a scoop neck into a turtleneck. I'd worn camisoles that she'd tug at until the fabric practically reached my collarbones.

My excitement about my dress — a $19 find in a sea of $200 dresses — was a diminishing as her disapproval rose.

"Well, why don't you try it on?" my mom suggested. Ah, a glimmer of hope, I thought.

I zipped up the gown and shuffled out to hear the verdict. Mom's face scrunched up like Lieutenant Columbo's as she solved the mystery of how to cover my adolescent cleavage.

"I have an idea!" Mom exclaimed, and she lifted up the tiny ruffled train from my dress and held two inches of it across my bust line.

"What do you think?" she asked.

I didn't respond. I was unimpressed at the notion of having my plunging neckline decorated with a tiny curtain to cover my cleavage.

"Let me just try it," she said. "You won't notice this little bit of fabric removed from the train and I'll sew it so it will blend right in. It will look like it was designed this way."

I was willing to try anything if it meant I could wear the dress to the dance.

When the alterations were complete, my mom was right. Somehow she was able to sew the extra fabric into the bust line as if it had been part of the original design. No one would ever notice — or so I thought. I was at the dance when a very voluptuous senior strutted onto the dance floor wearing the same dress. Well, not the *exact* same dress. Hers did not include a modesty panel.

I remember thinking on the dance floor how embarrassed and upset I should have been. But I wasn't. Instead, all I felt was cared for and loved. I had a mother who, when faced with something that made her uncomfortable, worked to find a way to keep me happy.

I'm twenty-eight years old now and my mom no longer tugs at my tops to cover up cleavage. Well, not all the time at least. But change, and stepping outside her comfort zone, is still a challenge for her. I especially stretched her comfort zone when I accepted a job in a city I'd always dreamed of moving to: New York.

"I guess I feel like once you move," she said, "you'll stay there and never come back."

I was sad to imagine this as a possibility. I assumed after having the experience of living in New York City for a few years, I'd eventually go home to Michigan.

Now after three years of working in New York City, I've been promoted twice at my job. I'm loving how convenient and active my life can be in the city compared to my rural zip code in Michigan, and I'm in a relationship with the most wonderful man. Will I ever go back to Michigan? The guilt I have for choosing to live 800 miles away from my family surfaced during a recent visit home. I felt like

I should be in Michigan with my family, especially my grandparents, so I could fully enjoy the time I have left with them.

"You should never feel guilty about living your life," my mom said to me. "You have so many great things happening for you in New York, and that's all your family wants for you."

"Plus," she continued. "Your time in New York isn't done. You still have more to accomplish there. You can't come back now!"

This woman who hates change strongly supports me living away from home, almost as strongly as she used to pull up my tank tops. My mom has always put my happiness first and has found a way to make my dreams come true, whether it's altering my formal dress or learning to live with me so far away. My happiness is her priority and I am grateful.

~Katelyn Stanis

Love Is Spelled Bev

If you just believe in me, I will love you endlessly.
~Mariah Carey

Our family had suffered many medical hardships that left us stressed and in poverty. My mom, Nancy, didn't want us to miss out so she let us spend time with others who could provide experiences that she couldn't give us. Sometimes this meant we ate dinners with other families or didn't celebrate our birthdays with her.

In my case, I often had dinner and played board games at my boyfriend Tommy's house. His mother Bev showered me with kindness and encouraged me to achieve greatness when I was a teenager.

She was compassionate and knew some of the difficulties my family faced. I remember her telling me, "Kelly, the one thing in life that can't ever be taken from you is an education. Pursue higher education to empower yourself. It's always comforting to know you can provide for yourself."

She not only encouraged me to work hard and achieve, but she also exposed me to the very things that could be gained through success. She did this by including me in her family outings, which often involved theater and fine dining. I remember being in awe of the fancy hotels with marble halls and crystal chandeliers. I was wide eyed and grateful for each new experience they shared with me.

When I turned eighteen and graduated from high school, Tommy and I got married. We had two wonderful years together until he died in a motorcycle accident.

Unfortunately, as part of my grieving process, I thought I should separate myself from Tommy's family, and that meant abandoning Bev. I wanted to be left alone with my pain.

The amazing thing was, just like my own mother's love, Bev's love for me remained steadfast. As I moved on with my life, attending college and striving for some of the very things she instilled in me, she watched from a distance and encouraged me. When I found love again, married, and had children she was right there. And I was ready to go back to her.

Bev welcomed my husband and children into her life with a compassionate and loving heart. Even when others questioned why she would welcome my new husband into her family, she says, "That is my Kelly and that was my son's Kelly. He would want her to be happy and loved, with my support."

More than twenty years have passed and I have seen that neither grief nor love have expiration dates or rigid rules. Just as Bev has room in her heart for me, my husband, and our children, they have room in their hearts for her. The kids call her "Aunt Bev."

I am truly the lucky one. I have the love of my mom, two mothers-in-law, and a wonderful husband, who accepts and respects that my past is part of my present. The funny thing is that both my mothers-in-law are named Beverly. I don't believe that is a coincidence; instead I see it as another one of love's miracles.

~Kelly Hennigan

Better than Cool

The more I live, the more I recognize that the teaching moments in my youth, especially those provided by my parents, have shaped my life and made me who I am.

~Robert D. Hales

Certain words always come to mind when I think of my mom. Honest and kind. A hardworking farmer's wife. She is definitely a lady who isn't afraid to get her hands dirty. However, there is one word I'm sure I never used to describe my mom: cool. Lord knows I wished for it — especially during my teen years.

My best friend had a cool mom. Patty's mom wore stonewashed jeans and sang along to Madonna. I wasn't sure *my* mom had even heard of Madonna.

Truth be told, Mom and I didn't have much in common. I loved checking out the latest styles at the mall. Shopping gave her a headache. I enjoyed traveling and exploring new places. She was a homebody. In high school, I was captain of the pom-pom squad. She played the accordion.

However, there was one thing I always appreciated about my mom: she was a fabulous listener. Every day I came home from school and told her about my day. I could tell her anything — the good, the bad and the boring. She always listened, even when I told her things she didn't want to hear. Like the night I went on my first date.

It was a double date, actually. Two popular boys had promised to take my friend and me to dinner and a movie. They pulled into the driveway and honked the horn. Of course my mom wasn't okay with that. She crossed her arms and gave me a look.

"If he wants to date you, he can come in and get you."

As it turned out, I should've left him in the driveway. The boy was a loser. The date didn't go well. Later that night I returned home and marched up the steps to Mom and Dad's bedroom.

"How was your night?" Mom stifled a yawn. Dad snored.

"Terrible," I said. "They didn't take us to dinner. We didn't see a movie. Someone got alcohol and they spent the entire night driving around back roads, drinking beer."

"What?" Dad mumbled, half asleep. Mom elbowed him.

"I swear I didn't drink," I said, plopping onto the bed. "I didn't want to drink. I just wanted to come home."

Thinking back, I'm surprised I even told her. After all, she had every right to be upset. Instead, she just listened. She didn't overreact. Dad never learned to master this skill. Mom did it well, time and time again. So I kept telling her stuff.

After high school I moved out on my own. I called my mom often, mostly for cooking advice. Dad liked to tease me when he answered the phone.

"Is Mom there? Is Mom there?" he huffed, acting offended. "Doesn't anyone ever want to talk to me?"

"Okay fine," I said. "I'll talk to you. How long does it take to hard-boil an egg?"

After a few seconds of silence, Dad cleared his throat. "Here's Mom."

Life went on. I went to college, got a job and met my future husband. Curt and I got married one beautiful day in May.

At the end of the ceremony, we faced the congregation and grinned as our pastor belted out an official introduction with his best preacher voice. "Ladies and gentlemen, I present to you Mr. and Mrs. Curtis Zeck."

There was something very symbolic about that moment. We had walked into that place on our own, but we would leave together. I squeezed Curt's arm as we took our first step back up the aisle.

As we approached the first row, I glanced at my mom. She looked lovely — even with damp eyes and a red splotchy face. As mother-of-the-bride she wanted to look pretty. I thought about how she had struggled to find the right dress. She didn't like to shop. She didn't like many of the current styles, yet she wanted to make sure I liked what she wore.

Within a few years, Curt and I were expecting our first baby.

My husband was wonderful, but sometimes a girl just needs her mom — even if she is about to become one herself.

Between contractions I picked up the phone.

"Mom, I'm scared," I said, whispering into the phone. "I don't think I can do this. I'm totally exhausted. This is just too hard."

Mom's tone was sympathetic, but firm. "I know it's hard, but you can do this. Labor lasts only so long and then it's over. Think about holding your sweet baby."

Six hours later I called Mom again. "She's here," I said, looking down at my beautiful baby girl. Mom was right. Joy had replaced pain.

It didn't take long to realize I had no idea how to care for a newborn. Thank goodness Mom was only a phone call away.

"The baby has a bumpy rash all over her tummy. Should I call the doctor?"

"Should I give her some cereal before putting her to bed?"

"How many diapers does a normal kid go through?"

Mom always warned me that babies grow quickly. The years flew by. Two more baby girls joined our family. Today, I can hardly believe I have three teenagers.

If ever I needed Mom's advice, it's now. It amazes me how Mom managed to keep her meltdowns to a minimum during my teen years. I needed to know her secret.

"So how'd you do it, Mom?" I asked. "I told you stuff, but you never freaked out. How did you keep your cool?"

Suddenly, I caught myself smiling. After all these years, I had described my mom, and I used the word "cool." So cool, in fact, I wanted to be like her.

"Oh, I definitely freaked out!" she said, laughing. "I just waited until later. I tried to stay calm when I was with you."

Now there's a skill I hope to master someday.

My mom never dressed in cute, trendy clothes or listened to popular music, but she always gave the best advice. She encouraged me through good times and bad. She's my lifelong friend.

Today I realize what a special gift that actually is. Not everyone can say their mom is their very best friend.

I can.

And I think that's pretty cool.

~Sheri Zeck

41

Box of Love

I remember my mother's prayers and they have always
followed me. They have clung to me all my life.
~Abraham Lincoln

When I was little I followed my mother around like a shadow, never leaving her side. I would bury my head full of curly brown hair into her chest whenever I met someone new.

When September of 1999 arrived, and I was starting preschool, I was nervous. The night before my first day my mother surprised me with a special gift. She sat at her vanity holding a rectangular box wrapped in faded paper with pastel flowers on it. It was no bigger than the palm of her hand. My big brown eyes grew wide at the sight of the little box. Was it a necklace? A bracelet?

"It must stay wrapped," my mother told me softly. The gift was neither a necklace nor a bracelet; inside was something of a much higher value than any piece of jewelry. "This box is full of my love," she said. Her grandmother had given her this box many years prior, when my mother was just a little girl. On the side of the box was a small poem written on paper that time had turned yellow. My mother read part of it aloud:

This is a very special gift that you can never see. Whenever you are lonely
or even feeling blue, just hold the box close and know that I think of you.

I stashed that box deep inside the front pocket of my new pink backpack. And the next day, when I sat alone on a tiny blue chair while all the other children played, I suddenly remembered that box. I could see its outline through the fabric. Just knowing it was there was enough to ease the loneliness and fear.

Day after day the box of love traveled to and from school with me. It took several months before it returned to its home safe inside my mother's closet. And now, I still carry that box of love with me wherever I go, in my heart. It provides the support that I need as I navigate my new world as an adult.

~Katelyn Mills

BEST MOM EVER!

Chapter 5

The Strength of a Mother

*There's something really empowering about going,
"Hell, I can do this! I can do this all!" That's the
wonderful thing about mothers, you can
because you must, and you just do.*
~Kate Winslet

42

Fifty-One Hours

*Mother love is the fuel that enables a normal
human being to do the impossible.*
~Marion C. Garretty

The brevity of the text message from my mother-in-law conveyed the urgency of the situation more than the words themselves did: "Come out now. Need you." I ran outside and found my wife collapsing in the driveway, speaking incoherently.

Time seemed to stand still, yet the minutes flew by in a blur. I remember calling 911. I remember running out front to meet the paramedics. I remember the baby crying. As my wife became less and less responsive, I remember watching the rise and fall of her chest, to make sure she was still breathing. I remember the ambulance, and the team that greeted us at the hospital.

A diagnosis came quickly — a hemorrhagic stroke in the basal ganglia, caused by post-partum preeclampsia. In plain terms, my wife developed a condition in the days following the birth of our son Oliver that caused her blood pressure to spike, ultimately resulting in a ruptured blood vessel deep in her brain.

As my wife lay in the ICU, paralyzed on one side and unable to speak, I sat next to her in a chair and researched her prognosis on the Internet. Though knowledge is supposed to make you feel empowered, everything I read deflated me. Her particular type and location of stroke was among the most serious — fatal more than half the time.

Survivors tended to have debilitating long-term deficits.

We had waited a long time for this life and I couldn't believe we were losing it so soon. More than twenty years after our first date, following years apart and a miraculous reunion, Amy and I had finally married. And then our little boy Oliver had arrived after what seemed like a relatively uneventful pregnancy. Our new little family had only been in place for fifty-one hours.

It was surreal. How could our dream slip away so quickly? How would I ever care for our baby alone? Could we ever return to the life we envisioned?

Amy slept most of those first few days — an effect of the trauma to her brain, as well as the medication being used to lower her blood pressure. With our newborn in the care of family, I sat at her bedside day and night — never really asleep, never really awake. Despite the dozens of wires and monitors hooked up to her, I still found myself continually watching to make sure she was breathing. With every breath, there was hope. She was still with us. She was still fighting.

The nurses brought a breast pump in from the adjacent maternity ward, and we began to pump milk and send it home to Oliver. Even when she was in the ICU, my amazing wife was still taking care of her baby.

As the days and nights passed, a miraculous thing happened. The bleeding in Amy's brain stopped. The swelling began to subside — and as it did, little by little, my wife returned to me. Sensation and movement came back on her weak side. Speech started to return. A relentless drive emerged from her weakened body — a drive to get stronger, to improve, to be Oliver's mom again.

Several days later, mother and baby were finally reunited in our home. It's an image I'll never forget. Amy, still wearing her ID bracelet from the ICU, holding her baby and crying tears of relief and joy. For his part, Oliver remained asleep, blissfully oblivious to all the drama.

The doctors said she was lucky. It would require months of rehabilitation but the life we had planned was still possible.

I sometimes wonder what I'll tell our son about those weeks. Thankfully, he won't remember any of it. He'll have no memory of his mom being rushed to the ER when he was just days old. He won't remember how worried everyone was, or how many different people held him while his mom recovered in the ICU.

By the time he's old enough to understand any of this, time will have already begun to dull our memories of it all. Time does that. But I'll make sure he always knows that his mom moved heaven and earth to get back to him. I'll tell him how she surpassed the doctors' expectations at every step. He'll know that she stood when they said she couldn't, and spoke when nobody expected. He'll know that her first sentence was, "I miss my baby."

To him, she'll just be "Mom." But he'll quickly figure out how amazing she is, and how lucky we are to have her in our lives. I'll make sure he always knows that she waited a long time to be his mother, and nothing was going to keep her away from him. Nothing. Not even a stroke.

So many moments will forever be burned into my memory. The image of Amy taking her first step or saying my name. The sight of her walking the last two steps from the wheelchair to the car on the day we brought her home, adamant that she was going to walk on her own.

Mostly though, I'll remember my incredible wife sending milk home for her baby. And I'll be reminded that — at her worst, fighting for her life in the ICU, before she could even talk or walk — even at that moment, she was still the best mother I've ever known.

~Rob L. Berry

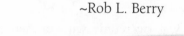

A Second Chance at Seventy-Eight

My mom is my hero. [She] inspired me to dream when
I was a kid, so anytime anyone inspires you to
dream, that's gotta be your hero.
~Tim McGraw

As Purcell's trumpet processional played, friends and family rose to their feet in honor of the radiant bride who gracefully made her way down the aisle. The bride looked dazzling in her cream-colored gown. It was adorned with tiny crystals that reflected the rays of light streaming through the windows. As she made her way past each pew, the bride warmly smiled at the guests, until her gaze finally rested upon the groom, whose eyes welled with tears.

In that moment, I was overcome with immense emotion. For the woman who walked down the aisle was not my daughter, or my sister, or a dear friend. Amazingly, this woman was my seventy-eight-year-old mother.

I never imagined that my mother would get remarried, particularly at such a late stage in life when many people struggle with health issues, financial insecurity, or a fundamental loss in purpose. Indeed, my mother had gone through her fair share of adversity. But unlike her peers, my mother was not done with living. She was once again demonstrating that you're never too old to chase a dream.

My mother first arrived in the United States from South Korea back in 1964 when she was just twenty-six years old. She planned to pursue a Ph.D. at the University of Kentucky. Although she came with only one hundred dollars in her pocket, my mother was filled with optimism and excitement for the future.

On a trip to Massachusetts, she visited my father, who had also immigrated to the States from South Korea in search of a better life and education. They had grown up together. My mother decided to stay in the city of Cambridge to be with my dad and to pursue her studies there.

With that one decision, her life took a drastic detour down a path fraught with unforeseeable challenges. As is often the case, her life became intermingled with both unbearable heartbreak and moments of boundless joy.

Shortly after their marriage, my father began to manifest symptoms of bipolar depression. At that time, not a lot was known about mental illness, and it was never discussed in Asian households.

It was confusing and distressing for my mother to routinely find my father unable to get out of bed or go to work. These long periods of depression were punctuated by manic phases, where my father incessantly labored on outlandish business ventures. Unable to sleep, my father went on spending sprees, abused alcohol in an effort to self-medicate, and even struck out in violence. This gentle man turned into a virtual stranger overnight.

To support our family, my mother was forced to work two full-time jobs during the day and night for several years. Despite the enormous pressures imposed by my father's illness, my mother's spirit never broke. Amidst her eighty-hour workweeks, my mother still came to my soccer games, sewed my school costumes, and surprised us with small gifts. We always knew we were loved.

It was no coincidence that my mother was born in the Year of the Tiger according to the Chinese zodiac. This is not to say my mother was a modern day tiger mom who demanded academic perfection from her children. No, my mother was a tiger who fiercely fought against the outside world while being utterly tender at home. No one could have guessed that the same woman who fended off the foreclosure of our home could sing so softly to us each night.

After almost two decades of marriage, my mother made the exceedingly difficult decision to separate from my father in order to protect our family. Ironically, while our family became a "broken" one to the outside world, this dramatic shift made each of us more whole, as my siblings and I were spared from further instability and outbursts from our father.

My mother could have completely collapsed under the burden of responsibility as a single mother to four children. However, she had greater plans for us all.

At the age of forty-six, my mother embarked on a new career in life insurance. While this was not the career she had imagined for herself as a young child, she chose this career since the earnings were entirely dependent on the agent's efforts and sales. My mother knew she could outwork almost anyone if it meant that we could attend college. I remember her working from dawn until dinnertime, when she would take a short break to eat with us. And then she would head back to the office until ten almost every single night.

My mother's herculean efforts paid off. Within five years of becoming an agent, she became the top salesperson in her company and broke all sales records, despite English being her second language. I watched in amazement as my mother transformed into a true professional who was repeatedly recognized with corporate awards and a queen-size income. I'll never forget the moment when my mother read an article in *The Boston Globe* and realized that she had earned more than the president of Boston University that year, a highly respected man with the doctorate degree she once desired. Although she never had to say a word, my mother drove home the message that someone could embark on a new career late in life and still wildly succeed.

During this time, I graduated from high school and college. And most fortunately, my father re-entered our lives after coming to terms with his own disease. Hard won acceptance and subsequent medical treatment fundamentally changed my father into a peaceful and contented man who cherished being with us.

Although they never remarried, my parents reconciled and stayed committed to each other until his death six years ago. People could not understand their continued closeness after all the trauma my mother had endured. But she still felt emotionally committed to this man with whom she had shared marital vows and grown children. Even on his deathbed, my mother was still loyally by my father's side.

Almost one year after my father's passing, an unexpected phone call altered my mother's life yet again. A mutual friend who had grown up with both of my parents in South Korea reached out to my mother. Although many decades had passed since they had gone to middle school together, he had secretly harbored a love for my mother all that time.

He never revealed his feelings to my mother until after my father's death. And in the few years that followed, my mother fell in love with this ebullient and intellectual man with whom she shared leisurely walks, competitive ping pong matches, and lively discussions about literature.

Which brings us to their wedding day.

Seeing my mother walk down the aisle stirred several contrasting emotions inside me. With each step forward, my mother created a different path for her future. It was an alternate ending to what I had expected, yet still full of promise and joy with a new companion who unconditionally offered his heart. This was enormously comforting.

I also admittedly felt profound loss for my father who had passed, and the countless opportunities that my parents had missed along the way due to mental illness that went untreated for so long.

But mostly, I felt immeasurable gratitude to my mother. With each step that she took, my mother showed me that second chances in life are indeed possible for those who keep the faith and continue moving forward.

~Pauline Koh-Banerjee

Unexpected Blessing

Life is what happens when you're
busy making other plans.
~John Lennon

My sobbing daughter stopped my world. "Mom, I'm pregnant." She had just finished her first semester of community college and she was only eighteen. Only a month before, I had let her move into an apartment near campus with two other students. It seemed so practical, relieving her of a long daily commute, and giving her more time and energy for studying and her part-time job. I knew that she was still dating her high school sweetheart. But, naïve as it sounds, I didn't see this coming.

There was no question she would keep the baby. While the dad would stay involved to some degree, she would be a single mom. And thus began the first day of the rest of our lives.

I told her that I would do everything I could to help her be a good mom. She could move back home, but she had to stay in school and keep working "until her contractions started." She could take one quarter off from school after the baby was born, and then go back full-time until she completed her degree. Then she would get a job and support herself and her child. She agreed.

Over the months, as her baby bump became a baby beach ball, reality began to sink in. She saw her peers moving in a direction that was no longer open to her. The plans and dreams she had just months before were no longer feasible. The overseas internship was gone, as was the promise of a job in San Francisco after graduation. She knew she needed to stay close to family for practical and emotional support, at least for some years to come.

Her social status changed. She was no longer the popular, carefree, spontaneous center of her social circle. She faced the judgment of friends and even some family members. It hurt. Friends drifted away. Even friends that stayed could not understand the changes in her life and the joy she wanted to share. There was sadness mixed with her excitement.

But she moved forward. The formerly self-absorbed, live-for-the-moment teenager began to think of someone besides herself. On top of work and school, she took birth and parenting classes. She ate healthy food. A crib appeared by her bed. The friends who stuck by her gave her a baby shower. Instead of modeling the newest fashion, she now held up baby clothes and marveled at the thought that her baby would be wearing them.

She and I grew closer. The mom who didn't know anything became the mom who knew everything. Of course I didn't, but she was scared and I became her safety net. We sat on the couch while she ate strawberries and pineapple (her daily craving), and talked about life and love and how everything was going to be okay.

And then it happened. We almost didn't make it to the hospital in time. Her uneven contractions led us to believe she wasn't in serious labor yet. She didn't want to go and then be sent home. Finally, I made an executive decision and loaded her in the car and off to the hospital we went. They settled her in a room. The nurse checked while Mia cried and asked if they were going to send her home. "Nope," the nurse said briskly, "you are going to have a baby!"

And so she did. Somehow my little 5'2" baby girl pushed out a big, slippery, healthy baby boy. I cried as they placed him on her stomach. He looked just like her. And in a miraculous transformation she became a mom.

As planned, she took a quarter off from college and spent, as any mom knows, exhausting days and sleepless nights falling in love.

When it was time to go back to school, she arranged childcare and set off with two backpacks, one with her books and the other with her breast pump. She called between classes to check on the little one, and required many photos texted to her throughout the day until she could get back home to him.

It wasn't easy. There were lots of tears and a few setbacks. But oh how she loved that child. I watched her come home so tired and then light up when she saw him, finding renewed energy to play and feed and rock him to sleep. She never rushed her time with him, even though she had homework to do after he went to sleep.

Everything she did now, she told me, was for him. She still had plans and dreams, but they were different plans and dreams — the plans and dreams of a mother, full of love and responsibility.

Two years later, she graduated. I held her son while she walked across the stage to get her diploma. Two days later she had a full-time job. As promised, she had finished her education and gotten a job.

I was so proud of her. And a bit in awe. She was a much better mother than I was at the beginning. I was older and more prepared, but still grew gradually into motherhood. Luckily, my children survived all my mistakes and ignorance. Where did she get that sense of command and confidence about raising her son? His paternal great-grandmother and I laughed with affection and admiration at how she made sure that we followed her instructions when he was in our care. New mothers much older than her sought her advice.

Her son is five now. Last year she married a wonderful man. He said that he fell in love with her when he watched her with her son. He fell in love with both of them. And they both fell in love with him.

What I initially saw as a tragic event in our lives has become our greatest blessing. My daughter is fulfilled and happy. So happy! As is her son, who, when asked who has the best mom ever, enthusiastically replies, "I do!"

~Galen Pearl

45

Cracks in the Clay

*My mother is my root, my foundation. She planted the
seed that I base my life on, and that is the belief
that the ability to achieve starts in your mind.*
~Michael Jordan

My three-and-a-half-year-old daughter's shoes keep slipping off because they can't contain her excitement. Her feet move too fast for the poor shoes to hold on. My eighteen-month-old son simply takes his off, but I can see the bare cement floor is cold for his toes. He lifts his arms for me to pick him up, and he too is squirming with eagerness. We're visiting my parents in rural Alabama, and today we get to play in my mom's pottery studio.

All the things they're told not to touch on a regular basis are finally available to them: the sponges, the stamps, the wedges, the clay itself. Choosing the color of the glaze is a decision my daughter makes with the utmost gravity. Her eyes are shining with pride.

My mom shows my daughter how to roll out the clay, how to make it pliable and then flat. Her new interest is slab pottery, so today we're making bowls.

"I can eat my cereal in my new bowl?" my daughter asks. We've told her yes already, but the idea of making something she gets to use is beyond exciting. She wants to be sure we won't change our minds.

We both nod — my mom behind her, guiding the rolling pin, while I help her little brother pick out the stamps he'll use. My daughter helps him choose the letters in his name to press into the clay. He picks out a dragonfly stamp and wonders what clay tastes like.

"All right, are y'all watching?" my mom asks as she scoots a mold the color and shape of a half-moon under the clay.

They crowd around her workstation as she shows them how to curl the sides, and how to use water to seal and smooth the edges. I step back to take a picture of the three heads bent together in this endeavor, my heart full to bursting at how they listen so attentively, the light catching on their baby curls.

When it's my turn, I realize it's harder than it looks. My bowl is misshapen and the kids giggle because theirs look better. I was paying attention to them more than my mom's instructions.

"Well, you should've seen the fairy tea sets your aunt and I used to make when we were little," I tell them. "Linlin would give us extra bits of clay; then we'd paint them with sparkly nail polish. Fairies loved 'em."

"I'm pretty sure I still have them," my mom says.

My daughter's eyes light up. My son is hungry, and since we're not letting him eat clay, he wants something else — blueberries from the bush outside. My mom lets them run to it, their short legs pumping in the grass, scaring up tiny bugs that catch the morning sunlight like flakes of gold confetti celebrating their presence.

The pottery wheel in the corner catches my eye and I walk over to it, the room suddenly silent without all the noise of two little children. It's a manual wheel. I give it a kick and it barely budges. My mom has a newer one now, but this is the one she used when my sister and I were little, when we'd make cups and saucers for fairies. It's been through floods, too heavy to move when we had to evacuate. I loved when we were young and she'd let us practice kick, our short legs stretching to reach. Then when our muscles started burning or we fell off the bench seat, she'd take over and it was like a queen taking her throne.

I look again at the picture I took with my phone and realize what a gift it is.

And to think it almost didn't happen.

The pottery wheel had stopped spinning for a while as her world turned to government-mandated testing and meetings and more paper-work that went along with her job. My sister and I were a handful, too, as we got older, trying to figure out who we wanted to be in the world. Sometimes we made bad decisions and that pain we caused diminished her creative spark.

She had to devote her time to molding and shaping us. She couldn't dedicate the time she needed to her craft.

Having her artistic outlet cut off was suffocating her. Her fingers ached for clay, for the ability to create something beautiful out of a lump.

She was cracking but hid it so well. Until she finally had enough. Thankfully, she knew herself well enough to know the cracks that needed to be filled could only be patched with clay. So she ordered some and bought glazes. She took classes to reacquaint herself with her lost creative side. Now I bring my own children to experience the joy of allowing creative talents to flourish.

I choose the glaze for my bowl that I'll never use. My art comes from my words, not from my hands. Then I join them outside by the blueberry bushes.

"Look at my tart face, Mommy!" My daughter grimaces comically. My son laughs so hard he falls down. I wrap my arm around my momma's waist and lay my head on her shoulder.

"I'm so proud of you," I whisper. "Thank you."

She smiles. "For what?"

But I can't put into words the fullness my heart feels, so I squeeze her tighter, then let go. I pop in a tart blueberry, a little pink on top near the stem, and scrunch my face in exaggeration as my kids laugh and laugh.

"For giving us this," I should've said. "For being the best mom ever."

~Candice Marley Conner

46

Amazing Amanda

Marriage made you family, love
made you my daughter.
~Author Unknown

N ot every woman would have been as optimistic as
      Amanda when she learned she might have a baby with
      Down syndrome. Amanda took it all in stride, even
      when the diagnosis was confirmed. She welcomed
Lilly with open arms.

When Amanda's husband admitted some months later that he
didn't love Lilly as much as he should because she was born with a
disability, Amanda moved on into the world of single parenting. Yet
those who met her for the first time were still astonished at her upbeat
energy and her ongoing optimism.

I met Amanda when Lilly was under a year old. From the moment
I held her and she laid her sweet little head on my shoulder I was
smitten. I wasn't just smitten with Lilly, though. I was quite taken with
Amanda, too. A young single mom with little money, she took a job
with a bus company so Lilly could accompany her to work. In between
work she juggled doctors' appointments — there were many — as well
as therapies to improve Lilly's chances for walking and speaking. She
did all this with a smile. I rarely heard her complain.

A few months later, Amanda began dating our middle son. That
meant we got to spend more time with her — and Lilly, too. We came to
think of them as family as we watched this amazing mother constantly

put Lilly ahead of herself. She pinched pennies and worked long hours, but Lilly never went without. Amanda did her research and found resources to provide the things she couldn't afford for her little girl. We were impressed with how she never complained and always smiled, even in the midst of frequent trips to doctors' offices and emergency rooms. Those first years with Lilly were filled with constant health crises.

When our son Jim proposed to Amanda we were thrilled.

Today Lilly is a happy, smart, quick-witted ten-year-old. The fruits of Amanda's — and for the past six years Jim's, too — parenting efforts are apparent when Lilly walks into a room. Articulate and sociable, she always asks, "How's your day?" She is so much like her wonderful mother.

Amanda's constant optimism hasn't wavered in the years we've known her. It's contagious, and has rubbed off on so many of our family members and friends. Amanda was truly blessed with the birth of Lilly, and we've been blessed by the presence of both of them in our lives.

~Kimberly Ripley

My Hero Doesn't Wear a Cape

*A hero is someone who has given his or her life
to something bigger than oneself.*
~Joseph Campbell

M y hero doesn't wear a cape, she doesn't have super-powers, and she can't fly, but she is the Best Mom Ever. She can wash clothes, clean the house, and still make time to deliver warm bacon and cheese sandwiches to my nephew at school.

When I was a young girl, my sister was the person I looked up to. Since our parents worked most of the time, my sister took care of me. She made sure that my homework was complete, my clothes were clean, and I ate dinner. She never complained. She simply took charge as she always does.

Ten years ago, while pregnant with my nephew, my sister was diagnosed with pericardium cardiomyopathy. This condition causes a galloping heartbeat, shortness of breath and eventually heart failure. My parents were presented with an option. If she delivered her baby early, her condition would improve, but the baby might not survive.

My parents made the decision to keep my sister on life support while she recovered from the illness that threatened to take her away from us. She spent nearly three months in Baltimore at the medical center. Miraculously, she recovered and delivered a healthy baby boy.

Armed with a pacemaker and nothing more than her strength and resolve, she has shown me what can be accomplished regardless of disability. Although she can't walk the entire grocery store without growing tired, this single mother cares for my autistic ten-year-old nephew and my sixteen-year-old nephew. She makes it look easy, but I know that it isn't.

She tries to hide her exhaustion, but I can hear it in her voice and see it in her slow gait. It is an inspiration watching her do all that she does with such severe health limitations. My hero is less than five feet tall and has a defibrillator keeping her alive. Nevertheless, she has been able to care for not only her two children, but also our parents, in a way that can only be described as selfless.

~Leah G. Reynolds

Two in One

*She has to have four arms, four legs, four eyes, two
hearts, and double the love. There is nothing
single about a single mom.*
~Mandy Hale

My mother and I have always been close. I like to think that our mother-daughter relationship has always been different from others. My father died of a drug overdose when I was three and my mother also became the father figure in my life.

Shortly after my father passed away my mother lost her job. She didn't know what to do. She decided to enroll in grad school. It was a struggle for her. She didn't have a job, she had to pay her tuition, and she was taking care of her young daughter (me).

Fast-forward six years. My mother earned a master's degree in psychology. She's currently working at a summer camp for children who have selective mutism, and yet somehow she still manages to make time for me. We joke around, play games, even binge-watch *Downton Abbey*. She's more than just a mom — she's a mom, a dad, a supporter, and a best friend, all in one.

My mom is the most inspiring woman I have ever met. She does everything. She goes above and beyond. My mom is the best mom *and* the best dad ever.

~Shannon Thompson, age 11

Superglue

A mother is she who can take the place of all others
but whose place no one else can take.
~Cardinal Mermillod

I remember closing the door on the station wagon to go into school that day. I also remember my mother calling me back to open and close it again, so I thought that I had just not closed it well enough. It wasn't until my mother picked me up from school that I realized it was something else. My mom's hand was wrapped in bandages and she had a splint on one of her fingers. When I asked her what had happened, she did not want to tell me, but I begged her to.

Of course she assured me that it wasn't my fault but I was devastated. I know I cried and that my mother probably cried, knowing I felt so bad. It would be a while, though, before I realized that a broken finger was not going to stop my supermom.

When I was in middle school, my father was working in the steel mills in Pennsylvania. He was laid off four times; each time the layoffs were just the beginning of the mill going out of business. During that time, my mother actually worked four jobs to keep food on the table. She was a schoolteacher, a newspaper reporter, a typing teacher at the local community college, and a server at the country club. Yet, we still lost our house.

It was devastating, but my parents made the most of it. With two weeks to move out, we found a small country house to rent a few miles away and moved everything in our Jeep. My mother even sat on the bottom of our eight-foot sofa, with the top hanging out the back of the Jeep. Her willingness to roll up her sleeves and do what was needed, with a smile on her face, really helped.

A few years later, I was in high school and she was still working several jobs while my dad worked as a night security guard. One night my mother returned from a meeting and was about to head back out to the newspaper to write up her story. She slipped on the wet steps to our deck, cutting open both knees. She was convinced that she could just change her pantyhose and continue on to the paper to file her story. We had to convince her to stay and called our father to come home and take her to the hospital. It required several stitches and bandages, which we thought might keep her down for a few days. Of course, she was up bright and early the next morning, going on with her work and that article; it was put in the next day with no further delay.

Less than two years later, my father got a job in Georgia, far away from our home in Pennsylvania. Despite our protests, my mother led the way, parenting us without him for several months and leading us in packing up our house for the movers. We left after my older sister's high school graduation ceremony, climbed in the car and took off for Georgia. My sister and I swore we would return north for college. We both ended up graduating from the University of Georgia and stayed home through college, which pleased our mother.

It was my mother who suggested that I call the handsome young man who had given me his number while riding the bus at college. I was not sure if I should, but her words, "Call him, you never know how you will meet your husband," were prophetic when I married that wonderful man less than a year later.

When my mother finally became an empty nester she tried to fill her life with work and church. At church, she heard about a beautiful young girl who needed a family. After discussing it, my parents realized that they did not like an empty house. They ended up adopting four more children over the next several years and hosting several foster children.

I soon realized how lucky I was to have such a strong, close family when my husband went hunting and never returned home. His body was found at the bottom of a tree, the broken tree stand lying beside him. That night seemed to last forever as my family drove across the state to be with me as I buried my soul mate. They continued to support me as I moved back home and went back to college to change careers as a way of dealing with my grief. When I had lived at home long enough, it was my mother who insisted that I move out and become independent again.

Several years later, as I came to realize that I would probably never remarry, my parents took in two young boys as foster children. The two tumbling towheads quickly won my heart and, when my parents decided that they were too old to adopt children that young, I decided that I would adopt them instead.

My parents fostered the boys until I was cleared to adopt and have supported me ever since, caring for the boys while I'm at work. Even though I am technically a single parent, I really am not. I have my parents, and especially my amazing mother, backing me up.

It was my mother's strength and determination that helped me become the strong woman and mother that I am today. She is also the superglue that has held my family together through many challenges. The love that she has given not only her biological children but her foster and adopted children and grandchildren is her legacy. I am thankful every day that I was born to such an amazing mother.

~Melissa Basinger Green

The Boxes in the Basement

*If the whole world were put into one scale,
and my mother in the other, the whole
world would kick the beam.*
~Henry Bickersteth

W e all have heroes, mentors, and people who have influenced us, encouraged us, and motivated us to reach new heights. Some of my personal heroes include political figures like Sir Winston Churchill, Thomas Jefferson, Abraham Lincoln, and Ronald Reagan. Some are sports stars like Peyton Manning, Walter Payton, Michael Jordan, and Pat Tillman. My other heroes and mentors are mostly people you do not know. One of them is named Gwen. She was my mother.

My journey began during an afternoon of spring-cleaning in my basement. It was late April, the week before Mother's Day 2015, when I was surveying the treasure trove of stuff that had collected over the years. As I began sorting through various artifacts and relics I had been hoarding, I encountered two tattered cardboard boxes. I suddenly recalled that I had inherited them from my late father four years before. I had never looked inside them.

My curiosity and anticipation were childlike as I rummaged through each box, realizing at some point that this "stuff" had belonged to my mom. The actual cardboard boxes themselves are not relevant. It was the small miracle that I found in one of them that changed my life. It reconnected me with my mom, who had died twenty years earlier.

There were pieces of costume jewelry, stuffed animals, old photographs, miscellaneous personal belongings, and a red spiral notebook in those boxes. I did not open the little red notebook at first and tossed it to the side as I continued to reflect upon my mom. Each item I found in these cardboard boxes brought back several memories of her. However, it was that little red notebook that kept speaking to me, so I finally opened it.

My mom had always been active and healthy. However, on Mother's Day in 1994 she appeared pale, fatigued, and very fragile. After a few weeks of doctor visits and tests, we got the bad news.

As I thumbed through the yellowing, discolored pages of that little red notebook, I realized I was reading Mom's cancer journal. She was reaching out to me, knowing that someday I would read her journal. She was still giving me advice, encouragement, strength, and motivation through her words.

Mom was an integral part of her patient groups and would often give support and advice to other patients who had little hope or faith in recovery. Mom always said you should not underestimate your power to influence others.

Mom reflected in her journal that the time you have to impact others and influence their lives is limited by the time you have here on earth. Mom was leading and influencing others even during a time when she was fighting for her own life.

Through all of the pain and mental anguish of chemotherapy, Mom wrote in her journal about the importance of keeping the faith and having confidence so that others would not lose hope. My mom found inspiration in the saying, "When you allow your confidence to shine, you unconsciously permit others to do the same."

Although Mom knew what she was up against with her future chemo treatments, she never lost her sense of humor or her positive outlook. She never stopped planning for the future and setting goals for herself, and that was evident in the pages of her journal, even though she got sicker and sicker as the year went on.

Unfortunately, I was on a business trip when my mother lost her battle. I had seen her two days before, at least, but I didn't get to say my official "goodbye" and tell her how much she meant to me on her final day. Her lessons have stuck with me, and I try to be as positive as she was and not let anyone's negativity define me. Mom would always say, "Someone else's perception of you does not have to become your reality."

That was my mom — a real role model.

~Skip Myers

BEST MOM EVER!

Chapter 6

A Grandmother's Love

*A grandmother is a little bit parent, a little bit
teacher, and a little bit best friend.*
~Author Unknown

She Understood

A grandma is warm hugs and sweet memories.
She remembers all of your accomplishments
and forgets all of your mistakes.
~Barbara Cage

I had been trying to have this conversation with my grandmother for a long time. Four months. Four months since I left the harsh streets of Brooklyn and the unaccepting, neglectful home of my father. Four months since my last period. I was fourteen years old and I didn't know much about anything, but I knew enough to realize I was pregnant.

I thought that maybe if I just forgot what happened, it would go away. I thought that maybe my belly would stop growing. That maybe I would stop throwing up and be able to eat again.

I had no idea how my grandmother would react. She had always been so loving when I was a young child. There were eleven of us grandchildren at the time but I felt like I had always been her favorite.

She had become a mother at the age of fifteen and I knew she always wanted so much more for me. So when I started to tell her, the words wouldn't come out. All I could do was cry. I ran from the small living room of the two-bedroom trailer that housed seven people, through the screen door and out on to the wooden front porch. It was an October night in North Carolina. It was cold out. Cold, now that was something I was used to.

I stood there crying and shaking. I stared out into the black sky;

the stars looked blurred through my tears. I heard the screen door creak open behind me. My grandmother stood beside me and placed her hand on my shoulder. She looked down at my bare feet, my toes purple from the chill of the night air, and asked, "Are you pregnant, honey?"

My anguish and terror spilled out in sobs as I muttered, "yes" over and over again. When I found enough courage to look into my grandmother's face, her brown eyes were glowing with warmth. She was smiling. She took my hand and guided me back inside. "You certainly can't be out in this cold with no shoes on your feet, dear. How about I run you a bath?"

My fears all melted away in that bath. It was the most peaceful place I had ever found myself. Afterward, my grandmother wrapped me inside her bathrobe. I had always loved that robe. Grandmother would wear it in the early mornings as she cooked breakfast and read the newspaper. I am not sure of the material, but it was fabulously soft.

It felt as though I was wrapped in warm clouds. I rubbed my arms, hugging myself, and began to look deep into the baby pink fabric of the robe. I was studying it so closely and for the first time since I realized the truth of my situation, I had a pleasant thought. I was thinking about what color my baby would wear.

My grandmother knew what I was thinking. She smiled and said, "Maybe we'll have us a baby girl."

I smiled back. "Maybe." That night my grandmother told me stories of pregnancy and birth. We laughed, we planned, and we figured out what my next steps should be. We talked about everything from prenatal vitamins to college funds for the baby. My grandmother told me the story of my birth and the first time she saw me in the bassinet through the glass window in the nursery. I had heard that story many times before, but tonight it was even more special.

I have often been told that being a parent does not come with a book of instructions. Well, for those of us who are lucky, we can find many answers in the words and actions of the women who came before us.

That October night in North Carolina was a pivotal moment that shaped my future. Grandmother's strength, acceptance, and guidance in that moment have always served as a motivating force in my life. There is nothing quite like a mother's love, except perhaps for one thing: the love of a grandmother.

~Patricia Dublin

52

The Phone Call

From there to here, from here to there,
funny things are everywhere.
~Dr. Seuss

I was walking to my next class when my grandmother called. I assumed it would be one of her usual "when are you coming over for dinner" phone calls. But instead I heard heavy breathing and her panicked tone as she started speaking. I started running to my car, ready to rush to her home, as I asked, "Grandma, what's wrong?"

"Oh honey, I can't find the damn Internet button again. I have LOST IT!" I stopped running. All of the horrible scenarios that had been running through my mind disappeared as I started to laugh and cry in the middle of the university quad. My grandma was yelling through the phone. "What's so funny? I can't get my e-mail. I can't check my Facebook! Honey, what do I do?"

This was not the first time that Grandma had called me in a panic about her computer. I remember one e-mail that contained more curse words than an actual explanation of the problem. She has always been an outspoken and honest woman, and I could not imagine life without her as one of my mentors. After I was able to compose myself and let her know that I was thankful she and Grandpa were both alive and well, I was able to walk her through the loss of her Internet "button."

Two minutes later, she was cheerful. "There it is! It's back! Oh, thank you, honey. What a relief!" The whole family knows that Grandma must never lose access to her e-mails, political websites, and Facebook for more than a few hours. Where would we be without her daily e-mails and comments on our Facebook posts — in all capital letters?

She says she uses ALL CAPS because she does not like holding down the shift button to capitalize. I say she is yelling. Every time I see her posts, I imagine Grandma screaming at the computer screen while typing. In reality, she is quite calm as she sits at the computer, usually listening to NPR while Grandpa watches westerns in the other room. But it doesn't stop me from laughing anyway. And my friends have had to get used to it. At first they thought some random elderly woman was yelling at them on Facebook.

Grandma is a character, to say the least, and one of the most intelligent, strong, self-confident women I have ever known. I may receive a few scary phone calls about her broken Internet or listen to her cursing her disobedient printer, but I am glad to be her technical help person, on the phone or in person. I'd actually be disappointed if that "damn Internet button" stopped disappearing on her.

~Emma Blandford

53

Understanding

*Grandmas hold our tiny hands for just a
little while, but our hearts forever.*
~Author Unknown

You always stole my thunder. You gave them everything they wanted. You never said no when they asked for anything: a second helping of dessert; candy before dinner; a few more minutes in the bath; money for the ice cream truck.

I struggled to show you respect and appreciation while trying to make sure you didn't spoil my children. I thought you would turn them into "selfish brats" by giving them everything they wanted. I thought they might never learn to wait, take turns, or share because you granted their wishes as soon as they opened their mouths and pointed.

You held each one of my babies long after he fell asleep. Didn't you understand they needed to learn to fall asleep on their own?

I resented you for buying the most expensive gifts on their birthdays and Christmas. How could I possibly compete with you? How do you think it feels to know that the very best presents, the ones they'll be the most excited and aglow about, are not from their parents?

They loved their afternoons with you. You made their favorite things for dinner — three different meals for three different boys. And you always had a little surprise — a present, candy, or a special treat. I didn't want them to associate you with gifts and sweets. I thought they should love you for you. I tried to tell you this, but you wouldn't listen. You continued to indulge them in every way possible.

I spent a lot of time wondering why you did all these things and how I could get you to ease up. I know grandmothers are supposed to "spoil the kids," then send them home, but you were… ridiculous.

Until you were gone.

I had to hold my boys and tell them that their grandma died. It didn't seem possible — you were supposed to be there for all the other special moments: proms, graduations, weddings. But they lost their grandma too soon and too suddenly. They were not ready to say goodbye to you.

During those years when I wished you'd stop spoiling them, I never thought about how much you loved them. How you showed it in every way possible: your cooking, the gifts, the sweets, your presence. The way you could recount every detail of a special moment, whether it was a perfect catch in the outfield or a sweet and slightly off-key note sung at a school concert. Your grandmotherly love for them knew no bounds. Your heart poured love from every place possible — your kitchen, your pocketbook, your words and your tireless arms.

It's pointless to dwell on regrets, but I often think about how I had it all wrong. I was so wrong in how I perceived your generosity. My kids, now in their teens, miss you dearly. And they don't miss your gifts or your money. They miss *you*. They miss running to greet you at the door and hugging you before you could step in. They miss looking up at the bleachers and seeing you, one of their biggest fans, smiling right at them. They miss talking to you and hearing your words of wisdom, encouragement, and love.

If I could speak to you one more time, I would tell you that every time I watch them arrive at a new milestone, and every time they amaze me with their perseverance, talents or triumphs, I think of you. And I wish they could have you back.

Come back and love them one last time, like no one else in the world but a grandmother could. Bring your sweets and surprises. Reward them with gifts for the smallest accomplishments. Painstakingly prepare their favorite meals. Take them anywhere they want to go. All and only because you love them.

Come back and see how much they've grown. Watch each boy becoming his own version of a young man. Be in awe with me as we admire how family, friendship, time, and love helped them grow so beautifully over the years.

The more I long for you to come back, though, the more I realize that in a way, you never left.

I understand now. I know that being their grandma gave you joy and purpose. Your love is a big part of who they are and what they will become as they grow. For this, and for every treat and gift, and every time I thought you were spoiling them, I thank you.

And I will wish a million times that you could do it all again.

~Tina Plantamura

The Blue Dress

We should all have one person who knows
how to bless us despite the evidence.
Grandmother was that person to me.
~Phyllis Theroux

My birthday fell during summer break so I never had the big parties that other kids had during the school year. The summer I turned ten I thought I was too old for a birthday party, but I was still feeling quite lonely on the big day.

That was, until I went upstairs to my room after breakfast. There, spread out on my bed, was the most beautiful dress I'd ever seen. It was pale blue, made of sheer nylon with tiny white, velvety flowers sprinkled over it. The dress had appeared as if by magic, and seemed to float above the bed, light and delicate.

Of course, magic had nothing to do with it. Grandma Ivanoff lived with us and she was a skilled seamstress. While I was out of the house each summer day, she'd worked on this wonderful gift in secret.

I loved that blue dress. I wore it for my school portrait when I graduated from sixth grade. It made me feel pretty and feminine, and I knew it brought out the blue in my eyes.

Yet what made this dress the most special was that it came from the hands of my grandmother. I picture her bending over the sewing machine in the summer heat of Washington, D.C., and I wonder how she hid the scraps and the dress while she was working on it.

Of course, I finally outgrew that beautiful dress. But I still have the sixth-grade graduation picture, and I will always treasure the memory of my grandmother and all the love that she put into that filmy blue dress.

~Michele Ivy Davis

Your Way, My Way

*Being a single parent is twice the work, twice the
stress and twice the tears but also twice the hugs,
twice the love and twice the pride.*
~Author Unknown

We'd barely gotten inside the building when the squeals started. "Look Grandma, come over here! We can touch the fish!" I scurried over to where my granddaughters had joined several other children who were sticking their hands in the water, feeling the stingrays. The employee on duty showed the girls how to place their hands gently in the pool. "Try it, Grandma," they said in unison, giggling with glee as they touched the creatures.

My son watched from a distance, allowing the girls their independence. If I'd been their mother, I'd have tagged along with the girls, supervising and making sure they followed the attendant's instructions, but my son preferred to watch from afar.

At that moment, I thought about my son and what life had dished out to him. He's the only parent the girls have. My son had always dreamed of a normal life with a wife, children, and a happy marriage that would last forever. Unfortunately, he'd watched his dreams come crashing down. In the end, he'd had to rescue and fight for his daughters, who had been in and out of foster homes after their mother couldn't take care of them. Throughout it all, my son had encouraged the girls to at least keep in touch with their mother, until she unexpectedly passed away.

The girls raced from exhibit to exhibit as we walked through the aquarium. It made me nervous. I fretted that a stranger might kidnap them, but it never bothered my son.

I thought about when my children were small, and how disciplined they had been. I could take them any place and they would stay next to me. Racing ahead wasn't allowed. Neither was screaming and yelling. However, I noticed that most of the other children at the aquarium were acting the same way as my granddaughters. Parents these days seemed more relaxed and willing to let their children run free.

Eventually we took a break. My son led his daughters to the snack bar to get something to eat while I rested my feet.

When I raised my son, we could never afford to buy goodies, whether it was at the zoo, the movies, or other places we visited. Instead I packed homemade snacks and juice. Did my granddaughters realize this was a special treat? Probably not.

Amid banana plants and humidity, we spent our time in a rainforest exhibit, watching the girls speed across a rope bridge. If my kids had crossed that many times I would have insisted they quit. However, my son let the girls race back and forth until they finally grew weary.

I figured we'd leave for home then. Nope. My son led the girls to the souvenir shop, where he told them they could each pick out a gift. My granddaughters surprised me with their thoughtfulness. They didn't ask if they could buy more than one item. Obviously they knew the rules. After they'd examined everything, they each chose a beautiful musical globe. My son didn't blink an eye, even though I knew he probably couldn't afford the gifts.

As we drove back to my mother's home, I glanced at my son and felt a warm rush of gratitude. In the back seat, my granddaughters merrily inspected their magical globes. They'd had a wonderful time.

While my son and I haven't always agreed on parenting styles, I know that one thing is certain. He is a wonderful father and mother combined. Single parenting is complicated, especially when there are hurdles along the way. Placing his hopes and dreams on the back burner, my son has never complained. Instead, he's plodded along, doing the best he can to take care of his two daughters, trying to make their lives as normal as possible. In my eyes, the "best" is all that any parent can do.

My heart goes out to all the fathers and mothers who raise their children alone. One day I hope my granddaughters appreciate the love and devotion my son has given them. His children come first. Life with his daughters is challenging, yet he faces each day with hope, a prayer, and unconditional love, because that's what the best parents do.

~Jill Burns

Forever Young

*It is only in adventure that some people succeed in
knowing themselves — in finding themselves.*
~André Gide

Grandma was a Disney guru. Having worked as a restaurant greeter in the Magic Kingdom as a "retirement gig," she knew all the rides, theme parks and insider information that added to the magical experience of Disney. Armed with an arsenal of Disney knowledge and an uncanny ability to beat the long lines, Grandma gave two of my brothers and me a Disney experience that has been etched in our memories.

Even though we were all in our early twenties, Brian, Eric and I were excited to spend the day with Grandma at Disney's Hollywood Studios. Although she was in her seventies, Grandma navigated the crowds swiftly as my brothers and I tried to keep up.

We arrived in the morning, just as the theme park opened its doors for the day. Grandma led the way and headed toward the popular rides to scope out the wait times. She had done this before, and we were speedwalking toward the park's newest ride: the Rock 'n' Roller Coaster Starring Aerosmith.

"Hurry up," Grandma said as we approached the line. "The wait isn't bad right now — forty minutes. It's only going to get longer as the day goes on."

For us, the forty-minute wait seemed reasonable, so we hopped in line while Grandma held our hats and sunglasses and waited for us at the ride's exit. The estimated wait time was right on target, and we got our adrenaline rush and were ready for the next ride; which Grandma had already scoped out.

"The wait time for Tower of Terror is only twenty minutes," Grandma said. "Let's go do that now."

Wait, did she mean "let's" as in "let us?"

"Gram, are you going on this one with us?" we asked.

Without even batting an eye, Grandma simply nodded her head and off we went. As we made our way through the line, we could see the camera flashes at the top. Now that we knew where to pose for the souvenir photo, we made a plan. We would make the *Home Alone* face with one hand on each cheek and our mouths open in horror. That was the plan anyway.

Things went awry once we actually got on the ride. With our safety belts holding us in place, we could feel the ride bringing us up, nearly 200 feet into the air. We held our hands to our cheeks as the doors opened to the outside and the ride made its first accelerated drop. The cameras flashed and we knew we had a hilarious souvenir-worthy photo.

"Let's look for our picture," I said as we exited the ride. "We had the pose timed perfectly."

Well, three out of four isn't bad. Grandma braved the ride, with an ear-to-ear grin, but she couldn't quite go hands-free. She clutched the safety bar as she giggled like a child each time the elevator descended.

They say a picture is worth a thousand words, but this photo was about one word: love. Grandma would go to any lengths (or heights) for her family.

~Sarah McCrobie

Grandma Power

Grandma always made you feel she had been waiting
to see just you all day and now the day was complete.
~Marcy DeMaree

I stood on tiptoe to reach the water flowing from the kitchen faucet. "Good job, Laurie. You are being so careful with the plates." My grandmother's approval felt as warm as the water.

She stood next to me in her white cotton blouse and flowered skirt, her shoulder pressed against mine. The stool I stood on made us the same height.

I was happy to be living with her. My parents were splitting up and she provided the medicine I needed: small tasks done together, making me feel useful. We picked flowers, emptied wastepaper baskets, and folded towels.

I had always wanted to be like her: cheerful, capable, and ready to share the apple pies she baked from scratch and the flowers she grew in her perennial garden.

After the dishes were done, I sat at her kitchen table with my math homework as she stood at the stove cooking.

"Grandmummy?"

"Yes, Laurie. What's on your mind?"

"Do you think Mom and Dad will get back together?"

"I don't know, sweetheart. But whatever happens, I want you to know that you're going to be all right. Your parents love you and you'll always have me."

I felt comforted. She had made me no promises, but somehow her honesty gave me courage. And she was there for me. I knew that was rock-solid truth.

The next day at school I was distracted, missing important explanations in math class that would make my homework impossible to do that night. Miss Dickerson, my fifth grade teacher, called me to her desk during free reading time. "Laurie, I heard your family is having some troubles and I want you to know I am praying for you. You're going to be all right."

I smiled and looked her straight in the eye and knew she meant it. *Two people. I have two people on my side*, I thought.

When I reached my grandmother's house that afternoon, she was waiting for me by the kitchen door.

"Come on in, sweetie. I made you some cinnamon toast."

I followed her into the warm room, putting down my heavy book bag and sighing with relief.

"I have some good news," she said, placing the plate of toast and cup of milk in front of me. "I went to see your mother today and she's gaining strength. I think she'll be up for a visit in a few days."

I closed my eyes and pictured my mom the last time I saw her, under the covers in her bed, pale, with her eyes closed. She hadn't heard me when I called her name. I sat for a long time on the front steps of our house. That's where Grandmummy found me when she came to check on us. I didn't understand what depression was at my young age, but I understood that my mom couldn't take care of me.

It wasn't until years later, when I had reached adulthood, that my grandmother confided to me that her own mother had sunk into a depression when she was young.

The weeks went by. I enjoyed the routine at Cackleberry Farm, as my grandmother's house was called. My weekly visits to my mom went okay. She could look at me now, and smile and call me by name with love in her voice. But she didn't get out of bed.

My dad came to see me at my grandmother's house. His beard and long hippie hair looked the same, but his eyes were sad.

"It's not fair," I told him reproachfully. "I need two parents, so I can go to the other one if one isn't helping me."

His silence hurt. But how was I to know that he was sparing me the pain of the details of a marriage falling apart?

My grandmother hugged him at the door — more evidence of her peace-loving nature as she continued to love her son-in-law.

After a month of her tender care, Grandmummy broke the news to me as she sat on the edge of my bed after nighttime prayers. "Your mom is ready for you to come home. I plan to drive you over after school tomorrow."

I cried out and hugged her tightly.

"I am always here, sweet Laurie. You must always feel free to come to see me."

My homecoming was a mixed experience because my mother struggled for a long time to find her emotional equilibrium. I took care of myself at times and learned resilience.

True to her word, my grandmother remained my best source of constant love. When I was old enough to ride my bike the six miles to her house, she welcomed my spontaneous appearances. She prayed for me. She hosted me overnight. And when she moved away she wrote me lengthy, newsy letters.

She also loved me, applauding my college graduation, offering her joyful presence at my wedding and expressing her excitement at the birth of each of my children.

I received the blessing of her long life, her cheerful heart, and her love until her passing at the age of 101. And I still carry her lessons with me as I pass them on to my own granddaughter.

~Laure Covert

A Hidden Hero

*I think a hero is any person really intent on
making this a better place for all people.*
~Maya Angelou

My grandma placed a comforting hand over mine but it did little to calm the quivering of my chin or the tears spilling down my cheeks. "I don't think you chose this, honey."

My grandmother is rough around the edges, brash, and painfully honest. She curses more than most teenagers and can outdrink a twenty-one-year-old. When I was five years old, she backed up the car at a fast food drive-thru to scream at the worker behind the glass because he didn't give her a napkin.

Grandma is loud, happy, and always laughing, but she can worry herself into a full-on panic in a matter of seconds and is never calm about anything. A long running joke in our family has always been "don't tell Grandma" whenever something bad happens for fear of her being worried into an early grave.

This woman loves harder and deeper than anyone I know. She has more pride in her kids and grandkids than anything else in her life (even when we don't deserve it). She has worked hard her whole life to earn everything she has. Nothing was ever handed to her, as she grew up with a lot of siblings and not much money. I respect my grandmother more than nearly anyone else in my life, which made this confession that much harder. I didn't want to disappoint her.

"I met her, didn't I?" asked Grandma. "The other day when you were here. The girl you had with you… I thought I noticed something between you."

I shifted on the barstool and attempted to sit higher as I picked at an invisible spot on the counter between us. "Yeah, she was with me."

Grandma hummed. I watched as her eyes glazed over and she tried to recall the girl I had brought to meet her the week before. I waited for the same questions I had from others. Is it a phase? What about when you had all those boyfriends? Were you faking it before? What about God? It's in the Bible. You might go to hell. Aren't you scared of that? Even in the 21st century, I had been bombarded with animosity and ignorance from people I loved. I had lost friends along the way, but I didn't want to lose any of my family. This was me. It was a piece of me I couldn't change.

"Well," she gave me a half smile, "like I said, I don't think you chose this. Nobody chooses to make their life more difficult."

I nodded along with her. She was right. I wish it was as easy as falling in love with Prince Charming and having two or three perfect children with him, but that's not the hand I was dealt.

"I'm sorry I didn't tell you sooner," I mumbled pathetically as my tears started to dry. "Not everyone has been accepting of it."

"Listen, honey," she leaned closer to ensure I was really hearing her this time. "It is nobody's business what you do in your own bedroom. Nobody's. I will always love you. I accept you, and I would love to meet her again."

My shoulders relaxed. She was the first person in my family to ask to meet the girl who would one day be my wife. She was the first person to give me unconditional acceptance. She never once questioned my relationship or sexuality. She never brought up religion, politics, or "family values" in regards to my relationship. Grandma helped me take the first real step toward loving and accepting myself.

In the weeks and months to come, the rest of the family followed suit. If Grandma was okay with it, so were they. More importantly, I grew more and more secure with myself as I realized I wouldn't want a different hand dealt to me, anyway. I never wanted a Prince Charming to begin with. I no longer felt guilty for being who I am.

There are a lot of things I don't know. I don't know if I'll live a long life or die young. I don't know if we should guide our lives by science or by faith. I don't know if the world will ever find peace.

But… I do know one thing without a doubt: heroes exist in the most unlikely of places. I went to my grandma's house that day expecting to be rejected. Expecting to have to explain myself. Expecting to come out on the other side feeling worse than I already did. Heroes don't always wear capes or uniforms. They don't always make their presence known. Sometimes the best heroes hide in the corners of our hearts and only come forward when we need them the most.

My grandma is a hero.

She accepted me without question and without judgment.

Someday, hopefully a long time from now, she'll be gone and I'll continue to tell this story to anybody who will listen. The story of my grandma and how the world is a little flatter without her but better because she was here.

~Allisa Bahney

A Bumpy Road to the Altar

*A daughter is a miracle that never
ceases to be miraculous.*
~Author Unknown

I collapsed in my chair as I tried to grasp what my daughter just told me. "Please tell me what you just said is *not* so!" My heart was pounding and my breathing shallow... and I was only the grandmother.

All the dreams my daughter had for her teenager had just flown out the window. What about college? What about her plans to travel? My granddaughter was only seventeen and hadn't even graduated high school. How would the family handle this? Was it really a disaster or was I overreacting?

My beloved granddaughter was pregnant. So what would happen next? Weeks of tears, hurt feelings and bewilderment filled our lives. Many friends and family members suggested putting the baby up for adoption. The answer that came back emphatically was that my granddaughter wanted this baby. No amount of prodding or pleading changed her mind. As her grandmother I felt helpless and frustrated. My heart was hurting for my daughter and breaking for my granddaughter.

Where was the father of this baby? What were his feelings about all this? It turns out he was there all along supporting the decision to keep the baby. As time passed it became apparent these young kids were really in love and most importantly, they wanted their child. But getting married? They were so young.

My daughter and her husband were determined to help these kids get it right. I stood back and watched miracles happen. I was extremely proud of my daughter and son-in-law for never giving up on this young couple. It appeared their faith was stronger than mine.

Because my granddaughter was a minor, she needed her parents' permission to marry. They told her she would have to finish high school first. This was easily accomplished, as she was home-schooled. Putting her nose to the grindstone helped make the first few months of pregnancy go faster. The reward was achieved with an early graduation.

As the kids began to work on their relationship it was apparent they needed help. Their immaturity had become a problem. Therefore, another stipulation before they could marry was counseling. Would they make it? If my daughter had any say, they would indeed.

How my daughter remained in control of her emotions throughout this ordeal was a wonder for me to witness. The strength my daughter displayed was impressive.

The birth of my great-grandson was a bittersweet occasion. It brought to the surface the unconditional love that was poured into the lives of my granddaughter and her fiancé. They learned that no matter what life brought them, the love that was given by my daughter and son-in-law made them resilient as individuals and stronger as a couple.

Watching from the outside was a learning experience for me as well. Though nothing about the marriage was traditional, it was a story with a happy ending. What began as shock, hurt and disappointment ended with a story about making choices, experiencing consequences, and finding grace along a bumpy road to the altar.

The strength of my daughter filled me with overflowing pride. Being a mother is not easy in the best of circumstances. The love and support she gave to my granddaughter and her new husband and baby were extraordinary. Keeping her marriage and family intact was most important and the results were wonderful. I so admire my daughter for how she made this all work. She's the best mom ever, in my opinion!

~Nancy Maggio

Coffee with Gran

*Grandmothers always have time to talk
and make you feel special.*
~Catherine Pulsifer

The smell of coffee always brings me back to my grand-mother's house. As a young, free-spirited child, I spent many weekends at her house. Fall, winter, spring, summer, I was there. She lived right across the river, so we would sometimes take the ferry to get to her house.

I enjoyed her way of living, which was simple and laid-back. She was a phenomenal painter so we often painted ceramics at her house. We also spent many days sitting on her patio, talking about life and the latest story I'd written. She was very supportive of my writing, telling me I had talent.

I remember one winter morning I woke up freezing, the floor as cold as ice. I put my slippers on, wrapped a blanket around myself, grabbed my Scooby-Doo stuffed animal, and dreamily made my way to the kitchen, following that coffee smell. Gran was fixing the usual breakfast: grits with cheese, buttered toast and, of course, a hot cup of coffee. I always felt safe there.

"Good morning, sweetie, want some breakfast?" she asked, as I plopped down in the chair at the table. As I ate breakfast and enjoyed my coffee with lots of milk, Gran drank cup after cup of coffee as well.

"So, how is the writing going, sweetie?" she asked, as we sat at the table after we finished eating breakfast.

"I stopped writing that story." I replied as I pulled my blanket closer to me, pouting.

"Why did you stop? You were working so hard on it."

"I don't know… I don't think I can do it." I said, my voice low and my eyes down.

"Honey… you have a talent for storytelling. That I know. I don't think you should give up. You can write, Paige. You have a great way with words, always have," Gran said. I looked up and met her eyes.

"You think so?"

"I know so. Please don't give up, Paige."

"Okay, I won't give up." I smiled.

"That's my sweet girl," Gran said, a smile on her face.

A lot of our conversations were over a cup of coffee. And we still meet for coffee and talk. I took Gran's advice and never stopped writing, and she is still my motivation. She taught me to never give up on my dreams. Writing is a part of me now. And while I'm writing, there is always a cup of coffee next to me.

~Paige N. Holmes

BEST MOM EVER!

My Role Model

Children have never been very good
at listening to their elders, but they have
never failed to imitate them.
~James Baldwin

Commencement

*Setting an example is not the main means of
influencing others; it is the only means.*
~Albert Einstein

"Which side of the cap does the tassel go on again?" Mom asked, brushing the strands off her face.

"On the right," I said, adjusting the little blue tuft on my own cap.

"What about my hood? Do I have it on correctly?" I turned around to see my mom scanning the line of students behind her, studying their outfits.

"Mom, for the hundredth time, your hood's fine. You're wearing it just like everyone else."

Mom scowled doubtfully. "Are you sure? The back doesn't feel right. Maybe it's not centered," she said, trying to readjust it.

I let out an exasperated sigh before facing forward again. *Some things never change*, I thought to myself, but I smiled.

It was June 2nd and the atmosphere was heady at Madison Square Garden, as hundreds of graduating students prepared for the upcoming commencement ceremony. Amidst the elated scholars eagerly taking selfies and posing for group photos stood my mother and me.

My mother is an immigrant who left her family in India twenty-five years ago to start a new one with my father in the United States. She was an aspiring teacher, and had been in the middle of her undergraduate career, when she conceived me and decided to move, dropping out of college to raise me, and later my sister, in the heart of New York City. Twenty-five years later, both of us were graduating with master's degrees in education. As we stood in line, clad in long purple gowns, waiting to enter the auditorium, I thought back to the experiences that got me there: the long hours I put into my job as a kindergarten teacher during the weekdays while attending classes in the evenings; the sleepless nights I spent studying for exams; and the weekends I dedicated to writing papers.

Suddenly, my thoughts were interrupted by the sound of a happy shriek and someone yelling my mother's name from further up the line. I leaned over to see who it was and watched as an unfamiliar woman about my age in a cap and gown waved and walked toward us.

"Mita! It's so nice to see you!" she exclaimed. "Congratulations on graduating!" My mother smiled back, but to my surprise began to turn red.

"Thanks, Sue. You look wonderful," mom replied before gesturing to me. "This is my son." Sue's eyes widened as I introduced myself.

"Oh wow. Your son is graduating, too?" she said incredulously. "That is so cute. You guys are getting your degrees at the same time. You must be so proud of him!" Mom gave a smile and nodded, her face still red. Sue turned to me and held out her camera. "Would you mind taking a picture of me with your mom?"

"Oh goodness, no," my mom said quickly with a nervous laugh, but Sue wouldn't have it. I could tell Mom was feeling very uncomfortable as she grimaced at the camera. After taking the photo, Sue gave Mom a quick hug and went back to her spot in line, shouting, "we finally made it!" That made Mom blush even more. What was going on?

"Do you see the line moving? How much longer do we have to wait out here?" she asked in a low voice.

"Don't worry. The line is starting to move now," I replied, taking a step forward. "Why were you so embarrassed to take that photo, Mom? Did something happen between you and Sue?" Mom shook her head and her face turned red again.

She was quiet for a few seconds and then she answered me.

"Because I am ashamed of how old I am and how long it took me to get here," she whispered. We had reached the entrance to the auditorium now, and before I could respond, we were directed to our seats. As we entered, I heard Sir Edward Elgar's famous tune, "Pomp and Circumstance," a staple at nearly every graduation event, as jubilant family members stood up and clapped, snapping pictures, shouting names, and waving furiously. I searched the crowd for my dad and sister, spotting them near the back of the auditorium as we sat in our seats.

As the ceremony began and the president proceeded to give her commencement address, I could not help but think about what my mom confided in me. Ashamed? Sitting next to her and seeing her in full regalia, I simply could not understand it. Here was a woman who left everything behind to start anew in a foreign land. A woman who devoted herself to supporting her husband, taking care of her children, and ensuring they received a good college education, all while holding down a full-time job and working toward the education she had halted all those years ago. I vividly recalled how she would apologize to my sister for not being able to bring her to a dance class because she had a test the following Monday. How she would clean up the dinner dishes and then open her textbooks well after my father went to bed. How she had to master English, which resulted in my sister and me having to read over her papers numerous times, much to our annoyance. I felt a tinge of guilt, remembering the times I complained.

Despite all odds, my mother had achieved one of her longtime goals. She would at last be able to teach her own class, and I could not be prouder of her.

At the end of the ceremony, the president conferred our degrees and the whole crowd burst into applause. I turned to my mother and gave her a hug, remembering all the sacrifices and all the struggles it took her. "I'm so proud of you, Mom," I whispered for her ears only. She hugged me tighter. "Me too."

My mother used to be ashamed of the fact that it took years for her to get her degree. I disagree. I told her that there was nothing to be ashamed of. If this isn't the definition of what it means to succeed as an immigrant in this country, then I don't know what is. As we left the auditorium together, I told her to keep her gown on at least until we reached the subway platform. My heart filled with gratitude and love as we walked arm in arm.

My parents always tell me there are few things in this world that are worth pursuing and that an education is one of them. But I think having a dream, and committing yourself to achieve it no matter what, is just as important. My mother is a prime example of that.

~Prithwijit Das

A Mom to Many

*Little souls find their way to you, whether they're
from your womb or someone else's.*
~Sheryl Crow

My parents began taking in foster children when I was twelve. Forty foster kids eventually passed through their home. Each one held a special place in our hearts, and each one knew without a doubt that he or she was loved and was truly part of our family.

Even as a sarcastic and unappreciative teenager, I knew something special was happening in our home. It wasn't easy to be a foster sister to kids who sometimes stole from me, ruined my possessions and invaded my space. But I also knew it wasn't easy for my parents, especially for my stay-at-home mother.

Not many moms would willingly and lovingly continue raising kids for half a century, but that's what my mom did. She started, as do most moms, with her own children, having two girls and a boy before her twenty-fifth birthday. Eleven years after the youngest of the original trio was born, along came a fourth child — me. I felt a bit like an only child when my older siblings left home for jobs and college.

That didn't last long, however, because that's when my parents felt the call to be foster parents. There were babies and preschoolers, tweens and teens, all of whom needed more than just food and shelter — they needed love and comfort and the chance to experience what makes a house a home. My parents gave them that and more.

Now that I'm a mother of my own, I marvel at how my mom related to these battered, bruised kids who had been treated so abominably by their own moms and dads (and other relatives). Many of these kids were sexually, physically, mentally, and verbally abused. Some of them had never eaten a meal with the entire family seated around a table. They had never had a space of their own in a house. They had never been unconditionally loved. Their backstories would break your heart.

Sometimes they arrived at my parents' house in the middle of the night with nothing but the clothes they were wearing. The luckier ones had a few belongings stuffed into a black trash bag. All of them were frightened and lonely, and many of them missed their parents.

Mama Jo would greet them at the door with her heart opened wide. She would settle them into our house as if they were her long-lost sons or daughters returning home. Everyone was treated like a full member of our family.

My mother taught them the things that most of us learn from growing up in normal, loving families — things like how to treat one another with kindness, how to do chores, and how to act at the dinner table. She advocated for them at school, but expected them to do their own schoolwork. She gave them hugs but meted out consequences when necessary. She prayed for them, and showed them how God cared for them as well.

She wasn't perfect, and she would be the first to admit she made mistakes. But the kids understood that she was someone who cared, who had their best interests at heart, and who was a safe haven in the storm of their lives.

Most of all, she gave them unconditional love and acceptance. My mom never allowed a child's current circumstances to dictate a child's future. She's a firm believer that people can change, and kids can too. That attitude, coupled with the amazing successes she and my father achieved with these foster children, led the local social services department to call my parents first with the most difficult cases.

My parents even adopted twins who had been foster kids in our home for several years before their biological mom and dad gave up their parental rights. The boy-girl twins were fourteen years younger than me, meaning my parents willingly extended their child-raising years to start again with preschoolers when I was graduating from high school.

I know my parents made a lasting difference in the lives of those foster children because we still keep in touch. The troubled ten-year-old boy who bounced back and forth from his mom's house to ours as a foster kid now has a successful military career. The abused teenage girl who had started to make unwise choices became a nurse who asked my father to walk her down the aisle when she got married. The sexually abused nine-year-old girl who developed an annoying personality to cope credits my mother for showing her she was loveable. Now she's married with children of her own.

When I reflect on the half century my mother spent raising kids, the majority of whom were not hers by birth, my heart overflows with love and gratitude for the example she set for me and countless others. I try to be as good a mother as she is. If more mothers were like Mama Jo, the world would indeed be a better place.

~Sarah Hamaker

Stinky Mary

There is an instinct in a woman to love most her own
child — and an instinct to make any child who
needs her love, her own.
~Robert Brault

I had hurried home after school, running the last half block to get there in time for whatever television show was playing in the afternoon. While I was happily munching on a snack, my mother was staring out the front window. "Marcia," she said, "who is that little girl walking past the house?"

Irritated by the interruption, I stood and looked out at the unkempt girl who was one of my fifth grade classmates. I groaned as I told my mother her name was Mary before turning away in disgust.

"I want you to invite her over tomorrow after school."

"What? I can't do that! She's stinky and nasty and nobody likes her. I can't have her come to my house!" Waving my pickle in the air for emphasis, I complained that my reputation would be ruined, that nobody would like me or play with me anymore. I was careful to reiterate the fact that she smelled like pee.

My mother was undaunted and insisted that I bring Mary home with me. I knew that no amount of arguing was going to change her mind, so I agreed.

The next day, I waited until school was out before I approached Mary. I stood under the trees just past the school grounds, and when she walked by, her head down, I called her name. She acted startled, as if I might hurt her. Other kids had. They had said mean things and even thrown garbage at her.

I looked around, making sure nobody was watching, and asked her if she wanted to come to my house and have a snack and meet my mom. She agreed and started giggling and dancing in circles around me. Her unfettered joy made me feel awkward.

Fortunately, I lived really close, so we only had to cross the street and pass four houses. She knew which one was mine and raced ahead and up the steps. I had to brush up against her to open the door, and the smell of stale urine wafted off her clothes. I know I wrinkled my nose, but whether she noticed or not, I am uncertain. I imagine she was used to the reaction.

We stepped through the door, and the scent of fresh baked cookies filled the air. Mom seldom baked, and since she was baking now, I could only conclude she had done it to impress my guest. My mother came out of the kitchen all smiles, and I introduced her to Mary. She didn't seem to notice the girl's pungent aroma as she led her into the kitchen, where cookies and milk were already laid out on the table.

I sat. I ate cookies. I listened to my mother ask question after question. My mother tried to include me in the conversation, but I had little to offer. I was just biding my time until stinky Mary got out of my house so we could open the windows.

Finally, the visit was over. I stood quickly, ready to usher her out the door, when my mother put her hand on my arm. "Honey," she said to me, "I have been sorting through your clothes today. I wonder if Mary and her younger sisters can use these clothes you've outgrown." She smiled encouragingly, glancing at Mary while she spoke.

The girl nodded and grinned. She smiled a lot that afternoon. I hadn't seen her do it much before, I realized. Then my mom pointed to three large bags stuffed with items that had recently been folded in my drawers or hanging in my closet. I was horrified. The kids at school had seen me wearing those clothes! If stinky Mary showed up wearing them, then everyone would know she had been here. I shifted uncomfortably, shooting daggers at my mother with my eyes.

My mother produced a wrapped up paper plate holding more cookies. "How about you take these home to your family?"

I looked at the three bags of clothes and the plate of cookies, and my heart sank. Mary lived two blocks down the street. I knew she couldn't possibly carry all that stuff home with her, and my dad had our car at work. My mother was setting me up.

Sure enough, my mother picked up two bags and handed them to me. That left Mary carrying the plate of cookies and the other bag. I was not happy, but it didn't matter. I had no choice. So, off we went down the street past all the houses where people lived and looked out their windows and could see me as I trudged past.

I'd never been to Mary's house. But as I stood on the sidewalk looking at the peeling paint and the dead lawn strewn with broken toys and pieces of garbage, I was shocked. I wasn't sure what to make of it. Warily, I followed her up the steps of the cracked cement porch and on into the front room. I was assailed by a stench that made my eyes water. Mary whispered that we had to be quiet as her mother worked nights and was sleeping. She put the things she carried on top of piles of unidentifiable paraphernalia that littered the couch. I did the same.

She dragged me off down the hallway to her bedroom, which held a double bed that she shared with her two sisters. The younger siblings sat on the floor playing quietly. It became obvious that these two small creatures were the source of the odor. The bed they all shared reeked of urine. I made my stay as short as possible, escaping her world and running back to my own.

I am not sure what my mother expected of me regarding Mary, but I never attempted to befriend her. I observed my mother, at different times over the remainder of my childhood, watch for the girl as she dragged herself home each afternoon. Mom would walk out on the porch, wave Mary over, and hand her plates or bags of food, and the occasional items of clothing.

As an adult looking back, I realize that Mom did her good works in secret, never mentioning them to a soul. She just helped where she could. I secretly admired my mother for her kindness toward my classmate. I just wish I had told her. She taught me a very important lesson about kindness and compassion.

~Marcia Wells

A Knockout Performance

Perfection is not attainable, but if we chase
perfection we can catch excellence.
~Vince Lombardi

I've been taking adult tap dance lessons for close to four years. As a textbook overachiever, I expected to be shuffling off to Buffalo like Ginger Rogers by now. In reality, my rhythm is pretty spotty, and I still haven't mastered basic steps like cramp rolls or drawbacks.

My tap teacher Howard calls me a "perfectionist," but that's just something he says to make me feel better. I don't need to be perfect but I do prefer to succeed rather than fail. It's not my fault. It's my mom's.

Ma is just under five feet tall and weighs less than 100 pounds. She grew up in Manhattan in the 1950s and she's a fighter. And what I mean is, she loves to fight with people. It might be because she was an only child and never got the chance to beat up a younger sibling. In fact, she claims that the reason she had me, even though, allegedly, my father never wanted a second child (she loves to remind me of that all the time), was so that my older brother, Chris, would be spared the pain of a lonely childhood like the one she endured at the hands of her cold mother. And of course, my brother was so grateful, he beat the living daylights out of me every chance he got.

Ma doesn't use physical force against her opponents. She's a master of verbal intimidation. Every time I talk to her on the phone she's at war with someone. "You wouldn't believe the gross malfeasance going on with our homeowners association, Hilary! They're so scared of me, I've been banned from the meetings!" Or, "The cable company tried to raise our bill. I called and said, 'Do you want my business? I only want to hear one word, yes or no.' They lowered my bill twenty dollars a month." And don't even get her started on politics. Needless to say, as a small child, I did everything in my power to stay on her good side. My strategy was to do well in school, and everything else, to avoid disappointing her.

When I was six years old, Ma signed me up for ballet lessons. After a month of classes, a recital was scheduled. The teacher kept it simple. We weren't expected to memorize the routine. Life was easier back then. There was no *Dance Moms* TV show or YouTube. Our parents had no illusions that we kids were on the road to stardom. They just wanted us out of their hair for an hour or two. So all we had to do was form a line behind the teacher like little ducklings following the mama duck. The teacher would start the dance and, if we got lost, we'd mimic her movements, or rather, shadow the student standing right in front of us.

The day of the recital, dressed in cotton candy pink leotards, tutus, and matching ballet flats, we got into a line on stage. Standing directly in front of me was my frenemy, Lisa Kaplan. Lisa, with thick black glasses and dirty blond hair, had an annoying habit of singing my name on the school bus over and over again, "Hil-a-ree Hatt-en-bach" "Hil-a-ree Hatt-en-bach," until I snapped and screamed "SHUT UP, LISA!" Let's just say, we had history.

At show time, the music began and everyone's tiny arms flew up into fifth position. Well, everyone's except Lisa Kaplan's. She stood staring into the abyss, twirling her hair, paralyzed with fear. I glared at her in disbelief. As an overachieving six-year-old, I didn't recognize what was clearly stage fright. All I saw was my arch nemesis ruining my chance to shine. I gave her a shove.

She snapped out of her daze and shoved me back. Fists and ballet slippers started to fly. I grabbed her bun and yanked. She pulled on my leotard. A scratching and shrieking fight ensued while dainty Chopin music plinked out of the speakers. The music came to a screeching halt and soon our very upset moms pulled us apart. Ma dragged me off stage and said, "That's it. I'm enrolling you in karate with your brother." The subtext being that my fighting skills could use some improvement.

Cut to a few years ago. My tap teacher organized a tap recital and I decided it was time to redeem myself and invite Ma. Two shows were planned and I'd be dancing in three numbers. The matinee went off without a hitch but Ma wasn't in attendance at that show. She came to the evening show and sat in a row of chairs directly on the stage. When the lights dimmed, the jazz horns and piano blared from the speakers. I flapped and shuffle-ball changed my way across the stage with ease. I looked over at Ma beaming. She was finally getting the recital she'd hoped for all those years ago. I felt giddy and elated to be the source of her pride and for a brief moment, a big smile spread across my face as I thought, *YES! I'm totally killing it!*

But the sheer joy must have caused a system overload. My brain turned into a black hole of nothingness and white noise. I lost my place in the routine and froze. I couldn't remember the steps that I'd done flawlessly just hours before at the matinee. With what I can only imagine was an Edvard Munch-ian look of horror on my face, I fumbled and bumbled on my feet. It was too late. Devastation had already enveloped my entire being. I morphed into Lisa Kaplan, terrified and paralyzed, desperate for someone to knock me out and end my misery.

After the show I skulked out from backstage and avoided eye contact. Ma, to her credit, went on and on about how I was the best one up there and said she didn't notice my mistakes. That should have been exactly what I wanted to hear. Even if I wasn't perfect, she was still proud of me. But it wasn't. I wanted to be exceptional for Ma.

Shortly after, I fell into a long period of PTTD — Post-Traumatic Tap Disorder. I barely attended class and refused to perform in the following year's recital. It's been a couple of years since that fateful night. I'm back in tap class and building up my confidence to perform in front of an audience again. I'm also back in therapy. My therapist tells me to let go of the expectation, which I can't help but think of as "quitting." And you know, Ma didn't sneak me into this world to become a quitter. So I'll keep on pushing myself to be the best I can be and blame Ma for it because the truth is, she makes me try harder.

~Hilary Hattenbach

Best Breakfast Ever

One good mother is worth a hundred schoolmasters.
~George Herbert

My dad worked in construction. His day started early and ended late. All he wanted to do was crash on the couch and relax when he got home. For the most part that was what he did. No one complained; we were just happy when he was home.

But one hot and muggy summer, when my parents' nineteenth anniversary was coming up, they made plans to go out, just the two of them. The big day finally arrived and Dad got home at seven. Mom had fed all five of us early. She was dressed in her finest and wearing his favorite pair of high heels when he came in. They kissed, as they always did, when he came through the kitchen and headed for the family room. It was obvious he was hot and tired.

"Honey, I just need a thirty-minute nap and then I'll get ready and we will go out to eat," he said as he sat down on the couch.

Mom was already on her way over to the couch to give him a fresh cup of hot coffee. She bent over and kissed him on the head and said, "I'll be ready whenever you are."

I knew how important this evening was to my mother, but before long Dad was fast asleep. Then I watched my mother do the strangest thing. She reached into the refrigerator and took out eggs and bacon. Soon she had a batch of biscuits baking in the oven. I never said a word. I just watched her.

Breakfast was my dad's favorite meal. Before my eyes she piled a plate full of his favorite foods. As she set another fresh cup of coffee on the end table she bent down and kissed him while whispering in his ear, "It's time to wake up, honey."

He ran his fingers through his head of natural curly snow-white hair and sat up on the edge of the couch. As he looked up he found my mom standing in front of him with his dinner. I will never forget the look of love that passed between them as they made eye contact.

"Honey, I promised you I would take you out to dinner and I meant it," he said sincerely.

Mom sat down beside him on the couch as he took the plate of food. She kissed him on the cheek. "I know you would, but I also know you've had a hard day and you're tired. What's important is that we are together. We can go out any time for dinner."

I was seventeen then, and that lesson in love is still with me today, five decades later. Dad died nineteen years ago and Mom lived into her nineties. One day, I found her holding a picture of Dad in her hands. I watched her kiss him and then, as she emerged from the cloud of dementia, I heard her say, "Baby, it won't be much longer until I can come home to heaven to be with you forever."

Three years ago, Mom entered heaven's gate to be greeted by the love of her life. When I miss them I just imagine how happy they are to be together again. Then a sweet peace and comfort falls over me, the same way I felt when I saw their tremendous love for each other on that night when my mother made my father a special anniversary breakfast for dinner.

~Sylvia J. King

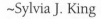

A Road Well Traveled

*If I have done anything in life worth attention, I feel
sure that I inherited the disposition from my mother.*
~Booker T. Washington

My parents got married right out of high school and started a family right away. My dad went to work in the oil fields, and soon accepted a job working overseas.

The money was great, but we only saw him every other month. My mom stayed home with her five children, essentially raising us alone. We had a place in the country with horses, dogs, chickens and a few head of cattle. Mom spent her time raising kids, sewing our clothes, cooking, cleaning and canning. She was very busy, but always made time for us. Of course, lots of mothers did things like that. But, Mom's greatest feat was yet to come.

When the oil business declined in the 1980s, my dad and most of his friends lost their jobs. Not long after that, other things began to go awry as well. The financial strain proved too much, and most of their friends ended up divorcing. The wives were at a loss as to how to manage without their large monthly paychecks.

But my mom was different. She helped out by working odd jobs and she learned to drive a semi-truck, so she could help my dad make more miles at his new job. But with three teenagers at home, she couldn't spend time on the road with him, so she decided to find a different kind of job.

Mom found an ad for the International Air Academy in Vancouver, Washington. She had always dreamed of working as a flight attendant, but had chosen a family over a career. She was intrigued with the idea that she might be able to work in the travel field after all. Having no idea how she would pay for the schooling, or even if she'd get a job, she took a leap of faith and dialed the number.

It wasn't easy, but she passed the entrance exam and was admitted to the three-month expedited training course. That was only half the battle, though, as she still needed the tuition. She finally got a loan to cover some of the expenses, and the president of the school gave her a personal loan to cover the rest.

As she perused her welcome packet, she realized there was a strict dress code, requiring professional dress each day. This was not something she had in her current wardrobe. And she also needed to see an eye doctor. Her older brother sent her enough money to purchase the clothes she needed and see an optometrist. And then she took her two youngest daughters — my sister and me — to Vancouver, where there was an apartment waiting for her in the family housing section.

The first day of class she was so nervous, I can remember her taking deep breaths and trying to calm herself before leaving. She was forty-five years old, and that made it a little intimidating to walk into a classroom full of twenty-year-olds and try to hold her own. But, she stood by her commitment and graduated at the top of her class.

Her first job as a travel agent was with a large agency in Aurora, Colorado. She felt great about her accomplishment and proud of the beautiful, high-rise building she worked in. I was so proud of what she had done. She'd found a way to rise above the curveball life had thrown at her, and instead of quitting as many of her friends had, she charged ahead and created a brand new career.

But, this story doesn't end there. Her company needed more people, and they were willing to train them on the job. So, two of my sisters went to work there as well. It would be three more years before I was old enough to join the ranks, but you better believe I took my turn as well. All in all, four of her five children became travel agents, and we often worked for the same company.

My Role Model | 217

This experience taught us a great deal about survival. We learned that it was never too late to start something new, to accomplish your dreams, and to rise above your current circumstances. Times haven't always been easy and we've moved quite a bit to follow jobs, but we've done whatever it takes.

I've had hard times in my own life, but because of the example set by this amazing woman, I went to college at the age of twenty-nine. It was late, but I had a great teacher, a wonderful role model, and a fantastic support system to help me on my way. If my mom hadn't set this example for me, I don't know where I'd be today. She is my inspiration for perseverance at any age.

~Stacie D. Williams

67

Magic Hands

If evolution really works, how come
mothers only have two hands?
~Milton Berle

My mother creates magic with her hands. Her fingers can coax slippery rose and lavender silk into a proper Princess Aurora dress for a dreaming four-year-old. She can embroider a hanging for my daughter's nursery, spending hours stitching tiny x's to fill in a smiling pink giraffe and his elephant friend. The next project might involve sewing and installing new curtains for my sister. Those magic hands hammer nails one moment and bead intricate necklaces the next.

Without her, I probably would have failed dozens of school assignments. Now, I can write stories all day long, and I can paint, but when it comes to anything remotely crafty, my fingers muddle up and my brain freezes.

My mother, bless her, never criticized or sighed when I asked for help with assignments. Even when given the task of a handmade book during grad school, she remained positive.

"All we have to do is measure the binding," my mother tried to explain. "You see, you sketch out what you want to do and where you want the pages to go like this." She demonstrated, drawing tiny neat squares across the page. "Then we find paper to back the text that matches the canvas paper you'll do the illustrations on. Of course, you'll need a border."

"For what?" I interrupted. My right eye was beginning to twitch.

"For the binding of course," she said patiently. Placing her hands together, she opened and closed them like a seam. "Then we'll need fillers and an inside cover as well before we drill holes through the backing to wind the ribbon through."

I blinked. "Can't we just glue some fabric on cardboard and staple it together?"

She opened her mouth, and closed it. "No."

I groaned.

"Don't worry." Her smile lit up the already sunny room. "It's easy."

"I just don't think this way," I told her.

"I know. But I do."

So my mother drove down from Austin once a week for a month to help me create a book to finish a master's degree she and my father were paying for. Not even a power outage one Sunday night could stop her. Under the pale glow of flashlights, my mother carefully taped the fifty pages of text I'd typed onto heavier, larger paper to match the dimensions of the paintings I'd done.

Of course, I got an A.

Without my mother, however, my academic career would have been a disaster. It was her hands that helped hot glue the puppets I needed for French class, her fingers that sewed the Little Red Riding Hood costume I wore as the lead in the first grade spring play. When my physics teacher decided the only way we were going to learn about circuits was to build a miniature house with working lighted rooms, my mom managed to not only wire the rooms, but decorate them so well *Good Housekeeping* could have done a photo shoot there. She used dollhouse furniture, of course.

When I was pregnant with my daughter, I sat in the doorway far enough from the fumes that she couldn't scold me as I watched her help my husband paint the nursery walls a pale pink.

"I wish I could do this stuff," I sighed.

"You're pregnant," my mother reminded me.

"No, I mean that I'm just not good at any of this," I whined. "I can't applique stockings like you can or make Halloween costumes like you did for me. I just have no patience. I get frustrated." I gestured to the careful detailing of a pillowcase she had embroidered for me in the guest bedroom next to the nursery. "I've tried and I've tried, but I get no joy out of sewing or decorating."

"You can cook," my husband said helpfully.

"You can't cook up a princess dress for Halloween," I wailed. "What if she wants to be a princess? I'll have to order something off Etsy!"

My mom stopped rolling paint and brushed a pink-stained hand across her cheek. "Honey, we do what we do out of love. I love to sew. I love to make arts and crafts. I love to decorate. For me, it was a joy to make the Christmas tree skirt under your tree, little dresses for you girls to wear, and pillows and dolls."

I blanched, imagining my own daughter coming to me with such requests.

"We all have our own talents," my mom continued. "You write, and you paint. You got a 4.0 in grad school, so you can easily help her with papers. I could never help you."

"She even helps me with business memos," my husband admitted. "And she helps the kids next door."

"We'll hang all the canvases you painted on her walls," my mom added helpfully. "So when she goes to sleep, she'll fall asleep looking at what you created for her."

"You can write her stories," my husband added. "Make little books for her."

"Not out of cloth," my mother chimed in quickly. "Don't try to recreate your childhood for her. Do what you can do to give her the best childhood you can. If you're happy, she'll be happy too." She gave me a playful swat. "Now get away from these fumes and go order us some dinner."

After calling in dinner, I lumbered up the stairs to my laptop. My mom was right. I might not be able to sew my daughter a Halloween costume, but I could do something just as nice. Opening up a new page, I began to type, "Dear Baby Girl…"

At twenty weeks, I started writing a letter to my daughter. Every month, I write her another letter and put it in a pink folder. Until she can read them, they'll wait for her. My paintings adorn her walls, and I've got plans to paint mermaids for her bathroom.

I may not be able to make her a costume like my mom did, but I can still give her the magical childhood my mom gave me.

I just need to use my hands.

~Miranda Koerner

68

Generous Miracles

*Start where you are. Use what you
have. Do what you can.*
~Arthur Ashe

She would give the shirt off her back to someone in need. My mother isn't perfect and our relationship has definitely had its ups and downs, but her generosity is something I have always admired.

When my parents divorced, I was just two years old. My stay-at-home mom was thrust into the working world, sometimes even working two jobs to provide for her three children. Her most obvious acts of generosity came in how she would deny herself to make sure we were provided for. We didn't have everything we wanted, but we always had what we needed.

Mom always reminded us that no matter how bad we thought things were, there were others who had it worse. We were struggling, but somehow she was still able to share what little we had with others, pulling off little miracles of giving.

My earliest memory of her generosity is from my elementary school years. I told her that a friend's parents were going through a difficult time and I didn't think my friend would be getting much for Christmas. I still don't know how she did it, but my mom dropped off a bag of toys for that girl at the school's front office. She still managed to provide a great Christmas for us, too, that year. My friend never knew the gifts came from my mom, because it was important to Mom that the girl believed the gifts were from her own parents.

In middle school, we were having a class trip and my best friend couldn't afford to go. When my mom found out, she offered to pay for the trip as long as my friend's parents could cover her personal expenses (food, souvenirs, etc.).

It was around this time I began to notice the many other things my mother did for those around her. Some gestures were small, like making a plate from our dinner and bringing it to an ill neighbor. Other gestures were blessings, such as the year she bought, hard boiled, and dyed hundreds of Easter eggs and donated them to a church she didn't even attend.

Most of my mother's generosity was anonymous. When a woman in our church was unexpectedly widowed, my mother snuck into service early every Sunday and left a small gift on the woman's regular seat. She never missed a co-worker's birthday or special occasion. She still donates to Salvation Army bell ringers, buys gifts for Angel Tree children, and puts money in the bucket when collections are being made.

Her example is her legacy, which has been passed on for generations. My sister, brother, and I have emulated her generosity. We each have our own ways in which we are called to help, almost always in anonymity, and always in sincerity. Donations of our time, goods, money… gifts, assistance, or even just a listening ear… these are all things rooted in the seeds my mother planted years ago. As we are all now parents, we are seeing this legacy continue in our own children.

~Gena McCown

My Mother, the Fighter

You never know how strong you are, until being
strong is the only choice you have.
~Bob Marley

During the twenty-seven years that I was blessed to have my mother, she spent most of her time battling multiple sclerosis, which was diagnosed at age forty-one. Multiple sclerosis is a neurological disorder that is characterized by exacerbations and remissions. It has no cure and each exacerbation is stronger than the one before. MS robbed my mother of her independence and her ability to walk, but she never stopped fighting to get better. In fact, she constantly confounded her neurologist by making strong recoveries after each attack. Her doctor had several patients with MS, but many of them only survived a few years after the onset of symptoms. My mother was still fighting after seventeen years.

My mother's MS struck for the final time in April 2005. Her breathing became compromised and she had to have a tracheotomy and use a respirator. Her doctors repeatedly tried to talk her out of such invasive procedures, but if medicine offered an option that could help her, she wanted it. Unfortunately, in September of that year she slipped into a coma. I hoped that she would make one of her legendary recoveries. However, the days turned into weeks and her doctors gathered my family for a meeting. We needed to decide if we wanted to let my mother stay in a coma indefinitely, or remove her respirator and begin hospice care.

I was my mother's health care proxy but I was only in my twenties. I wanted help so I spoke with the neurologist who had treated my mother for the past seventeen years. I had a frank conversation with him about how MS progresses as a disease and where my mother fit on that timeline. I also sought advice from my pastor, and a paternal aunt and uncle who were very close to me.

I prayed and hoped that my mother, the fighter, would return. She was only fifty-eight. During her life she had been a pianist, a writer, a lecturer, and most importantly, she was a fighter. She was also my best friend.

When I thought about how hard she'd fought to keep MS at bay, I wondered if I even had a right to consider removing her from life support. Wouldn't she have wanted her fight to continue? However, if she did awake from her coma, I asked myself, what kind of world would she return to? I had to look at her quality of life. Her MS had progressed to the point where it was preventing her lungs from functioning. If she did awake from her coma, she would have to use a respirator for the rest of her life and multiple sclerosis would continue to attack her body. Her vital signs also revealed that as she lingered in a coma, her body was beginning to fail.

Growing up, I always sought my mother's wisdom any time I had to make an important decision in life. I couldn't do that this time. However, after days of soul searching, I knew the best decision I could make for her was to let her go. I instructed my mother's doctors to remove her from her respirator. I knew that once they did this, she would not survive long. However, for the first time in weeks, I was able to sleep soundly. I was confident that I had made the right decision.

Normally my mother was the fighter in our family; however, during her final days, it was my time to fight. I had to fight fear; I had to fight hurt; I had to fight doubt. I had to find the courage and confidence to make the best decision for someone who had put her trust in me.

This time I heartbreakingly realized that I wasn't supposed to fight to keep her here. I was supposed to fight to let her go.

~Peyton Woodson Cooper

She Ran a Good Race

*You've got to get up every morning with determination
if you're going to go to bed with satisfaction.*
~George Lorimer

My friend completed a 5K in October 2015 with the help of her daughter Jan, her son-in-law Rod, and two of their good friends. What's so remarkable about that, you might be asking? My friend Irma Koehneke was ninety-eight and completely blind!

Here's how it all started. Rod and Jan are veteran marathon walkers. Over the years, Irma had been listening to them talk about their races and how they trained for them. One day, Jan mentioned that she was thinking about walking the St. Joe's 5K in Neenah, Wisconsin, a race to benefit the Saint Joseph Food Pantry. Irma decided she would do it too, and one month before the big event, she started training by walking the halls at her care facility. One person walked with Irma, while another staff member followed behind with the wheelchair, just in case she needed to rest.

On the day of the event, Irma and her support team lined up at the start line. Irma walked across the start line and then alternated between being pushed in her chair for 100 yards and walking 100 feet. Along the route, people cheered, "Go Irma!" Sixty-two minutes later Irma and her crew walked across the finish line. What an experience! But the best was yet to come.

After finishing the race, all the participants were treated to a brunch provided by the sponsors of the race. Hundreds of athletes gathered in the hotel for the awarding of the medals. Of course, Irma was given one in recognition of her accomplishment as "first place" in her age category.

Much to her surprise, Irma was invited to the podium to say a few words. She opened her remarks by saying, "I always ask God why he still has me on this earth. Well, I'm here to get the word out — Jesus loves you and He has died for you."

You could have heard a pin drop in that cavernous room. Irma made a few more heartfelt remarks before going back to her table. She touched many lives that day.

For several weeks after the race, people called to congratulate Irma, and two people interviewed her for magazines. Her photos made it onto Facebook, too. Irma is well known as the widow of the former president of Concordia University Chicago, where her daughter Jan went to college as well, so she served as an inspiration not only to her own family, but to all the young college students who learned of her feat. It was a wonderful mother-daughter experience.

~Judy Mickelson

BEST MOM EVER!

Chapter 8

By Heart, Not by Blood

*You've never turned me away and you've always
made me feel like you wanted to be a part of my
life. Thank You! I grow more and more proud
each day to call you "Mom!"*
~Author Unknown

Meant to Be

Biology is the least of what makes someone a mother.
~Oprah Winfrey

I was fourteen when I learned that my mom was not my "real" mom. She actually told me on the day of my fourteenth birthday, explaining that I was now old enough to know the truth.

Mom had been working at the local CVS pharmacy and it was her week to open up as part of the morning shift. It was before 7 a.m. when she discovered a shopping cart from the adjacent dollar store parked in the pharmacy's entrance.

Quietly sleeping in the cart was a newborn baby wrapped in a soiled blue blanket. Nobody was around; the parking lot was empty. She opened the store, turned off the alarm, and called the police. While she waited, she checked to be sure that the baby was dry and comfortable. She carried him around the store, holding him to her warm body.

The police and the child services person arrived together and insisted on taking the baby to the hospital. My mom went with them. Even though the authorities kept telling her that it was none of her concern, she stayed there for two days. She badgered the nurses, the police and the child services representative, whose job it was to care for the baby, for information and demanded updates on their success in finding the baby's mother. They would come to learn, as I have, that when my mom is on a mission nothing gets in her way.

My mom couldn't have kids of her own, and she and my dad

had been approved for adoption. My appearance was a sign so strong that she was relentless in her conviction that I was sent to her by a higher power. Her sheer determination and total ignorance of the law somehow convinced a judge that she could keep me while the official paperwork for my adoption was completed.

Knowing that she's not my birth mother hasn't changed anything. It has only made me more appreciative of her. She said I was welcome to try to find my biological mother if I wanted, but no one could find her when I was born so I think a search would be a waste of time.

I do find myself looking at my mom differently once in a while because it's hard to believe that she's *not* my birth mother. We both have blue eyes and blond hair, and she's often mistaken for my older sister because we look so much alike. Neither of us likes broccoli. We are both left-handed, we both whistle in tune, we both have perfect pitch, and we both play the piano. We laugh or cry at the same movies, and we often share the same dreams. I may have trouble finding a girlfriend because I'll compare them all to my mom, and they'll all fall short. I have several friends who have nothing in common with their biological parents; it's uncanny how similar I am to my adoptive ones.

Now it may be easy to explain all these similar traits as coincidence or parental influence — it's certainly not heredity — but I had to draw the line on wishful conjecture when I discovered that my mom was born with a slight deformity called a hammer toe on her left foot. You guessed it, I have one too, and it's the same toe on the same foot! Explain that if you can.

~Derek H.

72

The Magic Formula

*There's nothing more vital to the bond you share with
someone than simply being there for them.*
~Suman Rai

I couldn't help her! My daughter was in the hospital, deep in
the throes of labor with her first child, and there were complications. Her doctor was willing to let her labor progress a
little longer, but there was a good chance they'd have to do a
C-section. The doctor said the decision was hers — whether to wait
it out or go into surgery immediately.

There was nothing I could say to help her because I'd never
given birth.

My daughter was part of the package when I married her widowed
father when she was twelve years old. I had never been a mother when
this almost teenager dropped into my life. She didn't come with an
instruction manual either. So what did I know about having a baby?

Now, nothing was going as planned. Bonnie had wanted to use
a midwife and have her baby at a birthing center. But here she was,
at the hospital, in labor and not dilating, plus she had developed a
fever. She needed to make a tough decision. Should she labor a little
longer or have the C-section?

I could see all her fears play across her face. And I had nothing
to offer her.

My husband and I stepped out of the room to allow my daughter
and son-in-law a chance to talk privately. As we were leaving, I leaned

over to her and said, "Trust your gut. You'll make the right decision." That was all of the motherly advice I had.

As we waited in the hallway, I felt like a mother in one way, because I didn't want to see my daughter hurting, anxious and afraid. On the other hand, I was helpless. I didn't know what it was like to be in labor and face the decision she was about to make. How could I support her when I had no idea what she was going through?

Some mother I was! Failing my daughter at the most critical moment of her life.

No one trains to be a parent. It's a learn-as-you-go position. There were many times when I was clueless and leaned on my husband to deal with an issue. There was no magic formula. Many times, I went by instinct alone.

That was what I encouraged Bonnie to do now, to trust her gut. But was that enough?

Finally, our son-in-law called us back into the room.

"I'm going to have the C-section." Bonnie announced. "I know my body, and with this fever, things are going to continue to spiral downward."

I grabbed her hand and nodded.

"It's time to get this baby out," she said, with more confidence than she probably felt.

My gut instinct said this was the right decision. Despite her own fear, I think Bonnie felt that, too. She was learning to trust her own instincts.

The doctor confirmed that she made the right decision. This baby wasn't going to come naturally.

Although nothing went according to their plans, a healthy baby girl was born, and Bonnie came through her first surgery with flying colors.

In the months that followed, my daughter adjusted to her role as a mom and I adjusted to mine as "Grammy." There wasn't much advice I could give her about raising an infant, so I could only show up when she needed me.

It still bothered me that I didn't have any sage advice and perfect words of wisdom for her, especially at the hospital. When I mentioned this to her, she had a quick answer. "Mom, everyone has told me what I should do, how I should eat, how to prepare and care for this baby."

I felt all the weight of my inadequacies, because I had told her nothing.

Then my daughter's next words broke through. "Because you *didn't* tell me what to do or how to do it, it was so much easier to be around you. You were my safe zone."

Safe zone? Me? Her words stunned me.

What I perceived as my weakness, my daughter perceived as strength, or at least, safety. What more could a mom want than to be the safe place for her daughter!

She confirmed this on her first Mother's Day, when she posted a note to me via social media:

As I celebrate my first Mother's Day as a mama, I want to wish the happiest of days to my awesome mom! You have set the bar so high over the years we've been mother and daughter; I hope I can give my daughter the grace, love, support and joy that you've given me every day since you said yes to being my mom. I love you!

Tears sprang to my eyes as I read her words. She loved and accepted me as a mom, just as I was.

There isn't a magic formula to motherhood, whether you're a parent by birth or marriage or adoption. I only needed to be there for her and support her.

Bonnie and I now choose to take our journey further, expanding beyond our mother and daughter roles. This time, I'm privileged to be Grammy to my sweet granddaughter and a safe haven for my daughter. We're on this new road together, believing in each other, learning, and trusting our instincts. And knowing that we love each other. That's our magic formula.

~Rebecca Yauger

73

Lady Pamela

*Families don't have to match. You don't have to look
like someone else to love them.*
~Leigh Anne Tuohy

I always tell people I have four mothers. My biological mother, my stepmother, my mother-in-law, and then there's Lady Pamela. I met Pam in ninth grade; she was my French teacher. I loved her immediately because she could make anyone laugh at any time, no matter the circumstances.

Our particular relationship strengthened after my mother left soon after I turned fifteen, and Pam's husband of over twenty years succumbed to cancer. We saw each other through these very difficult times. One of the most amazing things to me was that although Pam stayed out of school to grieve for a few months, when she came back, she was still able to bring laughter to those around her. I knew then that I would always love this woman. I stayed in her French classes through all four years of high school, and continued to visit her during my five years in the military. I'd become a single mom to my beautiful daughter, Sarah, during my time in the service, and she became known as Grammie Pammie from then on.

After I got out of the service, I moved back to our hometown where I met, fell in love with, and married my husband. Pam offered her home to us for the wedding. Our wedding was in her backyard, which happened to be by a beautiful lake. A few months later, she offered her home to us again to have our baby shower for our daughter, Lily.

Pam has been retired from teaching for a number of years now, and spends her time traveling the world, writing memoirs about her life, and attending conferences for the original Pan Am flight attendants. She may have taught French for years, but that is the tip of the iceberg when it comes to who this woman is, the students' lives she touched, the friends she made, and the two adopted granddaughters she has through us. Thank you, Lady Pamela, for being my friend, my confidante, and my personal hero.

~Rose Robson

What We Are
Because of Each Other

Of all the gifts that life has to offer, a loving
mother is the greatest of them all.
~Author Unknown

A short, chunky woman with dyed strawberry blond hair pushed open my apartment door with the words, "Getting moved in?" My first-ever landlady had dropped in for a visit.

"Yes," I answered, "and I'm about settled." I had left the horrors of my childhood home that morning, tucking my possessions into the back seat and trunk of my friend's car. My few clothes now hung in a white wooden closet that wrapped around the chimney that passed through my room. I had rented one of the furnished "apartments" that had been fashioned from the second floor of this huge farmhouse. My "apartment" was really a bedroom with an old range and a refrigerator added to it.

"Bathroom is down the hall. Wash your dishes in the sink. Remember you share with two other tenants, so don't clutter it up with your stuff. They're both older ladies who go to bed early, so time your bath later in the evening; you'll get along fine. And, whenever he's here," she pointed to my friend, "your door is open."

She reiterated all the other house rules she'd explained when I took the apartment. Her right eye looked directly at me while her left seemed to look all around the room. I later learned she had a lazy eye as a child so the left only saw light. But, that day I felt she was looking inside me as well as evaluating my possessions.

"Did you make the bed?" she asked. My puzzled expression led her to lift the spread and reveal the bare mattress beneath. "You don't have bedding," she stated, then disappeared down the staircase.

"I've never had a bed before," I told my friend. He already knew.

She returned with a set of sheets and a pillowcase. "You can use these." I wondered to myself if I could figure out how to make a bed properly, then decided to wait until she left. I just thanked her.

But she didn't leave. Instead she continued asking questions. Each of my answers resulted in her disappearing and reappearing with household items I didn't know I needed.

Ever since I saw the apartment, I had been mesmerized by the vision of my own little space: the single bed in the corner next to the tall window; the low windowsill big enough to sit in with a view of the sky; the mirrored dressing table with cabinets on each side; the painted white table that overlooked Union Park. I was a little frightened by the gas stove on the inside wall because it had to be lit with a match. Beside it were a dry sink and a cupboard next to a short refrigerator.

By the time my landlady was satisfied that I was truly settled she had "lent" me two saucepans, a small iron skillet, a toaster, and an alarm clock. "You don't want to be late for school," she said as she put it in my hand.

The following Wednesday evening she yelled up the stairs: "Patty, what are you doing? I'm going to the grocery store. You wanna come?"

Since my only transportation consisted of my two legs and a bicycle, I answered, "Sure; when are you going?"

"In about five minutes; come on down when you're ready."

At the bottom of my stairs was a hallway with three doors, all leading into her home. I tried two. They were locked. I opened the third and walked through, then stood quietly just inside.

"We're not going to get anywhere with you standing there — come on; let's get going," was her invitation. The rooms in her home were expansive. I peeked in to the dining room. I saw a long dark dining table and a ceiling-to-floor bay window covered in white lace. Next to it was the huge, wood-paneled kitchen with a door that led outside.

She drove us to three different grocery stores that evening, explaining that prices for various items were better at one and vegetables were fresher at another. I carefully picked out the least expensive of whatever I needed.

When we returned home, her husband had a fresh pot of coffee for us. "Won't you stay for a cup of coffee?" she asked while he poked through the sacks of groceries in search of his fig cookies. And so began our Wednesday night outings.

After a few weeks I knew where she kept everything and would put her groceries away for her when we got home. Our Wednesday night outings expanded from groceries to clothing shopping and eventually to fabric stores for things we needed for projects we were doing together. "Dad," as she called her husband, began teasing us about our shopping. "You two go and spend my gas money even when you don't buy anything," he'd quip.

The door to her part of the house was permanently open after the second week I lived there. And by the third, she had me call her "Mom." Her invitation to come down always started with "Patty what are you doing?" It was almost always accompanied by the scent of something fresh — coffee, homemade bread, soup, chili, or fried chicken. Late night TV watching, Sunday brunches, and "Patty just come down anytime," were added to the Wednesday shopping trips. She was always doing something interesting and seemed to enjoy having me along.

"Take this pan of rolls and set it on the furnace grate to rise." "Take this thing and pull those jars out of the boiling water so I can put peaches in them." If I said, "I can't do that," she responded with, "Who told you you couldn't?" which set me to wondering why I thought I couldn't and eventually broke that cycle. When I asked, "What are you making?" as her sewing machine whirred, she responded with sewing lessons, which eventually revealed a natural talent I didn't know I had.

Dad's early comments about our Wednesday nights were prophetic. They became so important to us that when my husband asked me to marry him, my answer was, "Only if I can keep my Wednesday nights with Mom." He said yes and I did too!

When I told Mom, she said, "Patty you didn't really say that, did you?" I answered, "Yes, and he agreed. Will you make my wedding dress?"

She became the mother I needed; I was the daughter she never had. When I got jittery before my wedding and wondered if I would turn out like my parents, she reassured me: "Patty, you're not your parents. You're you. You love him. He loves you. Don't let fear cheat you out of what you two deserve. You have something special. Have you told him your fears? When you have fears or problems, don't come to me. Go to him. Always talk to one another. You two will be fine."

At twenty-three I became a married woman. As the years passed, Mom's hairstyle changed from a dyed strawberry blond bun to a snow-white Afro. I became the designated driver for our Wednesday outings. It was funny how Mom lost her ability to estimate distances once she turned over the car keys to me. "Just a ways up north out of town" would turn out to be a two-hour drive that she explained away with "You didn't go the way I told you."

We moved from her kitchen to mine for baking bread or canning peaches. I became the parent at times, explaining to her cataract surgeon her fears and that his work must result in her being able to continue her sewing and reading. It was my hand steadying hers in the recovery room. She awoke from her open-heart surgery with her hand in mine.

During the last years of her life, her youngest son and I shared in her care. Like true brother and sister we had good-natured "Mom always liked you best" battles. I wished I'd been born to her; he wished for the closeness that can only be shared by a mother and daughter.

His greatest compliment: "Patty, I'm thankful for what you both are because of each other."

Me too. Thanks, Mom!

~Patricia Voyce

75

Sacrifice

A Birthmother puts the needs of her child
above the wants of her heart.
~Skye Hardwick

I watch her grow
through a Facebook page,
her first steps,
first everything,
all through videos.
Seeing her eyes,
the same as mine,
wishing she were in my arms.
Her laugh,
strange to me,
echoes through speakers
across distance to reach my ears.
Her mother,
her real mother,
the one she'll grow to know,
smiling back,
a picture perfect love
that I sacrificed
to give her a life,

her mother a life,
they wouldn't have otherwise.

~Penny C.

76

Step by Stepmom

It's not the blood you share that makes you a mother...
It's the heart you share with one another.
~Patty Rase Hopson

M y wife, Diana, didn't know what she was signing up for when she married me eleven years ago at the age of forty-one. She knew she was getting three stepchildren, but she had no idea how much being a stepmother was going to test her patience and stretch her wisdom.

Diana had met my children, accidentally, on our second date. We were to meet at my house before going to the drive-in. However, my kids' mother was late picking them up, so they were still in the driveway when Diana arrived. Diana would have been content to drive around the block a time or two, but it was too late. She had been spotted.

My two boys—Anthony, then ten, and Gregory, then eight—politely shook her hand. However, my daughter Kimberly, who was only two, just gave Diana the lizard-eye from the car seat in her mother's car and didn't say a word.

Fortunately, it didn't take long for Kim to warm up to Diana. Oddly enough, their first real bonding experience was potty training. Kim was proving difficult to train, which was frustrating me because the boys had been so easy. Like most little girls, Kim was all about the Disney princesses, so Diana had the brilliant idea of buying Disney princess underwear for Kim.

The first time Kim peed on Cinderella, she was upset, but soon got over it. However, when she pooped on Sleeping Beauty, her "MOST FAVORITEST" princess, she was absolutely distraught. Potty training problem solved!

Our wedding in June of 2005 was as festive as we could hope for. Anthony and Greg (then twelve and almost ten) stood up with me at the wedding, looking all manly in their junior-size tuxedos. And Kimberly, my princess, was our flower girl, three weeks shy of her fourth birthday. Despite being so small, Kim knew what was going on, because immediately following the conclusion of the ceremony, Kim shouted, "Now I have *two* mommies!"

Kim tried to call Diana "Mommy" once a few days later. By the dubious look on her face though, we could tell that she didn't think it sounded right. Without a word being spoken by anyone, it was understood that the kids would just call Diana by her first name, which they still do to this day. Diana approved of this, mainly for the reason that their mother was still very much in the picture, and Diana had no intention of taking her place.

To say that living the life of a stepmother was an adjustment for Diana was an understatement. Though this was my second marriage, it was her first, and she had been single for a long time. She was used to a quiet house, an active social life, coming and going as she pleased, and eating cereal for dinner at least three nights a week. Now she had to make the whiplash transition to things like sibling conflict, parent-teacher conferences, picky eaters, and being home on the weekends when I had the kids.

Any joint custody situation is going to involve different parenting styles between the two households. Children, like rivers, will take the path of least resistance. Therefore, if one parent doesn't push them to do chores or to behave a certain way, they won't. Then, when the other parent does expect these things, there will be weeping and gnashing of teeth.

Diana grew up in a very traditional country home, where kids did their chores, respected their parents, went to church every Sunday and didn't expect to get anything without working hard for it. While I grew up with similar values, the splintering of my first marriage made it impractical, if not impossible, for me to pass those values along to my own kids during their formative years. Diana didn't give up though. Even if it didn't bother the kids that their rooms were messy, or their homework wasn't done, or the dishwasher needed emptying, or they smelled because they hadn't showered in three days, if it bothered Diana, she would let them hear about it, early and often, until the problem was corrected.

Naturally, the kids resented all of this nagging and correction, since they didn't get it at their mom's house. Over the years, though, they learned to appreciate other things about Diana. One of these things was Diana's love of vacations.

Diana decided that we should take a major vacation with the kids every other year. These trips have included Cedar Point, New Orleans, Disney World, Gatlinburg, Gulf Shores, and even a cruise to Mexico. As much as she enjoys the traveling, what Diana really cherishes is making memories with the kids. She was there for Anthony's first roller coaster ride, Greg's first ocean swim, and Kimberly's thirteenth birthday in Cozumel, just to name a few.

The boys each ended up moving in with us when they reached college age, and Kim joined us full-time at the age of fourteen. Despite the fact that Diana still nagged about little things like chores, as well as big things like who they were dating, the kids grew to appreciate her wisdom in these matters.

Through all of this, though, I find it strange that Diana still does not consider herself a mother, since the kids still have their mother. The kids see it differently, though. The year that Anthony turned eighteen, he got Diana a very nice card for Mother's Day. He told her, "You didn't give birth to me, but you did raise me, and I wouldn't be who I am today without you."

That's the truth. Anthony is married now and finishing college. Greg is also finishing his degree. He lives with us, and although he used to be a slob, his room is now the neatest in the house.

Kim is now a sophomore in high school. Being the rebel of the family, she has had the most conflict with Diana by far, be it about her clothes, her hair, her taste in music, her boyfriends, her unusual eating habits, or her addiction to social media. Diana stays the course, though, and refuses to give up on her. Little by little, as Kim grows, we can see Diana's patience and wisdom beginning to pay dividends.

All stepmoms should get a medal, but when I think about how my kids might have turned out without Diana's influence in their lives, I think my wife deserves three.

~M. Scott Coffman

Right from the Start

A daughter is one of the most beautiful
gifts this world has to give.
~Laurel Atherton

The babies came out of the back room one at a time. Kind orphanage workers carried them to their new moms. They were dressed adorably in colorful garments, but they were screaming and crying. The chorus of crying babies and the faces of the smiling, but anxious parents created an unforgettable movie-worthy scene.

A woman called out my new daughter's Chinese name and my heart jumped. I walked much too quickly to the front of the room as my wife followed. A woman handed me a cute baby wearing blue pajamas and said, "Look, she's not crying!" My wife held the video camera and captured the moment.

We took the nineteen-month-old baby to the back of the room and sat on a bench. Our daughter grabbed hold of her new mother. My wife smiled for the first time in months and then her eyes filled with tears and her mouth quivered. My legs weakened and I sat down, wiping my own eyes.

My wife held our baby tightly as I filmed them. And just like a movie, it was love at first sight. The baby in the blue pajamas had found her mother, the woman who would raise her and always love her. My brave wife, who had just recovered from open-heart surgery, had found her daughter, the child who would make all her days meaningful.

Yes, I captured the entire scene on camera, but I don't actually need to replay it because the moment is always with me. It is a moment that lifts me up when I'm down. It is a moment that inspires me today and tomorrow — my favorite moment.

Yesterday, when my wife came home from work, our nearly eleven-year-old daughter ran to the door. The preteen girl and her mother lovingly embraced, just like they were reliving that first meeting nine years ago. As I watched them my legs weakened and I sat down and wiped my eyes.

~Louis De Lauro

The Chosen Daughter

Memory is a way of holding onto the things you love,
the things you are, the things you never want to lose.
~From the television show The Wonder Years

I never got the chance to tell you how much I loved you and appreciated you for doing what you did for me. It took me a while to get to this point. I had to grow up and mature to understand the sacrifices you made.

I now fully understand that being a mother has nothing to do with birthing a child. I spent a good part of my childhood hating you for "abandoning" me, and hating my biological mother for giving me up. I didn't really appreciate you for being the mother who chose me.

It wasn't easy. In 1970, you and your husband were estranged, so essentially, you were a single black female who wanted to give me a good home. You knew my biological family through work... knew my situation. You were my savior. You petitioned the court three times. The first time they told you no, and you could have given up. No one would have blamed you for giving up after they told you no a second time. But you kept going back, and every time they closed the door in your face, you found a way to re-open it. You would not be denied.

The courts granted your wish the third time and made us family. You became my mother... the only mother I have ever known. Life was wonderful with you. You brought me home to a lovely two-story house in an upper middle class mixed neighborhood with a white and pink nursery and a beautiful handmade white crib. I had the best of everything — clothes, toys, bikes, a dog, and even a pool. You were very active in the community and you exposed me to that at an early age. I attended meetings and fundraisers with you, and learned about giving back at an early age.

You'd left Mississippi about fifteen years earlier. You realized that you wanted a better life than the one in the poor Mississippi Delta town of Lula. You didn't have much formal education, but you were a smart, hardworking, beautiful and charming woman who knew how to succeed. You had determination and a dream, and the wherewithal to make it all happen. And that you did, starting your own cleaning business and winning corporate contracts.

You also had an appreciation for fine furniture, knick-knacks, and antiques, and turned that into a business. You were multitasking before it became a thing. You taught yourself to read better, and knew the key to my success was going to be a good education. I heard about college before I even got to preschool, and knew I'd be headed to Indiana University. You loved to put me in front of the TV to watch *Sesame Street* and *Electric Company*. At the store, you bought me books instead of candy, and I learned the alphabet, shapes, colors, numbers and the name of the President before I knew my full name.

I was spoiled and you could never tell me no. I don't remember ever being disciplined but I'm sure it happened and was likely done with love. Because that's what I remember the most: being loved. That, and your big personality, and your arms giving me lots of hugs. I expected life with you to just get better with time. But of all the things we had together, that's the one thing we didn't have. Time.

November 13, 1976. I will never forget that day. I didn't know where you were and relatives were showing up. Nobody was answering my questions. And then I saw the newspaper. You were on page one of the Metro section, lying on a gurney. You had been in a car accident. The car had hit an embankment in the snow and gone airborne. When it landed, your legs and your chest were crushed. My brother was in the car with you and your arm was across his chest in a protective manner. Your other arm was broken. He didn't have a scratch on him but you had internal injuries. I read that it took them an hour to get you out of that mangled piece of metal with the Jaws of Life. I will never forget reading "a tired, but relieved, Mary Taylor was rushed to the hospital…." And that's when I figured out where you were. At the same hospital where you found me.

I rode to the hospital with family, but they wouldn't let me go in. I was only six, but I felt like I was sixteen. I remember looking up at that tall building and wondering which one of the windows belonged to your room. You were in intensive care and it was clear that you wouldn't make it. Even then, according to all accounts, you were worried about me. Wondered who would raise your little girl. You died later that day.

I had a rough life after you died. I had to move to the same state you left, and not much had changed. I went from a two-story house in a nice neighborhood to living in abject poverty in a two-room shack on a former plantation. Your younger sister never adopted me but became my legal guardian, as I was a ward of the state. She abused me for the next eleven years. I cried almost every day for the first year I lived there. I didn't go to the bathroom for almost a week because I was scared of going in that outhouse. We didn't even have running water.

I know that wasn't the life you wanted for me, and I want you to know that your deathbed prayers got me through and helped me succeed. I graduated as valedictorian from high school and *summa cum laude* from college (third in my class). Today, I am a licensed CPA in Texas. I work for a global company and I own a business, following in your entrepreneurial spirit. I am married, and I do so much community service, I know you would be proud. But my biggest accomplishment to date is being called Mom by a six-year-old. I am raising her with the same foundation you gave me. Most importantly, I'm raising her with the same love you showed me. And I can't seem to tell her no, either.

~Sheila Taylor-Clark

79

So Much More than a Mother-in-Law

Family isn't always blood. It's the people in
your life who want you in theirs.
~Author Unknown

The dictionary defines mother-in-law as the mother of one's husband or wife. Mother-in-law, however, often has a negative connotation. I've heard women refer to their mothers-in-law as monster-in-law and other even worse names.

But that's not *my* mother-in-law. I met Barbara when I was just seventeen. I was fortunate to meet her under casual circumstances, as I felt no pressure to impress her. Her son and I were just friends and not dating. In fact, the first time I went to her home, I leaned against the kitchen counter and broke a piece of the counter tile. Barbara and I shared our first good laugh together.

For two years, Barbara and I saw each other on a regular basis, as I was at her home quite often. We would sit and chat, share recipes, and look through photo albums of my husband as a baby. We would just, well, hang out. Like friends.

In addition to being just my friend though, she was (excuse me for saying this, Barbara) my "elder." I had great respect for her. I looked to her for advice and wisdom and was appreciative of what she had to offer. I learned a lot from her by the example she set.

Two years later, her son and I began officially dating. Luckily, it wasn't weird. It was a natural transition.

After her son and I got engaged, Barbara and I hung out even more. We talked (a lot), cooked together, and even went shopping and out to lunch. She then brought out her wedding photo albums and we pored over them for hours, smiling, giggling, and swapping stories: her experience versus my hopes.

Twenty-seven years later, Barbara and I are closer than ever. We've had many experiences most mothers- and daughters-in-law will never be fortunate enough to share. We've been on vacations together, we've shared beauty tips, we've driven sports cars over 100 miles per hour. We've been on paddleboat rides and train trips. We've gone together to weddings, funerals, and everything in between.

Five years ago, I had a son. Pregnancy, childbirth, new motherhood and now school have proven to be a learning curve for me (and my husband). My own mother, having passed away several years ago, is not around to teach me about parenting or to offer words of wisdom and encouragement. Luckily for me, I have Barbara. With the birth of my son, we became bonded forever! Barbara is the one I call for advice. She's the one person who can get my son to eat anything. She's also the person I ask to talk to my son when he's being so incorrigible I can't handle him.

Barbara reminds me I'm doing a great job and is great at gently offering a suggestion every now and then. I remind her that she is doing a great job, too, and I occasionally offer her a suggestion as well.

We both talk. We both listen. We both respect. We both love. And that's why Barbara isn't just my mother-in-law; she's my friend and adviser and the mom I can rely on for everything.

~Crescent LoMonaco

80

Divine Timing

Whether your children are yours through biology or
adoption, they are yours through love.
~Sadia Rebecca Rodriguez

R uby was visiting the doctor again with one of her many illnesses. She had seen a woman with black hair and Native American features come out as she entered, but she didn't think much of it until later. She was more focused on the sound of a crying baby inside the office.

A two-year-old child had been left with the receptionist. She was covered in boils, malnourished, and in so much pain that she couldn't stop crying. Ruby, ignoring the doctor's warnings that the little girl wouldn't live through the night, took her home. She decided that she could keep this child alive and she wasn't going to let anyone tell her otherwise.

Ruby stayed up all night with that baby, who was in so much pain that even a light touch would cause her to scream. No matter how little sleep Ruby had, she was not going to leave the baby girl's side.

Not only did the little girl live through the night, but she healed through the next few months. Ruby and her husband Don decided to adopt the little girl they had nursed back to health.

The father of the child, Frederick, emerged, but it seemed he only wanted money from his baby's new parents. The judge put a quick stop to that by ordering that Frederick have no contact with the new family. If he dared contact them, he would be put in jail.

Frederick's wife Nellie, the woman Ruby had seen leaving the doctor's office, stayed silent. The story eventually came out. The night before she left her baby at the doctor's office, she had been trying to comfort her. She knew her baby was sick, no matter how much she assured her other children that she would be all right. Her husband Frederick had had enough of the crying and told her to get rid of the baby or he would kill it.

Nellie dropped off her baby at the doctor to save her life. She didn't know what else to do. This was a long time ago, before there were resources available to help mothers in this kind of situation.

That little baby became my mother. We didn't find out her birth-mother's part of the story until 2014 when we met Fred, Nellie's son, the uncle I never knew I had. He had always thought the baby was adopted by the doctor. Nellie died in 2011, long before we had the chance to talk to her. We didn't get the chance to thank her for giving my mom a second chance by letting my grandparents adopt her.

~Ellicia Dawn

To the Friend Who Mothered Me

Being a mother is an attitude, not a biological relation.
~Robert A. Heinlein

For the days when I do not believe
I have the resilience, courage and strength
For the days I don't trust in myself
You do, and you remind me every day
You remind me when I think the sun won't shine
And that dreams are as forged as fairy tales
That there is light in everything around me
And with hope and faith I can prevail
You are strength just in and of yourself
You are unconditional love
You are a shoulder; a friend I don't take for granted
And forever and always you're a wonderful hug
Thanks for being a friend
Thanks for doing the job of a mom
You may not be mine for real
But you still hold the same exact spot
And for that I am grateful and beyond overjoyed
Wishing you the very best on this Mother's Day

Love always the girl you didn't birth
But is your child anyway

~Kimberly Edwards

BEST MOM EVER!

Maternal Miracles

*Blessed is a mother that would give up part of
her soul for her children's happiness.*
~Shannon L. Alder

No Questions Asked

God could not be everywhere and
therefore he made mothers.
~Jewish Proverb

My mom had reluctantly agreed to accompany Dad and us kids on a weekend camping trip in Pennsylvania's Amish Country when I was ten years old. We were lucky to rent a raised wooden tent platform during that rainy spring weekend. That put us safe and dry three feet off the damp ground. Dad supervised as my three siblings and I erected the tent. Then we all piled back into our station wagon for a day of sightseeing.

There wasn't much to see, as the rain had closed most of the local historic sites. We did stop at an Amish farm that advertised tours of the barn, petting the animals, and a snack of homemade donuts and fresh milk. Mom stayed outside in the drizzle while my father accompanied us into the barns. When we told Mom that we had petted the cows she insisted we wash our hands before eating our still warm, cinnamon-sugar donuts. Her caution may have been well founded, but by the time we washed our hands our warm donuts had gone cold.

It was not a great start to our trip, but we thought that Mom was overreacting when she woke us the next morning an hour before dawn. "George," she informed my father, "we have to go, now."

"Is something wrong?" my father asked groggily. "Are the kids okay? Are you okay? Can we leave later, after breakfast?"

"No," she insisted. "We have to leave now." We immediately decamped, carting our sleeping bags and army cots to the car. The tent, much heavier now that the canvas was wet from hours of rain, was the last item to be carried by all hands to the car. We dumped it onto the open rear deck with a mighty crash. It took a second or two for us to realize that the crashing sound came not from dropping the tent into the car but from the huge tree that inexplicably fell over and crushed the tent platform we had vacated moments before. We stared aghast at the carnage, and then at my nonplussed mother. Without any visible reaction, she said, "Get in the car, kids."

The following summer witnessed another display of Mom's uncanny maternal instincts. I remember Mom carrying me into our doctor's office because I was too weak to walk. I'm told that the doctor's diagnosis was "just a summer virus." That off-the-cuff assessment did not satisfy Mom's instincts whatsoever. She brought me to a medical laboratory and coolly instructed the technician to draw and analyze a specimen of my blood. He demurred, rightfully claiming he could not do so without a physician's orders. But he had never been confronted by my mother's will. He did as he was told, no further questions asked.

My blood specimen was quickly drawn and analyzed. The technician returned to instruct Mom to take me immediately to the nearest emergency room. Within a few hours my abdomen was opened and the ruptured appendix was removed. Subsequently I spent a hot summer convalescing and bored, but alive. No one asked how she knew. She just did.

Two decades later I was working as a registered nurse in the same emergency room that I had passed through as a critically ill eleven-year-old. Working double shifts was never a hardship because my profession was my true calling. Because I was proficient and professional I was often assigned to instruct newbie nurses, and sometimes physicians, in the arts and procedures of that chaotic setting.

One winter afternoon, at the change of shifts after my first eight hours, an ambulance arrived without prior notice with a patient in full cardiac arrest. I directed the EMTs to bring the patient into our "crash room" and called out a hospital-wide page to assemble the "code blue" team. Within seconds a crowd of clinicians of all types surrounded the stretcher, each carrying out his or her task. A young resident physician stepped close to the patient, a defibrillator paddle in each hand. She badly misplaced them on the patient's chest, which resulted in electrical burns but no restoration of the patient's heart rhythm.

I cursed under my breath with frustration. "Give me the paddles. Charge me up. Everyone step back from the stretcher," I ordered. I'd performed this life-saving procedure many times; I knew exactly how to effectively and safely carry it out. Unfortunately for me, the resident did not. She wanted to see how it was done so she stepped up close — too close — as I pulled the defibrillator's trigger. In that instant she mistakenly pushed me against the stretcher's metal railing.

Several things happened simultaneously. I became the unlucky recipient of 360 painful joules of electricity that bolted up my arms, made my eardrums tingle, and stopped my heart. The patient, who had not received the second electrical shock, died. And my mother, vacationing with my father in Florida, turned to him and said frantically, "Call Tommy, he's in the ER, something's wrong!" He did as he was told but he couldn't get through to anyone because the pandemonium in that emergency room reached new levels as the staff worked to save one of its own, me.

Late in her life I let my curiosity get the better of me. "Hey, Mom," I asked, "How did you do that? How'd you always know when something was going wrong?"

"It's not my job to wonder how or why, Tommy," she replied with a coy shrug. "It's just my job to do it." No further questions asked, none answered.

~Thom Schwarz

Serendipity

Being a mother means that your heart is no longer
yours; it wanders wherever your children do.
~Author Unknown

I sat on the rolled out white paper, my bare legs swinging off the edge of the examining table. While I waited, I examined the patterned wallpaper — green embryo-shaped swirls on a cream background.

"Apropos," I mumbled.

An abrupt knock caused me to jump. The door opened quickly as Dr. Graham stepped into the office, his kind smile reassuring.

"Hiya, Jen," he began. "So, we got the results back…" (Was it me or was that smile looking a little more forced?) "I'm afraid you're infertile."

Well. That was blunt. Wham, bam, you're sterile, Ma'am.

His expression remained calm and kind. *How could he be so composed? So unaffected? Where was the back rubbing? And why did he have embryos adorning his examining room walls? That was just cruel.*

And so it began.

The drive home was a blur of blind driving, loud wailing, and a heartbroken apology to the baby I couldn't have. My car was on autopilot as my newfound identity steered me home and into despair so deep that my whole body ached.

As time passed my husband and I began to entertain the possibility of adoption, but it was all too overwhelming. Instead, I pushed through the days, facing each monthly cycle with weepiness, anger, wine… or all of the above.

Then one day I decided I needed a puppy. I'd always loved dogs and had a couple growing up, so this made sense to me. My focus subtly shifted; I desperately needed something to give my love to, to fill the void. Unfortunately, I faced another obstacle. We'd signed a lease that forbade pets.

My husband, however, was on a mission. Unabashedly he pulled the "Infertile Card" and convinced our landlord to make an exception to his own rules: once he did, a fissure appeared in the dark clouds that surrounded me. I had something to look forward to! A puppy would never take the place of a baby, but I needed a home for the stash of love I'd built up for my unborn child.

The first thing I did was call my mother with the news.

She lived nearby and had helplessly shared in my burden of infertility as only a mother could. My news brought her relief and happiness; she was pleased to hear that my husband and I would be starting our search for a puppy the following weekend.

That plan, however, went out the window the next morning. Waiting another four days to begin our search required far too much discipline, so I took a day off from work and set out on my mission, alone. The Connecticut Humane Society was located in a nearby town, which also happened to be the same town where my mother lived. I knew it unlikely that I'd find an available puppy my first time looking, but I had to try. Off I went without a word to my husband, my mother or anyone.

Walking down the aisle alongside the cages was heartbreaking. I tried not to look into the eyes of any of the sad, precious creatures so desperate to be loved. I felt a kinship with them and a terrible betrayal within myself for bypassing them, but I needed a puppy. A baby of another kind…

He was in the third stall. As soon as he saw me he wagged his tail shyly and then sat up on his hind legs, reaching his paws through the bars of the cage and wrapping them around my hand. It was love at first sight. A young girl and her mother were behind me, approaching the cage moments after me. The child was telling her mother that she wanted this same puppy. I ignored them as they lingered, hoping, no doubt, that I would walk away.

I wouldn't move. I waited until one of the attendants came out to check on us and then told her that I'd be taking this dog. A twinge of guilt struck me as I put my needs before the little girl, but this was *my* dog. I was smitten.

They took us into a room where I completed the necessary paperwork. I pulled out my checkbook to pay, the final step before I could bring my sweet puppy home.

"I'm sorry, we don't take checks, Ma'am," the attendant said flatly.

This was the 1980s — we didn't have debit cards and at that point I only had one credit card, which I rarely carried. No problem: I'd run into town and take the money out of the bank.

"I'm sorry, we don't hold the animals for anyone," she added.

I looked through the window and saw the puppy stalkers still wandering around. I couldn't leave — they would get *my* puppy as soon as I left! Trying not to panic I asked if I could use their phone, as this was pre–cell phones. I called my mother, who lived only a few miles away, but there was no answer. I tried my girlfriend. Same result. I began to feel desperate and was fighting back tears when I heard her....

"Jen?"

That voice that I loved and knew so well came from behind me. I turned to see my beautiful mother standing in the doorway, smiling and looking surprised.

"Mom!"

Relief flowed in the form of tears. I couldn't believe that she was there — at the Humane Society of all places — and that she'd arrived just in time. She was on her way to the grocery store, she explained, and for "some reason" wound up taking a turn that brought her completely out of her way... and right past the Humane Society. It was then that she noticed what she thought was my car. Fortunately, she'd decided to come in and check.

My mother paid the attendant in cash and we walked out side-by-side, with my puppy in my arms. I've often thought about that day and how my mother appeared like an angel out of nowhere, a gift of divine intervention. Because of her and my sweet pup, Clancy, I was able to find hope again, which helped me through some difficult days. And Clancy wound up being a wonderful "sibling" to his baby sister, Erin, to whom I gave birth the following year!

~M.J. Shea

That Stolen Day

Life is not measured by the number of breaths we take,
but by the moments that take our breath away.
~Maya Angelou

My mother was on a first-name basis with the school faculty within a month of me starting kindergarten. I am convinced she must have set a Guinness World Record for the number of parent-teacher conferences held in a single school year.

It started when she let her six-year-old pick out her own wardrobe. Three days in a row, I went to school proudly dressed like the 1980's gold-medal gymnast Mary Lou Retton. Wearing pink leotards under a maroon one-piece swimsuit and leg warmers, I was the epitome of coolness. In *my* mind at least.

The school, however, was not impressed and sent a polite note home stating that I should wear something a bit more appropriate for school. They were right, my mother reasoned. So, we stepped up our fashion game and I dressed like Cyndi Lauper for two consecutive days before a parent-teacher conference was called. It would be the first of many.

I wasn't necessarily a precocious child, but my mother was a very strong-willed lady and a notorious procrastinator, and I often got in trouble because of it. Things like late permission slips and missing lunch money, or her advice — "It really is okay not to sleep at naptime. Your teachers won't mind." — plagued me. There was always something, and often my mother was the underlying cause.

So when she randomly showed up on a warm fall day in first grade announcing a family emergency, my teachers thought nothing of it. I grabbed my Smurfs lunchbox and raced after her. The hallways were a sea of autumnal color, covered in art made by young and clumsy hands. Orange paper plates transformed into crooked jack-o-lanterns and a dozen variations of black cats cut from inky construction paper hissed at passers-by. To this day, fall and all the colors that accompany it trigger warm memories of my mother.

I kept whispering, "What's wrong?" but she just kept walking and she wouldn't answer me. As we reached her little white and blue–pinstriped Ford Ranger (which she had already wrecked twice), I was shaking with fear. As a frequent visitor to the ER at a young age, I was well aware that the word "emergency" meant something bad and painful that usually involved needles and shots.

As we closed the doors of her truck, she grabbed my hand and said, "The emergency is that I missed my daughter." And then she told me that we were going to the lake, one of our favorite mother-daughter activities. I opened my mouth to cheer but before I got one gleeful screech out, she slapped my thigh, hard!

I was shocked and I started bawling. We rounded the corner of my school and drove past a row of windows filled with the curious faces of my classmates, noses pressed up against the glass. What they saw was my face contorted with sobs, howling just one word to my mother: "Why?" I'm quite sure they thought, "Wow. That must be some kind of emergency."

Once we were safely out of sight, my mother pulled over and hugged me tight, apologizing for what she'd done. She said, "I'm sorry I slapped you, but if we came around that corner and all of your classmates and your teacher saw you cheering and clapping they would have known."

That stolen day at the lake remains one of the best days of my life. After I stopped crying, we got happy meals at McDonald's. We fed Cheetos to the squirrels. We splashed and played in the blue-green lake water, still warm enough in the Texas fall to swim in. We flew a kite and got it stuck in a tree. And we laughed until our cheeks hurt.

I didn't ask the burning question on my mind. Was it really okay to skip school and play hooky with my mother at the lake? Wasn't that breaking the rules?

Yes, of course it was—but my mother knew that sometimes rules needed to be bent. Even broken.

They say a mother's intuition is one of the most powerful forces in the world, and I am convinced that's true. My mother died that November, a little over a month after our trip to the lake, after a terrible accident resulted in septic shock.

My mother knew something that no one else did that day when she took me to the lake. Somehow, deep in her soul, she knew that her time with me was short. And she was willing to bend a few rules to get one more laugh with me, to get one more hug... to get one more day at the lake.

A month after my mother died, I remember sitting under the Christmas tree, horribly sad that we wouldn't be able to exchange gifts anymore. But even in death, my mother came to the rescue. Normally, she waited until the last minute for everything. Except that year. She had secretly bought our presents in October and although she was gone—her love and her lessons weren't.

Those lessons live on in my heart to this day. Trust your heart. Your instinct is smarter than you give it credit for. Find something every day that makes you laugh until your cheeks hurt. Don't be so afraid of what everyone else thinks. If you want to dress like Mary Lou Retton, by all means girl—go for it!

~Kristi Adams

Mom's Dream House

The more a daughter knows the details of her
mother's life, the stronger the daughter.
~Anita Diamant

I was visiting Mom in Philadelphia where she and my stepfather lived. We were having a cup of coffee when she asked, "Did I ever tell you about the time I bought a house for a dollar?"

"No, I think I would remember that," I answered, wondering why I had never heard this amazing story before.

She must have realized how badly I needed hope that afternoon almost two decades ago. My job in Christian media was rewarding, but I worked lots of hours for little pay. After paying our monthly bills, there wasn't much left over. My son Zach was already a teenager. I didn't see any way that I would ever make enough money to buy a house for us.

My mother understood the importance of a home of your own. She and my father had purchased a couple together, before her heart was broken when their marriage fell apart. When this happened, Mom was in her early forties with seven children, five still living at home ranging in age from nine months to sixteen years. She once wrote, "The days did not hold any certainty—except the absolute certainty that I must start a new life after twenty-three years of marriage."

The year before my parents separated, I had moved into my first apartment, trying to escape the impending family doom. Being a self-involved teenager, I had no idea how greatly my mother was suffering or how courageously she dealt with all the obstacles she faced.

Her only income was a meager stipend as a church organist, because she had quit her job as a school music teacher when my youngest brother Jeremy was born. Mom's savings account had a balance of just $250, but in the divorce settlement she would eventually receive child support and possession of the family home — an older house filled with painful memories in a deteriorating neighborhood where she no longer wanted to live.

Mom's friend Eileen was a real estate agent who sympathized with her dream of wanting a new beginning in a safer neighborhood. Yet she also knew that Mom's limited income would prevent her from getting a bank loan.

Despite this, my mother told me, "Eileen called me one morning and suggested we go look at homes that afternoon. She considered this an outing, but I believed it was house hunting… she took us to a two-bedroom home on a boulevard street. The home, although well-constructed, was dirty and neglected — but it had a lovely living room, dining room, family room, one full bath and two half baths. There was a large attic with a pull-down stairway."

My then sixteen-year-old brother happened to go along on this house-hunting excursion. Already handy with tools, Greg said he thought he could convert the attic into the two additional bedrooms the family would require.

His offer cinched the deal for Mom. Eileen didn't have the heart to inform her soon-to-be divorced friend that she was certain no bank would finance the plan.

Instead she wrote up the purchase agreement, later explaining, "I didn't want to see you cry, so I thought I'd let the banker give you the bad news." After completing the paperwork, Eileen asked, "Do you have a dollar, Glenna? There has to be a down payment and one dollar will make it a binding contract." Mom handed Eileen the dollar bill, and eagerly signed the contract.

The following morning, my mother provided the bank's loan officer with the property's address. "I jog every morning and go by that house," he said. "It needs some work, but it is a well-built home in an excellent area."

The banker never asked about my mother's income, just her profession. "I imagine you would like a blanket mortgage until the divorce and house sale are final," he suggested. My mother quickly agreed.

Eileen was flabbergasted when Mom called to tell her the exciting news. "I now know the Lord means for you to have that home," she said with astonishment.

By sharing this miraculous story, my mother was trying to give me hope that "God's plans are greater than any plans we could imagine."

I thought of her one-dollar house often. Still, my life took a different turn when a few years after Zach grew up and moved out, I married a then forty-nine-year-old school administrator named Larry. Larry was a lifelong bachelor who had never had children. We weren't able to purchase a home because his career required three moves during the next decade.

Mom adored Larry, and she never gave up on trying to find a way for us to buy a home of our own. Then, in the fall of 2010, our seventy-eight-year-old beloved matriarch died suddenly. My desire to be a homeowner seemed to die with her.

It was resurrected in January 2013, when Larry's job finally allowed us to put down roots. We compiled a list of features we would like in our dream house. Two months later, I noticed an Internet listing for a property that was nearly an identical match. It was even in our price range.

I called Jeff, our real estate agent, right away. "It's already one of three houses you're going to be seeing this weekend," Jeff said encouragingly. This seemed like more than a coincidence, since we were searching in three different Ohio cities.

When we pulled into the driveway, I sensed that this brick ranch belonged to us. As the agent unlocked the front door, I didn't see the stained carpet or dingy walls; instead I saw God's gift to a woman who had always wanted a home.

I fought back tears of gratitude, while my husband's eyes widened in amazement at the house that fit our wish list and budget almost perfectly. Larry loved the property, but he left the decision up to me.

My brother Don, who is a real estate agent in Florida, told me that if I really wanted the property, I should decide quickly. It was a great buy, and someone else could snatch it up. Yet fear immobilized me, so I sat with my open Bible debating whether to agree to the owner's final offer. That's when I noticed some papers stuck in the back of the Bible.

It was an e-mail from Mom sent a decade earlier containing pages of advice about buying a home. I had forgotten that I had printed it out, or even kept it until then. That e-mail was all the incentive I needed to close the deal.

In April 2013, Larry and I signed papers that made me a first-time homeowner in my fifties. A little elbow grease, fresh paint, and some new carpet made it our own. I like to believe there's a window in Heaven where my mother can see my little dream house, the answer to her decades of prayers.

~Christina Ryan Claypool

My Dear "Deer" Mom

Perhaps they are not stars, but rather openings in
heaven where the love of our lost ones pours
through and shines down upon us to
let us know they are happy.
~Eskimo Proverb

The deer had been visiting my back yard for years. They always hung out in the very back of the yard, as far away from the house as possible. I loved to watch these beautiful creatures from the window of my dining room, and I was always careful not to spook them since they are very timid around people. However, there were times when my husband Dave or I would walk into the back yard not realizing the deer were there. As soon as the deer noticed us, they would became very nervous and quickly run away.

My mom also loved the deer. I used to call her whenever the deer were visiting, and I would send pictures to her cell phone so that she could see them, too. Her voice would be filled with such excitement and I could just imagine the big smile on her face. Talking about the deer and seeing the deer made her so happy! It became a fond ritual of ours to enjoy the beauty of the deer in my back yard together.

When my mom passed I lost my faith. I was in a very dark place emotionally and spiritually. I was incredibly angry and could not understand why God took my beautiful mom away from our family and from all of her friends who cherished and loved her. She was the most kind, warmhearted and selfless person you could ever know. It wasn't fair that she was gone. I have never experienced such excruciating pain as the loss of my mom.

The last several months of her life were spent in a hospital bed. She was bedridden and couldn't walk. After she passed, I couldn't get over the anger and sadness I felt about her suffering. I constantly questioned the injustice of it all.

One night, I was trying to relax and had fallen asleep on the couch while watching TV. When I woke up, I started thinking about my mom again, crying so hard I began hyperventilating. I couldn't get my anxiety under control. I was still so upset over what she had endured at the end.

Suddenly, Dave and I noticed that the motion light in the back yard had turned on. We thought that the deer might be there. Dave walked to the dining room window to look outside. He did not see any deer, and then the motion light turned off.

For some reason, I got up from the couch and looked out the living room window. I knew the deer never went in the front yard, because they didn't like to be so close to the house. But something compelled me to look anyway.

My face was very close to the window when all of a sudden I saw a beautiful deer walk alongside the garage from the back of the house, turn into our driveway, walk under the front awning and stop. The deer then turned its body and face toward the window and stood there looking straight at me. I was in awe! This beautiful deer just stood and stared at me for several minutes, her nose practically touching the window. It felt as though she were smiling at me as she bobbled her head and flicked her tail, never taking her eyes off me.

At the very moment I noticed the deer walking toward me, I stopped crying and started smiling. And at the very moment the deer turned to look at me in the window, I felt an enormous sense of peace and calm come over me, like nothing I'd ever felt before. For the first time since my mom passed I believed she was okay and that she was still with me. And if those several moments of the deer looking in the window at me were not incredible enough, the deer then turned and ran into the front yard and started playing in the snow! It was then that I also realized my mom was no longer in pain or unable to walk. She could not only walk again, but she could jump and run.

Two more deer came out of nowhere to join in the fun, and all three deer were jumping and playing in the snow together. They looked so carefree. It was an amazing sight! I believe my mom wanted to reassure me that she had been reunited with her family in the afterlife and that she was happy and free.

Since then I've had more deer sightings when I've needed them most. The deer appear at times when I am missing my mom or when I start worrying about her again. And each and every time the deer show up, I feel my mom's love comforting me.

Seeing the deer has lifted the dark cloud of sadness, anger, and grief I had been under and allowed me to start healing. And, knowing that my mom and I shared such special moments during those earlier times when the deer would visit my back yard, it thrills me to know that I have a continuing connection with her through the deer who visit me today.

~Kim Goodrich

Mother-Daughter Connection

*When I tell you I love you I don't say it out of habit or
to make conversation. I say it to remind you that
you are the best thing that ever happened to me.*
~Author Unknown

W hen I awoke on that dreary, rainy Monday morning in August, it never occurred to me that in a few hours the day would turn completely dark. My husband had taken a vacation day, and my younger son asked if we could go shopping for a newly released video game.

After my son found his game, I proposed we stop for lunch and eat in the ShopRite café area. No one knew why I made this suggestion; it was at least a half-hour drive from where we were, and the rain was coming down in buckets. My husband wasn't enthused with my idea, but went along with it anyway. For some reason I felt drawn to make that stop at ShopRite.

As we were walking around ShopRite deciding what to eat, we ran into my parents. I didn't know they would be there. The five of us found what we wanted for lunch and sat together as we ate. My mother shared a story about something she watched on television, and then rested her head on my shoulder. I placed my arm around her and asked, "Ma, are you tired?" She didn't respond, so in a louder tone I asked again; there was still no response. Keeping my left arm around her, I turned and with my right hand tapped her gently on the face and began screaming, "Ma! Ma!" Hysterical, I yelled across the table to my husband, "Call 911!"

The ambulance came and I rode in the passenger seat while my husband followed behind with my father and son. Now I knew why I had felt compelled to go out of our way to have lunch at ShopRite.

As my mother was fighting to stay alive in the back of the vehicle, my mind was racing faster than the ambulance. Did I tell her enough how much I loved her? Would there be another chance to tell her? Why was I short with her on the phone yesterday? So what if she had already told me that story once before, I should've listened without complaining.

By the time the ambulance reached the hospital, my mother was semi-conscious but her vital signs were poor. In my purse, I carried her list of medications so I gave them to the emergency room nurse and then filled out all the paperwork while the staff tended to my mother. She had a series of tests scheduled, including blood tests, a CT scan, and an EKG.

My mother appeared so fragile and uncertain of her surroundings. It was hard to see her hooked up to all those devices and intravenous lines. Was her life flashing through her mind like a family video?

I know what I was remembering — all the times she cared for me. The time she drove me to the hospital for a tetanus shot after I rode my bicycle into a rusty wheelbarrow, and the many times she brought me trays of ginger ale and cherry Jell-O when I was sick with mumps, measles, stomach viruses, and so much more.

I thought about how she would walk my sister and me to school when we didn't have a car, then walk across town to work, and then walk back to pick us up at 3:00. If she was tired, she never let on. After school, she made us homemade eggnog with milk, chocolate syrup and whole eggs. She baked the best cinnamon coffee cake from scratch. I wondered if I had ever told her that.

So many memories of her sacrifices were racing through my mind. So many occasions when she took care of us and put us first. I wished

I could have displayed even more gratitude than I had as a child, but of course children don't think ahead that way.

After undergoing tests, and receiving continuous care, Mom appeared fully conscious, but no diagnosis or prognosis was offered about her condition. She had to stay the night for further observation and monitoring of her heart. When told this, Mom began shaking like a young child afraid of being left alone in the dark. I asked the nurse if I could stay with my mother overnight, and was given the okay.

That night the roles were reversed; I was the one by my mother's bedside, nurturing and caring for her. We joked and I told my mother, "This wasn't how I planned a girls' night out." I sat up straight with my legs stretched across another chair watching my mother sleep through the night. The next morning my mother thanked me. She explained how at first she was afraid of dying during the night, but with me by her side, she knew she would live to see another day. She had additional tests scheduled, and it was concluded that Mom needed a pacemaker.

That was six years ago, and my mother is still with us. I talk with her every day and we make plans for lunch, doctor and hair appointments, walks in the park, shopping, or just going for a bran muffin and decaf tea. It's not what we do that's important, it's that we do it together.

I don't know what guided me to that ShopRite six years ago — God, a guardian angel, sixth sense, gut feeling or intuition — perhaps they're all the same thing. What matters is that we got our second chance, and I am enjoying every day of it with my mother.

~Valerie Testa Almquist

The Mother's Ring

Don't grieve. Anything you lose
comes round in another form.
~Rumi

M y mom had twelve children with my dad, and oh, how she loved each and every one of her kids. My father gave her a ring that she cherished — a "mother's ring" with all twelve of her children's birthstones. It was so beautiful and I am sure every time she looked at it and saw those stones sparkle, she felt again the newness of each baby she had brought into the world.

I was very close to my mother, as I handled most of her care the last few years of her life, so I knew how much she loved that ring. After she died, we couldn't find the ring at the nursing home where she lived. I thought that one of my sisters had it, but I wished that I could see it again. It was a meaningful link to my mother and represented the love she had for all of us.

I had a hard time dealing with the loss of my mother. I cried daily even months after she was gone. One afternoon, a year after her death, I was sitting home alone, crying again. Suddenly, I felt a gentle, comforting touch on my back. And then my phone, which had been out of service for the past two days, began to ring. I was quite startled, as it had been so unexpected after two days of silence.

It was the social worker from the nursing home my mother had lived in. She said they had found something belonging to my mom and she asked me to come and get it.

I made my way to the nursing home and was handed a small envelope. Inside was my mom's ring—that very special one with the twelve birthstones. I fell to my knees and cried.

I took that ring's appearance as a sign that my mother was telling me to stop being so sad for her because she had moved on. The social worker told me that she didn't know how it was not noticed for so long, as the safe it was found in was cleaned out on a regular basis.

Personally, I think Mom had something to do with it.

~Eleanor OToole

On My Biggest Fan

Smile… heaven is watching.
~African Proverb

I lost my mom four months ago today. A lot of the time I forget she's really, really gone. I get lost in work and conversations during the day and I forget that I won't be finding a silly comment from her as I scroll through Facebook, that we won't be going on another one of our shopping sprees, that I won't be seeing her any time soon.

But then I remember… and it hits hard.

One of the last conversations my mom and I had was about my overall wellbeing. I was complaining to her about how I felt bored — unfulfilled — during the week. Like I'd stopped making time for myself to do things that I really enjoyed. Sure, my life was pretty good, but sometimes I'd get caught up in the mundane routine of wake up – go to work – go to the gym – make dinner – eat dinner – go to bed. And when I was finally in bed I was wide awake, panicking that I'd just breezed through another day without much really happening.

Mom told me I should pick up tennis again. "Join a USTA team and get back into it! I always love watching you play," she said. I told her I'd think about it… but in my mind it seemed like way too much work. I hadn't picked up a racket in what seemed like years and I didn't really like playing with people I didn't know… and going online and filling out forms? Eh, probably not gonna happen. I left her that day practically forgetting we had even talked about the idea.

Mom went into a coma just hours after that conversation. She died the next day.

Flash-forward a couple of months. Tennis practically fell into my lap: my co-worker heard I used to play and she asked me if I'd like to hit after work. I said yes and we played, and even though I was rusty it was fun to be back on the court. The next day my co-worker's friend contacted me and asked if I would join her USTA team. I said yes and the following week I was playing my first match. It felt good — I was thrilled to be doing something Mom had wanted me to do and, as she had suspected, it made me a happier person.

This past Monday I played the most competitive match I've played since high school. We lost the first set 0–6. Great, I thought... another loss. But then something happened, and we won the second set 7–5.

We were losing 5–6 in the tiebreaker for the third set when I saw a crowd forming above us upstairs. And in the corner of my eye I caught a glimpse of someone I thought I knew.

My heart fluttered: *Mom's here!* I thought. Just as quickly as my heart jumped for joy thinking my biggest fan came to cheer me on, it sank. I realized that the lady with the short hair, who from a distance looked strikingly like Mom, was not her. I remembered that Mom died four months ago. In the midst of this match I had completely forgotten that she was gone.

I'm unsure how I didn't fall apart right there on the court. We ended up winning the tiebreaker, 10–8.

Driving home that night I thought a lot about Mom. I thought about how I'll never have her "cheering me on" again — at tennis matches or through work accomplishments or during life milestones. I thought about how unfair it was for her. Mom was my brother's, my dad's and my biggest fan. She'd give up anything to be at Lee's show or Dad's jam sessions or my tennis match. And she'd always be there after, smiling no matter the outcome, telling us how proud she was.

But then I thought about what I'm writing now. Tennis didn't just fall into my lap... someone wrapped it up in pretty paper, put a perfect bow on it, and neatly placed it there. I didn't just stumble back into tennis; someone helped me get there. I didn't lose that match, because someone helped me find the strength to win.

Mom might not be here with me every day. She won't be cheering me on at my next life event and she won't have words of encouragement for me at the end of it.

But maybe she'll lead me there. Maybe she'll help me get to where I need to be, and get me through the things I can't quite get through by myself.

After all, fans don't just stop cheering. Right?

~Georgia Putney

90

A Sign from Above

*"There is no death. People only die when we forget
them," my mother explained shortly before she
left me. "If you can remember me, I will
be with you always."*
~Isabel Allende

On August 4th, 2015 my mom sent me a text letting me
know that she went to the ER with some chest pain,
but not to worry. I told her I would be right there but
she knew I worked the graveyard shift and told me to
get some sleep, that it was probably nothing. As I was heading out the
door, I texted her, "Just let me love you!"

When I arrived at the hospital I knew this time was different.
My mom had a very long history of health issues related to Marfan
syndrome. But each doctor visit was routine in her eyes. So routine, in
fact, that she had asked me to smuggle in a Diet Coke and snickerdoodle
cookies for her. She wasn't allowed to eat in case they needed to do
surgery, but I still tried to find her those snickerdoodles. I couldn't
find any but I promised I would and I'd have them in my purse ready
for her when she was allowed to eat again.

The ER doctor at our local hospital in eastern Washington State
wanted to send my mom to Seattle via flight. My heart sank. She
refused the flight because she was worried about the cost. I told her
that nobody cared what it cost and we just wanted her to be well.
This was the first time I saw my mom cry about her health. She was

usually as tough as nails.

I called my stepdad and told him he had to come. He was working three hours away but immediately got in his car and came home. Mom was already on her way to Seattle via ambulance.

My stepdad and I drove to Seattle to join her, and believe it or not, I kept looking for snickerdoodles, to no avail. By the next day, Mom was in a great hospital and she was allowed to eat anything she wanted.

She was insistent I find her snickerdoodles but I still couldn't find any.

The next morning they took her for a CT scan. My stepdad and I waited in her room; not too worried, as this had become routine for us and she was already looking better. However, when the nursing assistant brought my mom back from her scan in a wheelchair she coded in the chair. My world stopped. They were able to revive her, but then she coded again, and this time nothing could bring her back.

My entire world crumbled.

I made my way from the fifth floor down to the outside world, as far away as I could get to make a few horrible phone calls.

When someone passes, the hospital brings a grief package to the family. Juice, snacks, and such. They don't want someone passing out from the shock.

As I sat on a curb outside, I was handed a bag of snacks from the grief package. Inside was a snickerdoodle cookie. I knew at that moment that my mom hadn't left me. Only her physical body was gone. She had finally found her snickerdoodle cookie and she had even found one for me, too. I knew she was going to be okay.

~Jamie D. Parker

BEST MOM EVER!

Chapter 10

A Mother's Legacy

*Children will not remember you for the
material things you provided, but for the
feeling that you cherished them.*
~Richard L. Evans

91

Harvest of Hope

*The love of gardening is a seed that
once sown never dies.*
~Gertrude Jekyll

The temperature was only in the low seventies that late September evening, and she was cold. I covered her small frame with a blanket as she sat there in the old wooden porch swing. My voice caught in my throat as I asked her if she was comfortable. I thought how strange it was for me to fuss over her this way and how my eighty-six-year-old mother had now become the mothered.

True to form, she said she was okay, but I knew that *I* wasn't okay. I knew we were starting to say goodbye to each other.

Earlier that day she had asked me to gather the seedpods from her flower garden. I brought them to her. As she reached to take them from me, I noticed how frail and small her hands were. How had I not noticed how frail they had become? When had her skin become so thin that I could almost see through it?

As she placed the pods on the blanket covering her lap, I thought how surreal it was for the two of us to be sitting here together on this glorious early autumn evening, visiting as we always did and talking as if nothing had changed. But *everything* had changed last week when the doctor had sat with us in that tiny room and discussed the test results — results that told us that she wouldn't be with us much longer.

Part of me wanted to scream out loud at how cruel and unfair life was. Part of me wanted to run away, to outrun the pain. But I couldn't. So I just sat there quietly beside her as she patiently began to separate the seeds from the pods. Small hands so like my own, worked deftly to finish her task, just as they had done with every task set before her.

I heard her explain how to store the seeds, and I remember her telling me how to wrap them up and when to take them out again for planting. She explained the depth to sow them and how far apart to place them from each other. We sat there together as the last rays of sun went over the hill, separating and wrapping and placing the round black seeds in a small cardboard box.

When we had finished our task, she looked lovingly at me with those soft brown eyes of hers that I knew so well. Her gaze never left mine as she purposefully passed the box to me for safekeeping.

I knew it was more than flower seeds she was giving me. She was trying to give me hope. Hope that there would again be flowers for me to enjoy, hope that after the winter of hurt that was coming soon, there would again be sun in my life. In preparing for a harvest that she knew she would never see, my mother was giving me one final gift — the lesson that life would go on and that after the rain, flowers of joy would bloom again in my world.

The cold winds of October blew harshly and the ground was cold the day we placed her there and said our goodbyes. Part of my heart went with her when she left. But the seeds remained. Tucked away where she had placed them, they remained through that first hard winter without her. Through the first Thanksgiving when her chair remained empty at our table. Through the first Christmas we didn't hear her sweet voice singing carols. Through the welcoming of the first new year I had ever known without her. Still the seeds remained in that cardboard box, wrapped tightly in a mother's love with her promise of a harvest of hope.

The robins appeared right on schedule to flit about in the warm spring sun. As if mocking the sadness within me, the earth around me once more exploded with possibility. I sat alone in her swing on a day when the soft sun couldn't quite cut the slight bite in the air. It was as if I heard her sweet voice in the breeze saying, "It's time. The hard hurt of winter is over and now, it's time. Time to plant the seeds for tomorrow's harvest." My hands shook a bit as I drew the cardboard box from its place in her bureau. How strange to think that her hands had touched it last. How bittersweet to think of the day that we had packed it away. But with all the strength, dignity and grace that I had learned from her, I knew what I must do.

And so I dug furrows in the rich brown earth. And I heard her voice gently reminding me how wide to dig the rows and how deep to plant the seeds. And so plant them I did, and they grew strong and beautiful like her, bringing me a harvest of hope… one last gift from my mother.

~Geneva France Coleman

Lessons in Lipstick

Mirror mirror on the wall, I am my mother after all.
~Author Unknown

"This is how you do your eyebrows," Mom said, lifting up an old toothbrush. "First, you brush them backwards," she said, doing so as I watched. "Then, you brush them straight up." Whisk, whisk, whisk. "And then, you knock them down." She smoothed her brows into place and smiled.

Before she married Dad and had the four of us, Mom was a model. When I was a teen getting ready for the big high school dance and she offered a make-up lesson, I listened.

"When you put on foundation," Mom said, tipping some Max Factor ivory out of its glass bottle and onto her fingers, "make sure you don't stop right at your jawline." Fingers moving smoothly over her skin, she lifted her chin. "You always want to look natural, so you don't want a line to show where your make-up starts and stops."

Over the years, I've probably watched Mom put on her "face" a million times. When I think of that foundation, I can still smell its lovely scent. For many years, until they quit making it in that bottle, I used it, too.

"Line your eyes like this." Mom leaned closer to the mirror, pulling the side of her eyelid gently, to make the skin taut. Then she skimmed the pencil on in one light stroke.

Even though Mom was beautiful and took care with her appearance every day, she was never conceited or vain. Looks weren't what really mattered in her book. She cared much more about less ephemeral qualities like honesty, loyalty, kindness, and compassion. But the night of the big dance, I wasn't thinking about any of those things.

"Always brown-black mascara for daytime," she stated. "Save black for evening events." She flicked the wand briskly, coating her lashes with a practiced hand. To this day, my mascara is brown-black, except for special evenings.

"With our complexion," she continued, "a soft coral color looks best." She twisted the sleek black tube in her hand, revealing a creamy bit of lipstick. "Red can look too harsh and darker shades don't look natural." She drew the color over her lips, top lip first, from the center out. She pressed her lips together just once. "There."

If I'd been willing to listen, of course, I could have learned lots of other important things from Mom. Like how to make that fabulous vegetable soup I still dream of, or Gramma's legendary Presbyterian stew. I could have mastered diapering a baby, or reupholstering a chair, or planting a summer garden.

Mom could have taught me to knit, if I'd only been willing to concentrate a little harder. There's an unfinished scarf in my closet, one Mom was making just for me. I'm thinking of taking a class so someday I can finish what she began.

But, in the meantime, every morning I look into the bathroom mirror and apply my make-up just the way Mom showed me years ago. Sometimes, in a trick of the light, I see her looking back. It's just me, of course, older now, with Mom's softer jawline and fuller cheeks. I'm so glad to find her there. That's when I smile, give her a wink and say, "Thanks, Mom."

~Kate Fellowes

The Gift of Illness

Motherhood: All love begins and ends there.
~Robert Browning

It's late afternoon; the sun is angling down
toward the west, bathing everything in a rich gold
that gilds house walls and dusty streets.
Even shadows take on warm taupe and tawny hues.
I'm ambling down a quiet lane heading for home — home!
My breath catches in my throat for a moment and
I stop just to savor the taste of that word on my tongue.
I am home…

I lean against a garden wall like an old friend
and gaze lovingly down the lane to where it
bends round a corner. I walked this self-same path
as a child, scuffing along, watching small puffs of dust rise
as I headed home to Mama and supper.
I would waltz in the door and Mama would hug me,
then scold me for the condition of my shoes before
sending me to wash up. It was a pattern that never failed:
dust in summer, snow in winter — Mama's reaction was always
the same, predictable as the sun rising over St. Martin's or
the leaves on the apple trees turning gold in September.
With Mama around, you always wore shoes;

you could be lounging about naked as a Botticelli cherub,
and Mama wouldn't object — as long as you were shoed.
I even remember her going to bed once or twice
with her own shoes on! I have sometimes wondered
if the naked human foot were somehow an affront
to her sense of order and rightness, something uncontrolled
and wanton. There must be a story there somewhere…

I smile in fond remembrance; I thought I knew her so well.
After all, she was Mama: baker of bread, washer of laundry,
and mistress of a thousand other details that kept us
safe, well fed and reasonably happy…
always busy, always doing, seldom sitting still, quick and flitting
as the small birds in the garden she so loved —
until that last illness that finally slowed her down,
then stopped her altogether…
It started out as just a cough, nothing serious,
but then she began puffing climbing the stairs
and had little energy for the myriad small things
that had filled her days and framed her life…
My last visit home had been to see her again
before we carried her to St. Martin's…

It had been a golden autumn day, warm and lush;
Onkel Fritz and Karl had brought her down into
the garden that morning, placing her gently
in a corner that would catch the sunlight all day.
I had pulled up an old wicker chair that Papa
had made and settled in, adjusting the blanket over her
while keeping an eye on Ethan, then a toddler,
as he lumbered about the garden like a minute bulldozer.
He would bring his small treasures and discoveries to us,
cooing in delight or babbling excitedly, saying things
only Mama seemed to fully understand…

That day passed slowly, like honey dripping from a comb.
Mama and I talked of everything, and nothing.
And sometimes we just sat in silence,
enjoying the moments we could share
because we still could share them…
Tante Luisa brought out lunch, then supper.
Ever practical Anna brought out the old tape recorder
to catch Mama's stories in her own voice.
When Ethan fell asleep on Mama's lap,
Anna carried him in for his nap.

People drifted in and out all day, stopping by to
share their time, their love and their memories.
In those hours I learned more about Mama than I had
in all the years previously. I came to know her not just
as my mother, but as Dorothea Mayerhoff:
how she got the scar on her right knee,
where she used to hide so Oma couldn't find her for chores,
how she and Papa would sneak off to St. Martin's
and make love in the sacristy because their parents
wanted to put off the wedding until after the harvest,
but no one objected to them going to church together.
Father Peter found them once, but as a young priest
he'd only made them bring flowers to the church in penance…
On and on her memories flowed: funny, tender,
sometimes somber, sometimes painful,
but always moving, always poignant — just like Mama.
It was her parting gift to us, this divulging of herself,
giving as she had always given…

The sun had set and the first stars were just peeping out
when we carried her back in. She was tiny and bird-light in our hands,
golden from the sun and rosy with reminiscence, eyes sparkling
and head high. We tucked her in and I sat by her bed for a bit
before she drifted off, holding those fragile fingers in mine.

By morning she was gone, a gentle smile on her lips,
her hands folded as if in prayer. Beside her
on the coverlet lay her well-thumbed Bible.
I didn't need to open it to know where she'd been reading…

Illness comes like a thief, breaking into our lives,
tossing aside our small plans and ransacking
the order we attempt to create around ourselves.
But illness can also come as an unrecognized guest,
forcing us to slow down, to step aside from the
frenetic pace of life and look at what we have;
to savor today because we know it won't last.
And the guest does not come empty-handed.

The gift of illness is the gift of time:
time to sit, to laugh, to remember;
time to hold hands, then let fingers slip apart
and come to rest in laps, on knees like open flowers;
time to hold, to cherish, to say goodbye…
The gift of illness is the recognition of mortality
and the preciousness of life, of love, of now.

Thank you, Mama.

~Deborah Kellogg

My Mother the Bag Lady

You can never guarantee you'll be the smartest
person in the room, but there is no excuse
for not being the most prepared.
~Brendan Paddick

I picked up the soft black and white tote bag and touched my face. If only I could kiss the owner one more time. Sorting out my mother's things after her death at age ninety overwhelmed me. Now what would I do with this bag with "Gladys" boldly written in red letters?

My mother loved purses and tote bags. As a child I would ask, "Do you have...?" Mom would dig into her leather purse that held Life Savers, tissues, pencils, paper, and safety pins. A piece of string and rubber bands were essential tools to have on hand. The purse even held a small sewing kit.

Some people might look at the black and white bag and say, "It's just a tote bag," but it was filled with memories for me. I remembered walking down the halls with "Gladys" on my arm. Weekly it went back and forth with me to the assisted living facility with drugstore items, extra snacks, and other things that Mom requested. The large size enabled me to bring clothes and toiletries during her frequent hospital stays. Now the treasured tote made me cry. I put it in a drawer to decide its fate later.

My memories of my mom seemed to revolve around bags. Earlier in my life, a bag held Sunday school teacher's lessons or minutes of the neighborhood garden club meetings. Another one held the Girl Scout leader's handbook and supplies to my childhood weekly scout group.

My mother, an artist, carried a green one that contained a small sketchpad, two artist pencils, and a separate eraser. She might find a cute dog, a small creek, or a beautiful flower to draw along the way. The sketch would later become an oil or watercolor painting.

My parents eventually moved into a senior retirement community in my city. Weekly, a red bag with black monogram initials accompanied her for phone duty at the senior complex. Mom could easily be entertained with a crossword puzzle or book—both of which she kept handy.

She loved to knit and demonstrated it by making gifts for the family. A bag with the logo of the senior complex contained knitting projects. Several seniors knitted blankets for the patients at St. Jude Children's Research Hospital in Memphis, Tennessee. Mom knitted hundreds of hats in multiple designs and colors. When she and the other knitters were featured on a local news program, Mom proudly showed off some of the finished hats.

When Mom started using a walker, she attached a black bag in front. On doctor visits it held a large-print book or a Kindle, which her granddaughter updated regularly. And let's not forget the small box of tissues, breath mints, a tablet of paper, pencil, water bottle, reading glasses, and sunglasses that filled the black bag.

Wherever she went as Gladys, Mom, or Grandma, my mother was ready. I seem to have inherited the trait. One year on a trip with two friends, I took twice as much luggage as they did combined. When I mentioned it, they answered, "We know when we travel with you, we can pack light because you bring everything we need." Or the time I went overseas and took an extra disposable camera—just in case. On the second day one of my fellow traveler's camera broke. And who came to the rescue? My closets contain many totes in colors and sizes that I have used in my own activities and trips. My mother taught me well.

One afternoon, I opened a drawer and saw the black and white bag again, still waiting for me to decide its fate. For several weeks I had been busy with the affairs of Mom's estate and I had forgotten about it. I pulled the bag out and gently ran my fingers down the sides. And then I felt something hard inside, something I hadn't noticed before. I pulled out a small golden pair of clip-on earrings in the shape of angels.

How did they get in there? I vaguely remembered them with all the other clip-on earrings months ago in Mom's jewelry box. Goosebumps ran up my arms. Sensing a heavenly connection, I could almost hear my mother say, "See, I was prepared for my final trip."

A black and white bag with gold earrings will be treasured in remembrance of the best bag lady I ever knew — my mother.

~Sharilynn Hunt

The Gift that Keeps on Giving

No matter what his rank or position may be,
the lover of books is the richest and the
happiest of the children of men.
~John Alfred Langford

Christmas was always my mom's favorite holiday. She never said so, but it was easy to see in the joy she derived from giving. She'd take days off from work to bake cookies and give most of them away. The thought she put into gifts was extraordinary, and she tried to surprise us with at least one completely unexpected item each year.

The greatest gift I ever received from her, however, was my love of reading. This is the gift I took with me to Iraq during my 2008-9 deployment. I managed to read a book each week. That meant I had to regularly mail books home to make room for new ones. Shipping typically took two weeks so I had to keep about a half dozen books in order to have something fresh. Even a small number of books can be burdensome when traveling to the other side of the world. Being stationed at three different Iraq bases over the course of that year made it even more so.

I still had more than three years left in my enlistment when I came home from Iraq so I knew I had one more deployment left. By Christmas 2009, e-readers were becoming less expensive. I asked my mom for one, a simple black and white device that would be seen as clunky and woefully outdated within a few years, but which served me well.

That e-reader bounced around the U.S. with me from the California desert to the hills of Kentucky and eventually to my little lakeside home in Michigan. It also traveled with me on my next trip to the other side of the world, this time to the snowy mountains of Afghanistan in January of 2011.

Because of that deployment's timing, I had asked my mom to resist temptation and not give me anything for the previous Christmas. There was no reason for me to expect that it would be her last Christmas. As I made my way home to bury her that spring, I brought my e-reader, trying to distract myself through delays and layovers. I never thought about it being the last gift she ever gave me.

About a week before Christmas 2015, a female friend asked me for some reading recommendations. She had been offered some free e-books, but her old smartphone wouldn't work as a reading device. Excitedly, I let her know I had a perfect gift for her, a paper book that seemed to perfectly suit her request. Unfortunately, there was a big problem with that. I had forgotten about giving away my extra copy a few days before, and the one I had had been personally signed for me. I felt guilty and scrambled to find another copy.

Then I remembered my old e-reader collecting dust in the corner. It already had access to the book I offered and several others that had been recommended to her. I hardly used it because I preferred paper books myself once I wasn't moving around so much. But I had kept the device because it was my mom's last gift to me. I paused only for a moment. My mom would've been proud of me for giving it away.

I sent that old e-reader to my friend on her birthday. She would take it with her as she traveled many miles to her family home for Christmas. Giving away my mom's last gift became an incredible gift to me, helping me to feel her spirit once again during her favorite holiday.

Had the story ended there, I would still be filled with joy. It was a gift that kept giving, though. My old e-reader is once again collecting dust in a corner of my house. It's a different house this time, one I bought with my friend the following summer. A picture of my mom hangs on the wall smiling at us, and I often smile back, thanking her for the generosity that has brought me so much joy.

~Drew Sheldon

Hazelnut Coffee
Sweetened with Faith

If the people we love are stolen from us, the way to
have them live on is to never stop loving them.
~James O'Barr

"Your mother is dying," the doctor said. "I doubt she has a month to live." His words paralyzed me as it confirmed all of my mother's suspicions that she had cancer. She was a knowledgeable, passionate nurse and a gifted diagnostician who knew the signs. She had complained for months that cancer was hiding in her body, but this was the first physician who proved her right.

While the doctor kept talking, I tuned out his voice and wondered why God chose this time, as there was no time left to try and save her. However, knowing my mom, if she had been told months ago, she would have subjected herself to every painful procedure imaginable and who knows if they would have worked anyway. My faith told me it was her time. God gave her no options. He wanted to take her home.

In her last job, she was the director of a nursing home, so she was very familiar with death and dying. While on her watch, no one ever died alone. She'd stay devotedly, holding their hands, whispering words of comfort and strength until their final breath was taken. She felt humbled to be at the closure of so many lives.

So, on that fateful Friday, I vowed to stay with her until the end.

She was my treasured lifeline and now, I had to be hers.

She wanted to rest in her bed, a big, old Craftmatic that once gave a "rise" to three generations all snuggled in together when she first purchased it years ago. Upon its arrival, she, my young daughter and I sat like peas in a pod testing its ups and downs, vibrations, temperature controls, and all its features, hysterically laughing like kids on an amusement park ride. I reminded her of that day as I tucked her in. She laughed, but felt she didn't have many more days to rest in her clunky adjustable bed. She had a gut feeling she was going to die soon. I had not shared the diagnosis or prognosis with her, but she was smart. She knew.

I left for a few moments to put on a pot of hazelnut-flavored coffee. As the scent circled its way to her room, it enticed her long-lost appetite. "What smells so delicious?" she asked.

"It's my favorite coffee Mom. Hazelnut," I answered.

She replied, "I've never tasted hazelnut coffee."

"Well, we'll take care of that tonight," I responded. I prepared a tray for her as she did when one of her four children was ill. A beautiful china cup and saucer, a small pot, cloth napkin, cookies and a fresh flower in a vase accompanied the cup of hazelnut coffee.

I trotted eagerly upstairs. I loved pleasing her. I put a tape in the cassette; her favorite music began to play. I opened the window to let the warm, summer breeze drift in and took my place on my father's side of the bed, which had been empty for twenty years.

She sipped the coffee slowly, savoring every drop, and then it began, five long hours of incredible, intense conversation, touching on subjects that lived deep in her soul, mind and heart. "How I love all of my babies," she cried, calling each one by name. She identified all of our weaknesses and strengths as though it was important for me to note.

Then, this woman, who never missed a Sunday mass, who wore her rosary beads down to tiny nubs, whose bedside prayer book was so worn and torn from use, blurted out how weak her faith really was. She questioned God's existence. She felt lost and frightened, wondering if Heaven existed and if she would be reunited with my dad and older brother.

She leaned against me, anxious, like a child afraid of the dark needing comfort from a parent. She knew my faith was much stronger than hers. It was a moment I will never forget. Now I had to find the words to give her strength, peace and comfort in her final hours.

"Mom," I said, "my faith is strong because you openly shared your love of God in every part of your life. My gift of faith is your gift of love to me." We cried and hugged. She made me promise that if anything happened to her, I would be there for the family. Coming from my mom, our matriarch, that was a surreal responsibility, but she assured me there was enough love in my heart to go around.

There was this long silence and then she spoke softly: "I'm dying. You don't need to say it. I know. It's something you feel. One day, when it's your time, you will understand the knowing." I didn't validate her thoughts. I told her she mustn't be afraid if it was God's Will. I assured her that my father and older brother would be waiting to embrace her. I prayed silently that her foundation of faith wouldn't fail her. She seemed more content, more trusting as she took her final sips of the hazelnut coffee.

"The coffee is sweet," I said.

"Sweetened with faith," she added with one of her radiant smiles. She rested her head comfortably on my shoulder like a tired, weathered sparrow whose wings had soared through many journeys but now accepted her final flight. I knew this was her moment of trust as she passed her matriarchal torch and was comfortable with its passing. My role was just beginning.

She died six days later, surrounded by family and friends, clutching her worn rosary beads. She only woke once, turning her head slightly, as though someone called her name. She opened her eyes, and then she shared a spark of life and a special smile reserved only for those she loved dearly. With her final breath she whispered my father and brother's name and then she was gone.

I took the worn rosary from her hand. It now rests next to my bedside, wrapped around my weathered prayer book in front of a picture of three generations of strong women: my mom, my daughter and me. Many nights, as I pray from the knobby plastic beads, I sip my hazelnut coffee. I'm grateful for those last, faith-filled hours with my mom, feeling her love. Those last moments with her have strengthened my faith, knowing one day, I too, with a trusting heart, will need to accept my final time and pass the matriarchal torch to my daughter.

~Lainie Belcastro

97

Shelter in a Storm

*My mother had a slender, small body, but a large
heart — a heart so large that everybody's
joys found welcome in it, and
hospitable accommodation.*
~Mark Twain

The rain started as I got into the car. The weather reflected the storm of emotions I felt. Three days earlier I had buried my mother. Now, as I prepared to go home, I knew I'd never return to this house again and find a parent waiting for me.

I saw the little family out of the corner of my eye through the haze of tears and a foggy window. The pungent aroma of funeral flowers was my only company, and they took up every seat. Steady traffic required that I wait, so I watched them make their way up the street in the pouring rain.

As they crossed the street, the tiny, young mother held one of the babies close to her, trying unsuccessfully to shield her from the rain. The father carried the other on his back. Rivulets of water running through his dreadlocks dripped into the face of the baby who held tightly to his neck.

I looked around the car as they passed in front of me. There was no room — flowers and knick-knacks from my mother's life filled every space in my car. Then I saw my mom's leopard print umbrella. I blew the horn, beckoning the father to come. His look of hope said he thought he had a ride.

A quick glance in the car revealed that my invitation was not to offer him a ride.

"Would you take this umbrella, please?" I asked.

"Oh, yes ma'am," he said softly. "Thank you." Then he hurried back to his waiting family.

The young mother quickly gathered her babies under the shelter of my mom's umbrella. For them the rain had stopped. They continued on their way with a souvenir of my mother's doing what it had always done for me, providing a cover of love.

~Trudie Nash

98

Mom Versus
the Three Stooges

There are many little ways to enlarge your child's
world. Love of books is the best of all.
~Jacqueline Kennedy Onassis

I tumbled down the school bus steps and dashed up the sidewalk, accompanied by my brother, Joe and my sister, Julie. Throwing open the front door, we spilled into the living room and switched on the television set.

"Well, how nice to see you, too," Mom said, appearing in the doorway. Our baby sister wriggled in her arms, anxious to be a part of the group. "Aren't you even going to say hello to your little sister?"

Cathy was an adorable baby with wispy blond curls and big brown eyes, but we were already absorbed in our latest discovery. Our after-school television show had begun airing another series and we couldn't get enough of these three funny guys. They entertained us from the moment they appeared on the screen. We cheered at their clumsy pratfalls and crowed with delight at their crazy antics. And a food fight, complete with whipped cream pies, caused us no end of laughter.

We'd never seen anything like *The Three Stooges* and after the first episode we were hooked. Nothing meant so much to us as getting home on time to watch our favorite show.

Despite Mom's admonishments and Dad's threats, the three of

us began to mimic the Stooges' outrageous behavior. We quoted our favorite Stooge sayings at odd moments, but especially during supper. If Mom prepared a dessert, one of us was bound to say, "I knew you were coming, so I baked a cake."

Grilled cheese sandwiches or macaroni and cheese? "Moe, Larry, the cheese! Moe, Larry, the cheese!"

We even learned a new word. That word was lummox. As in, "You big lummox, get out of my chair."

Mom had her own saying. "No more Stooges!"

Our affair with the Stooges might have continued, for Mom was close to overwhelmed with three school age kids, a baby, and a household, but with the decline of our table manners and an attempted food fight involving peas and mashed potatoes, she decided to take action.

Mom declared war on *The Three Stooges*.

It was a sneak attack. One afternoon we came home to find Mom at the door. "Come on out to the kitchen, kids. I've fixed sandwiches and you can tell me all about your day."

"What kind of sandwiches?"

"Egg salad."

Whatever Mom used to make egg salad was magical, transporting the regular sandwich to something heavenly. And she'd even sliced off the crusts! We sat down for a yummy after-school feast.

Mom questioned us about our school activities while we took our places around the kitchen table. Joe recounted the details of his geography test, I pulled out my almost-finished book report and Julie began selecting pictures from a stack of magazines for an art project. Even baby Cathy participated, as we took turns holding her on our laps.

Before we knew it, an hour had slipped by. And so had an episode of *The Three Stooges*.

Distracting us worked at first, but we quickly became wise to Mom's tactics. If Mom fixed sandwiches or even if she baked brownies, we gobbled them down and sneaked back to the living room in time to catch at least the last few minutes of *The Three Stooges*.

A full-out attack was Mom's next strategy. She marched into the living room and shut off the television. Right in the middle of a Stooges bank robbery.

We protested. We begged. We made promises of finished chores and finished homework and no more soda pop except for weekends.

But Mom was adamant. She shushed us with a look that would have made even Moe shake in his shoes. She plopped Cathy in her playpen and sat down on the couch. Then she picked up a book from the end table.

My brother groaned. My sister and I hung our heads. I liked to read, but even I didn't believe for one minute that any book had the ability to replace an episode of *The Three Stooges*.

"This was my favorite book when I was your age," Mom said. "I loved it and I know you will, too."

Oh no. Not only was she going to read us a book, but this was a *really old* book. A book from when *she* was a kid!

The book was large and thick, much bigger than the paperback mysteries that Mom tried to read whenever she got a chance. The colorful cover of the book was full of movement. The little girl with dark curls and rosy cheeks cavorted down a dirt path with two goats, a bouquet of pink and yellow wildflowers in one hand. A boy with a stick in his hand and a red cap on his head followed behind her while a snow-covered mountain rose in the blue background.

"The name of this book is *Heidi*," my mom announced.

I won't say we were captivated. Not at first. We cast longing glances at the blank television screen and fidgeted, playing with our shoelaces and poking at one another. Mom ignored us, already absorbed in the story of a little girl who became abandoned on the top of a mountain with a gruff old man. And after a few minutes, Mom's calm voice and the story stirred my imagination so that I no longer reacted when my brother shot a paper wad in my direction.

"That's the end of Chapter One," Mom said as she closed the book. "Time to start your homework."

I looked up in surprise. I'd been picturing the mountaintop hut and the wind blowing through the old fir trees. "Wait," I said. "What happens next? Does Heidi have to stay on the mountain with her grouchy grandfather?"

Mom just shook her head, a glint in her eye. "You'll find out tomorrow when I read the next chapter."

Perhaps it was the loving way in which she cradled the old book in her hands or how Mom developed a different voice for each character that grabbed our attention, but by the end of Chapter Three we were enthralled. We didn't poke and we didn't fidget. We just listened as Mom read about Heidi. How thrilled she was with the beauty of the mountains and the crimson snow. Her growing friendship with Peter and how she won over Grandfather. Little Swan and Little Bear, the goats. When Heidi was forced to leave the mountain to help care for Clara, I was devastated.

For a little while, I despised pretty, blond Clara. Even if she had to spend her life in a wheelchair.

Reading aloud was one of the best gifts my mom ever gave us. For me, it meant leaving behind the world of school and homework and the worries of whether or not I'd ever be a part of the popular group. Settled on the living room rug with a big pillow, I would close my eyes and go hiking with Heidi and Peter in the mountains. Instead of fretting over my hideous new glasses, I concerned myself with Clara's frail health, wondering if she'd ever walk and if Heidi would ever go home to her mountaintop.

To this day, whenever I pick up a book, I think of my mom. I always open the book to the title page and in my head, it's her voice I hear, announcing the title and "Chapter One." Because of Mom, as I read a book, I'm able to picture the characters and the settings and the action as if I had a movie screen in my head. Because of her, I developed a lifetime habit of reading that has given me countless hours of imagination and introspection and joy. Something that not even the Three Stooges could hope to accomplish.

~Monica Morris

The Sewing Machine

Sewing mends the soul.
~Author Unknown

For years, Mom's sewing machine sat in the corner of our dining room. Occasionally it hummed until almost mealtime as Mom created a variety of items. At a time when my parents did not have much money, I had beautiful dresses to wear to school and church because of Mom's creativity in remaking old dresses from her sisters. Our household snuggled under warm quilts at night, pieced together with scraps of cloth and tied to keep the batting securely in place.

My mom sewed tiny outfits for my Barbie doll, too. She made ball gowns, dresses and sportswear. She even splurged and bought Barbie trademark tiny buttons and trim to adorn these creations. I thought I had the best wardrobe any Barbie doll owner could want. My friends reinforced this idea when they longed for some of my mom's outfits for their dolls.

Eventually I outgrew playing with dolls and I packed away those tiny homemade treasures. I wasn't as excited about my own homemade clothing, and as Easter approached one year I begged for a store-bought dress. I never thought about the cost of a dress or my parents' finances. I just wanted to be like all the other girls.

My mom offered to take me shopping, to the fabric store for material and a new pattern, from which she could make me a very stylish, up-to-date dress. I continued to beg and plead to go to the store and try on ready-made dresses. My parents surprised me one Saturday morning by offering to go shopping for the dress I longed for instead of to the fabric store. I could hardly wait to begin trying on dresses.

We arrived at a department store in our city and found racks of sale merchandise. Although limited to this section, rather than every rack in the store, I happily chose a few outfits to try on. Mom patiently helped me narrow the selection until only one remained. The fashionable two-piece suit made me feel grown up. I admired myself in the full-length mirror and proclaimed it perfect. My father paid for the purchase and I proudly carried the dress box home, never thinking of the sacrifice it might have involved for my parents.

I looked at the still attached price tag as I prepared to cut it off. Snip! Done deal! Now I could wear it and not take it back. I dressed for Easter Sunday church service in my new outfit, adding a pretty scarf to give it some color. Mom gave an approving look when I came downstairs. I felt like I could float all the way to church in my store-bought Easter attire.

A few weeks later I approached my mom at her sewing machine, where she created yet another necessary item for our household. "Mom," I began in a quiet voice, "I've been thinking and I bet you could have made me three dresses for the price of the one you bought me."

She nodded her head. "Probably could have bought material for at least that many I think."

"Mom, I don't want to buy any more dresses. I really like this one and thank you for it but from now on we'll do it your way — fabric store for material I like and new patterns as styles change. You make really nice things."

Mom smiled and nodded her assent.

Years passed. Each year my wardrobe consisted of dresses my mom lovingly made for me. Sometimes my friends liked my clothes more than their own and I puffed with pride at my mom's ability to create amazing things from a pile of material, a bit of thread, some fabulous trim and her trusty sewing machine in the corner of the dining room. As my high school graduation approached, I never suggested a shopping trip to any place but the fabric store. I proudly wore my mom's creation as I received my diploma and at the celebrations that followed.

Mom and Dad moved a few times after I finished high school, but in every place they lived, except the last apartment, the sewing machine had a special place. Mom continued to sew warm quilts to tuck in her grandchildren, outfits for the granddaughters, and throw pillows to decorate our homes. We never knew what might come from that trusty sewing machine.

Mom passed away and we treasure the items that she sewed for us. The sewing machine now sits in one of her granddaughter's homes, but nothing we make seems to equal what Mom herself created for three generations of our family.

~Carol Elaine Harrison

The Easter Egg Hunts

If you want your children to turn out well, spend twice
as much time with them and half as much money.
~Abigail Van Buren

I grew up with my parents and three siblings, and money was tight. On a day-to-day basis, I didn't notice that the bread was a day old or that desserts or snacks were few and far between. Unless the electricity went off (which it often did), I wasn't aware of our financial status except during the holidays. Friends would be off skiing during Christmas vacation, while my siblings and I would take cardboard boxes from the Dumpster and slide down the local hills. Friends would mention going to the Caribbean during spring break while we spent the week playing with our local cousins. When my friends were wearing store-bought Halloween costumes, my siblings and I made our own by decorating our winter pajamas.

While I knew there were differences between my friends' celebrations and ours, I always felt ahead of the pack when it came to Easter. We didn't have the money for fancy clothes, ornate Easter baskets, or trips abroad. Instead, my mother outdid everyone I knew, and she started a tradition that I still maintain today.

She wrote Easter clues that rhymed and put a clue in each egg. She would then hide the eggs, and the next day, the four of us kids would go on the hunt. My mother would grab our poor Beagle, Tica, and dip her front paws in mud to create "Easter Bunny prints" and then she would read the first clue of the hunt. The clues always rhymed and were subtle enough to keep us guessing. For example, this clue led us to the sage bush in the back yard:

Keep that smile on your face
No pushing or shoving during the race
Outside again and look around
A sage clue is looking to be found.

She typically had ten clues, with the last one leading us to our basket, which was often a decorated paper lunch bag that contained an orange, a pair of socks (or some other necessity), and a small selection of jellybeans. She always made sure that she included a black jellybean. She would say that while most people didn't like that flavor, it was her favorite.

She would have us raise our black jellybeans in the air and she would make a toast, "Let this jellybean remind us that we should open our heads and hearts to different things, and now we should open our mouths to this jellybean." We would all pop them in our mouths and say, "Amen."

The other part of our Easter tradition was the money hunt. She would get sixteen plastic eggs and put coins in each of them. She would hide them around the yard while we were supposedly not looking. When the time came, she would remind us that we were each entitled to find four eggs. You would have thought we were searching for gold with all of the laughing, pushing, and intensity as we raced to find our four eggs.

We took our eggs inside, opened each one with gleeful shouts when we saw a quarter and tiny moans when we saw a penny. We each had to do the math to determine who had the most money. She always made sure that we each had at least one dollar in total. Then the weekend after Easter, when all of the Easter items went on sale, she would take us to a dollar store and let us shop for our own gifts.

We had these Easter hunts every year as I was growing up. When I graduated from college, moved away, and had my daughter, my mother came through for me again. My daughter was three and I was working as a freelance writer. I was so busy that I didn't prepare any clues. The day before Easter, I went to the mailbox and inside was a small box that contained four plastic eggs and clues that my mother wrote based on the location of various things in my house.

Not a year has gone by since that I have not continued the tradition. I still have the clues, the money hunt, and the black jellybean. In addition, the year that my mother passed away, I also added a golden egg to the hunt and told my daughter that my mother was shining her love and light on her. That egg has been the most sought after prize my daughter ever asked for.

~Judith Fitzsimmons

Her Smile

I wondered if my smile was as big as hers.
Maybe as big. But not as beautiful.
~Benjamin Alire Sáenz

Glancing up
Into the car mirror
Or brushing my teeth,
Sometimes, I catch a glimpse of it.
Sometimes, the tears cascade down my cheeks,
Or they just well up in the windows
Of my soul.
But I wouldn't trade those moments
For a million dollars.
I love seeing her smile —
Our smile.
It's one of the simple things
That holds us
Together
While we're apart.
I miss her every day.
But her smile —
With all its warmth,
Compassion,
Tenderness
And dear silliness —

Comforts my soul.
I thank God
It's there when I'm
Glancing up
Into the car mirror
Or brushing my teeth.
It's beautiful...

~Christina Galeone

Meet Our Contributors

Kristi Adams is a travel writer for Europe's *Stars and Stripes*, and an adjunct professor for the University of Maryland School of Architecture. An Air Force veteran, Kristi lives in Germany with her husband and the world's neediest rescue cat. She's currently working on her debut young adult novel.

Valerie Testa Almquist is the author of *Look Back Move Forward*, an inspirational, historical fiction adventure. She has a Master of Arts in Education and Human Services, and plans to continue writing inspirational books. She is married with two sons and resides in New Jersey. She enjoys family time, music, and dance.

Amy Anderson is an author who enjoys reading and writing nearly any genre. When she's not immersed in a book, she loves spending time with her family, rock climbing, cooking, and looking for new stories.

Mary Anglin-Coulter works as a full-time freelance writer and graphic designer. She lives in Bardstown, KY, with her wife and three daughters, lovingly referring to their home as the Estrogen House. She obtained her bachelor's degree from Bellarmine University. This is her fifth story published in the *Chicken Soup for the Soul* series.

Allisa Bahney received her BA in English Language and Literature, with minors in Creative Writing and Film Studies, from the University of Northern Iowa in 2009. She lives with her wife in Iowa and teaches high school English. Allisa enjoys traveling, boating, writing, and working with kids and animals. She hopes to someday be a successful screenwriter.

Lainie Belcastro has many titles in the arts, but her most treasured title is mom to her daughter Nika. As trademarked storytellers, Mrs. Terra Cotta Pots & Twig, they plant dreams for children with their first book coming soon! She is thrilled to be a member of the Chicken Soup for the Soul inspiring family! Believe!

Rob Berry is a graduate of California State University, Bakersfield. He and his wife Amy have three sons. He enjoys cycling, hockey, and spending time with his family.

S.L. Blake was born and raised in Northern California and now lives wherever the Army sends her active duty husband. She loves giraffes, chocolate, and reading. She spends her time writing novels and raising her two biggest fans.

Emma Blandford has hopes of traveling to as many countries and states as possible, and learning from new cultures along the way. She currently spends most of her time outside of work caring for her adopted mix-breed puppy and trying as many new ways to cook vegan foods as possible.

Jan Bono's new cozy mystery series set on the southwest Washington coast is now available! She's also published five humorous personal experience collections, two poetry chapbooks, nine one-act plays, a dinner theater play, and has written for magazines ranging from *Guideposts* to *Woman's World*. Learn more at JanBonoBooks.com.

Jill Burns lives in the mountains of West Virginia with her wonderful family. She's a retired piano teacher and performer. She enjoys writing, music, gardening, nature, and spending time with her grandchildren.

Penny C. is an aspiring writer.

Elynne Chaplik-Aleskow is a Pushcart Prize-nominated author of *My Gift of Now*, which was named one of the 25 Most Inspirational Books of 2015 by *Conversations* magazine. Elynne is founding general manager of WYCC-TV/PBS and Distinguished Professor Emeritus of Wright College in Chicago. Her husband Richard is her muse.

Penelope Childers is a published author and enjoys life-changing true stories. She and her husband live in Fresno, CA. Penelope dedicates her story "Last Gift" to her inspirational mother, Lorene Penrod.

Christina Ryan Claypool is an Amy and Ohio APME award-winning journalist and speaker with a Master of Ministry degree from Mount Vernon Nazarene University. Her inspirational novel, *Secrets of the Pastor's Wife*, will be released soon. Learn more at christinaryanclaypool.com.

M. Scott Coffman lives in Central Illinois with his wife and two of his three kids, the oldest having married and moved on. By day, he works at an insurance agency. By night, he writes his blog, *Truth Mission*, and is the author of *Do You CARE?* (with James P. Rousey) and the upcoming epic sci-fi series, *The Servant Saga*.

Geneva Coleman is a freelance writer from Eastern Kentucky. She and her husband, Mike, have four adult sons and three grandchildren. She credits her inspiration to write to her parents, Joe and Opal France, and the confidence to write to her husband and most supportive fan, Mike.

Candice Marley Conner loves all fairy tales, and has to take turns with her six-year-old daughter and three-year-old son on who gets to be the evil villain. She lives at the bottom of Alabama where the antebellum lady dips her toes into the Gulf of Mexico.

Peyton Woodson Cooper writes Christian fiction, inspirational nonfiction and children's books. She offers simple stories, told well. She feels that we live in a Twitter and Facebook world and attention spans are short; that's why her novellas and short stories offer quick reads for the busy reader. Let her books inspire you.

Laure Covert is a long-time resident of Pennsylvania where she juggles freelance writing, interpreting Spanish, and teaching English as a Second Language. Her favorite job is being a mom to her three adult children and a grandmother to her granddaughter Lily. Books and birds are her two personal passions.

Prithwijit Das received his Bachelor of Arts from Cornell University, and Master of Science in Education from Hunter College of the City University of New York in 2016. A native New Yorker, Prithwijit has taught kindergarten in the Bronx and plans to continue working with children and families in the city he grew up in.

Michele Ivy Davis is a freelance writer and photographer. Her stories and articles have appeared in a variety of magazines, newspapers, and law enforcement publications, and her debut novel, *Evangeline Brown and the Cadillac Motel*, received national and international awards. Learn more at MicheleIvyDavis.com.

The youngest of six kids, **Ellicia Dawn** grew up in a small town that some would consider the end of the world. She began writing in high school, making it her preferred outlet for her thoughts and dreams. A book lover, she is now pursuing a career in writing novels.

Louis De Lauro has taught elementary school for twenty-five years. He is the Founder and Board President of the charity Juggling Life. He is a computer teacher, a chess coach, and a juggler. He adores his wife Krista and daughter Ava, who was adopted from China in 2005. Louis writes inspirational stories and poems daily.

Jonathan Doll, Ph.D. is an education leader who has worked internationally and at the state level. He's an advocate of social justice and equity and earned his Ph.D. from Texas A&M University in curriculum and instruction, with an emphasis in ESL. He writes a *Huffington Post* blog about education issues. E-mail him at jonathan.doll@gmail.com.

Patricia Dublin received her Bachelor of Nursing and Associate of Arts, with honors, from Austin Peay State University. She has four daughters and is married to her loving and supportive husband Sergeant Troy Dublin. She enjoys cruising and writing, and this is the first story she has ever submitted to be published.

Chava Dumas is a doula, writer, public speaker, and health crisis support counselor. She is a wife, mother, and grandma who believes a sense of humor is essential! She is the author of *Preparing for Pesach... B'simchah! 40 Lifesaving Lessons to Help You Make It to the Finish Line.* Learn more at chavaddoula.com.

Emily Dupree enjoys living in agriculture country and divides her time between gardening, traveling, preparing taxes at H&R Block, and reading. Her first short story for a class assignment won a creative writing competition and was subsequently published in 2007. She plans to write children's and young adult fiction.

Kim Edwards is an aspiring writer who enjoys helping people in her free time, watching *Ellen*, and playing with her cat Colton. She is a home health aide at Hospicare, finding new ways to give back by caring for others. Her struggles with depression and an eating disorder are what inspired her writing. She is now studying Psychology.

Barbara Farland is an accomplished writer, creative thinker, wife, and momó. She loves being able to wear all these hats at once through her short stories, blog posts, poetry, and books. As a communications expert by trade, she believes "stories make us, and stories make us known." Learn more at barbarafarland.com.

Leila Feliciano received her Bachelor of Arts and Master of Communications degrees from Western New England University in 2012 and 2016 respectively. She lives in Puerto Rico. Leila enjoys reading, yoga, music, movies, and writing poetry. She hopes to one day publish her own book of poetry.

Kate Fellowes credits her success as a writer to early encouragement from her mom. She writes mystery novels, romantic short stories, essays, and poetry. Kate loves animals and books, and the feel of a pen scratching over paper. She blogs about work and life at katefellowes. wordpress.com.

Judith Fitzsimmons is an author, yoga instructor, aromatherapist, and most importantly, a mom. She lives with her adopted cat Parker in Franklin, TN, near her beautiful daughter Chelsea.

Marianne Fosnow has been an avid reader and fan of the *Chicken Soup for the Soul* series for many years. She is proud to have stories included in *Chicken Soup for the Soul: The Spirit of America* and *Chicken Soup for the Soul: Curvy & Confident*. She lives in Fort Mill, SC.

Major Jody Fuller is a comedian, speaker, writer, and soldier with three tours of duty in Iraq. As a lifetime stutterer, he's an advocate for stuttering awareness. Jody has worked with some of the biggest names in comedy and has entertained troops in fourteen countries around the world. Jody lives in Alabama with his dog and cat.

Christina Galeone is a freelance journalist. She writes regularly for Beliefnet, *Community Advocate*, *Worcester Telegram & Gazette*, *The Yankee Xpress*, and *The Catholic Free Press*. She's grateful to be a part of the Chicken Soup for the Soul family and grateful to be able to honor her selfless, beautiful, loving mom, Barbara, in this way.

Kim Goodrich was inspired to write her story while she was mourning the loss of her beloved mom, Marlene. Kim has always had a passion for writing and found that writing about her experience was healing. She is grateful for her mom's unconditional love, which gave her the courage to write and submit her story.

Melissa Basinger Green received her Bachelor of Science in Secondary Science Education from the University of Georgia in 1995 and her Bachelor of Arts in Drama and Theatre from the University of Georgia in 2001. She currently resides in Georgia and works as a 911 dispatcher. She has two teenage sons.

Derek H. is the author of several novels and a collection of short stories. His books are widely read and are available on Amazon.com.

Barbara E. Haley, an educator and reading interventionist, lives in San Antonio, TX, and enjoys writing at IHOP and spending time with her grandchildren. She has published devotions on living with chronic pain and three juvenile chapter books. Learn more at barbarahaleybooks.com.

A freelance writer and editor, **Sarah Hamaker** has written *Ending Sibling Rivalry* and *Hired @ Home*. Her stories have appeared in previous *Chicken Soup for the Soul* books, and she's a frequent blogger for *The Washington Post's* "On Parenting." Sarah lives in Virginia with her husband and four children.

Carol Elaine Harrison writes to her mother and father, Joe and Opal France, and her grandmother, Ethel Lee. She credits the confidence to write to her most supportive fan, her husband, Mike.

Hilary Hattenbach, a writer and marketing strategist living in Los Angeles, is the co-author of *The Kitchen Decoded Cookbook* (Skyhorse 2104.) An aspiring tap dancer and joyologist, her work has been published in *Entropy* and *The Eastsider*. She's working on a collection of personal essays for publication.

Christy Heitger-Ewing, an award-winning writer and columnist who writes human interest stories for national, regional, and local magazines, has contributed to a dozen anthologies and is the author of *Cabin Glory: Amusing Tales of Time Spent at the Family Retreat* (cabinglory.com). She lives in Indiana with her husband and two sons.

Kelly Hennigan loves being able to share her writing with others. She thanks her mom, Nancy Sanderson, for believing in her writing. Nancy always patiently listened when Kelly shared her latest prose. She treasures her mother and asks all who read this to please pray for her mom's healing from lung cancer and Crohn's disease.

Julie Hornok's stories have appeared in several publications and websites, and this is her fifth appearance in the *Chicken Soup for the Soul* series. When she is not busy driving her three kids all around town, she loves to teach yoga and support families living with autism. Learn more at juliehornok.com.

Allison Howell has been published twice before in the *Chicken Soup for the Soul* series and writes a bi-monthly column for her local newspaper, *The Frontiersman*. She enjoys reading, community theater, and outdoor fun in Alaska with her husband and children.

Sharilynn Hunt is a retired medical social worker and founder of New Creation Realities Ministry, a teaching and prayer ministry. She authored *Prevailing Prayer*, a training manual for prayer groups. She writes devotionals and her new 31-day devotional book, *Grace Overcomes Today*, will be released this year.

Karla James is a devoted wife and mother of two beautiful boys. She is an elementary educator with fifteen years of experience. Karla enjoys spending time with her family, traveling, and writing.

Deborah Kellogg has a BA and MA in German, and is finishing another MA in English. She is a tenured professor in German at Normandale

Community College in Bloomington, MN. She has three children and two grandchildren. She loves traveling, writing, biking, and anything having to do with the German.

Anna Sofia Kendall is the author of *College PaperBuddy*, a guide for writing academic papers. She has also previously been published in the *Chicken Soup for the Soul* series and various journal articles. She isn't a mom in the traditional sense, but is "turtle mom" to the world's coolest box turtle, Monèt. E-mail her at anna@collegepaperbuddy.com.

Sylvia J. King is a sixty-nine-year-old author enjoying retirement. Writing has been a lifelong love. She keeps herself busy by being the learning coach for five online, home-schooled children through the K12 program.

Miranda Koerner received her bachelor's degree in journalism from Baylor University in 2006 and has been working as a writer and a journalist ever since. She will graduate with her master's in education and creative writing in May 2017. She lives with her daughter, Adrielle, her husband, Ben, and two Chihuahuas, Bitty and Bear.

Pauline Koh-Banerjee is a former tenure-track professor turned full-time mom and freelance writer living in California. When not shuttling her kids around town, Pauline can be found volunteering in the classroom, working out in the weight room, or coaching youth soccer.

Crescent LoMonaco used her knowledge from years working behind the chair and owning a hair salon to write the "Ask a Stylist" column for the *Santa Barbara Independent*. She is a frequent contributor to the *Chicken Soup for the Soul* series. She lives on the California coast with her husband and son.

Originally from upstate New York, **Linda Lou** is a humor writer and stand-up comic who has made Las Vegas her home since 2003. Her

Amazon bestselling memoir, *Bastard Husband: A Love Story*, is a hilarious account of her experience starting over in Sin City after a mid-life divorce.

Nancy Maggio is a native of California, where she received her teaching credential in music. Now retired, she lives in Leisure World Seal Beach and still enjoys singing with two different groups. She is also active in creative writing and theater groups. Nancy writes nonfiction stories from life changing experiences.

Tina Wagner Mattern is a Portland, OR writer/hairstylist/wife/mother. She has been blessed with not one, but two, awesome mothers, the one who gave birth to her and the one who adopted her at the age of seven. This will be her eleventh story published in the *Chicken Soup for the Soul* series. E-mail her at tinamattern@earthlink.net.

Gena McCown is a women's ministry coach, public speaker, and writer from South Florida. Married for over eighteen years to her husband Justin, they have been blessed with three daughters. Gena has a heart for serving women, and sharing messages of hope, love, and forgiveness.

Sarah McCrobie has contributed to multiple *Chicken Soup for the Soul* books. A native of Oswego, NY, Sarah enjoys photography, writing and making memories with her family in the small port city she calls home. She holds a bachelor's degree in journalism from SUNY Oswego and does public relations work in an academic setting.

Judy Mickelson enjoys visiting shut-ins and being a hospice volunteer. She reads voraciously, travels widely, plays bridge, and has been a "Foreign Friendship Family" for twenty years. She would like to thank Jan Bathke, who is Irma's daughter and Judy's friend, along with her friend, Barb Frailing, for their help in writing the story.

Katelyn Mills is currently pursuing her bachelor's degree in psychology and her master's degree in elementary/special education. She has a passion for teaching, writing, traveling, and fitness.

Monica Morris writes from her century-old farmhouse where she lives with her husband, Joe, one dog and three cats. She is a regular contributor to *Guideposts* and is at work on her second book, a historical novel set during the Civil War.

Skip Myers is a leading security industry expert and speaker specializing in fraud prevention and risk analysis. He resides in Atlanta, GA with his wife and family.

Trudie Nash, a retired educator, has worked for over forty years with the Greenville County School District. She received her Bachelor of Arts degree from Winston-Salem State University and her Master's of Education from Columbia College. She is the grandmother of three of the world's most adorable children.

Julie Osborne is a former editor, feature writer, and columnist for Current Publishing in Carmel, IN. She recently launched into the freelance world with her blog *Tales of Oz* at julieosborne.com. Her best friend is a rescue dog whose name happened to be Toto when they met. E-mail her at info@julieosborne.com.

Gordon Osmond is a graduate of Columbia College and Columbia Law School. He is the author of eight produced stage plays, three published novels, and three published nonfiction books about English, his life, and sports. He loves dogs, cats, and select humans. E-mail him at fertile1@aol.com.

Eleanor OToole was born and raised in northwest Connecticut along with eleven siblings. Her writing is inspired by people and life events. Eleanor works in a private school and loves reading, baseball, and the beach. She shares her home with the love of her life, Joe, and a sixteen-year-old cat named Mandy.

Nancy Emmick Panko is a retired pediatric nurse who began writing her real life experiences at the urging of a friend. She is a seven-time contributor to the *Chicken Soup for the Soul* series and is the author of the inspirational novel, *Guiding Missal*. Nancy and her husband live in North Carolina near their two children and four grandchildren.

Jamie D. Parker wrote her story after the passing of her mother. She misses her greatly.

Galen Pearl lives in the Pacific Northwest, close to her five kids and two grandchildren. She is the author of the book *10 Steps to Finding Your Happy Place (and Staying There)*, and of the blog *No Way Cafe*, found at galenpearl.blogspot.com. E-mail her at galenpearl@gmail.com.

Tina Plantamura is a writer at heart and a seamstress by trade. She lives on the New Jersey Shore with her husband, three sons, and two black cats. Tina hopes to publish her first novel soon.

Sandra Plawski retired in 2015 after forty-five years of traveling and being self-employed in the jewelry and exotic water plant business. She and her husband live on a farm in rural Colorado. She enjoys nature, her cat Jet, and stargazing at night, when she gets ideas for her writing to inspire people of all ages.

Connie Kaseweter Pullen lives in rural Sandy, OR, near her five children and several grandchildren. She earned her Bachelor of Arts degree at the University of Portland in 2006, with a double major in Psychology and Sociology. Connie enjoys writing, photography, and exploring nature. E-mail her at MyGrandmaPullen@aol.com.

Georgia Putney received her Bachelor of Arts in English from the University of Virginia in 2013. She currently resides in her hometown in Virginia where she works at an advertising agency. When she's not working, Georgia enjoys reading and writing, playing tennis, and being with friends and family.

Leah Reynolds received her Master of Science degree in 2009 from the University of Maryland. She is married with two boys and is an author of psychological thrillers and nonfiction novels. Leah enjoys writing, traveling, reading books of all genres and spending time with her family.

Terri Rilea simply enjoys writing. Writing is one way to share our life's experiences and to keep those memories alive. It has been a lifelong dream of hers to become published. That dream came true when the *Chicken Soup for the Soul* series decided to publish this story. She is beyond delighted!

Kimberly Ripley is a freelance writer and published author from New Hampshire. She is a married mom of five grown children and a couple of extras. Her favorite role is that of Nana to Lilly and Aiden.

Rose Robson is a Coast Guard veteran turned stay-at-home mother of two wonderful daughters, Sarah and Lily. She is married to the love of her life James, and they chose to make their home in Rose's hometown of Newnan, GA. Rose recently completed her BA in Criminology in 2016 and is currently enjoying life with her family.

Thom Schwarz, RN, is approaching the decade mark of his hospice and palliative care nursing work and forty years as a registered nurse. He thinks it's time to retire and write his historical novel, *The Keeper and His Wives*, set in New England in 1887-88.

M.J. Shea is a freelance writer in Clinton, CT. She and her husband enjoy kayaking, antiquing, biking, and frequent walks to the shore. M.J. recently left a lengthy career with the judicial branch of the State of Connecticut to pursue her dream of writing and illustrating children's books.

Drew Sheldon was raised by a single mother in a time and place where that was highly unusual. That led him to follow an uncommon path through life and he's now aspiring to be the kind of writer his mother would like. He lives in the Pacific Northwest with his girlfriend and their blended family of fur-babies.

Alison Shelton received her Bachelor of Arts in English, a Master's degree and taught high school English for thirty years. Now retired, she enjoys her family, two dogs and a variety of craft projects. She writes for an association magazine and, occasionally, for other periodicals.

Katelyn Stanis grew up in Michigan and has been writing since she was in second grade. She currently resides in Jersey City and enjoys running, barre dance classes, and cooking. Katelyn writes inspirational stories for young women. For partnership inquiries, contact Katelyn at katelyn.stanis@gmail.com.

Noelle Sterne received her Ph.D. from Columbia University and has published over 400 essays, writing craft and spiritual articles, and fiction. Her book, *Challenges in Writing Your Dissertation*, evolved from her coaching practice with struggling graduate students. Her book, *Trust Your Life*, helps readers release regrets and reach lifelong yearnings.

Dawn Storey is a wife, mother, and a systems specialist. A spiritual seeker, she dreams of writing books that inspire readers. Her first book, *Discussions with My Best Self: Journaling to the Soul Within*, is a result of her passion for metaphysics and her love of journaling. Learn more at DawnJStorey.blogspot.com.

Sheila Taylor-Clark received her BBA, with highest honors, from Jackson State University in 1993. She is a CPA who enjoys traveling, fine dining, and blogging. Sheila is married to Nate and is a mom to McKenzie. A two-time breast cancer survivor, she plans to write her first novel soon. E-mail her at shaycpa@msn.com.

Shannon Thompson is a middle school student who is active in her community. She loves drama, choir and all things music. Shannon plans to pursue a career in musical theater and performing arts, attending a prestigious musical college like Juilliard or American Academy of Dramatic Arts.

Tanya J. Tyler is a freelance writer and editor living in Lexington, KY. She is also an ordained minister in the Christian church, Disciples of Christ, and has served churches in Kentucky and Illinois.

Patricia Voyce writes from her home in Pleasant Hill, IA.

Bev Walters is retired and lives in Kansas with her husband and children. She is from a large family and writes about growing up and hopes to write her life story within the next three years. Writing has been her lifelong passion.

Marcia Wells taught middle and high school students for twenty years. After encouraging her students to reach for their dreams, she decided to retire early to pursue her own. She has written two young adult fantasy novels. She and her husband live in Eastern Washington. Marcia enjoys family, skiing, and snorkeling.

Stacie D. Williams received her BA in English and Writing in 2012, and her MA degree in English in 2016. She enjoys spending time in the country, reading, cross-stitch, working on crafts, and writing. Stacie currently resides in Southern Oregon with her mother. She plans to write full-time in the future.

Margie Williamson has degrees from the University of Georgia and the New Orleans Baptist Theological Seminary. She works as a writer and editor and writer of Life Bible Study Curriculum. She loves to travel, spend time with her family and friends, and bury herself in a good book. Her greatest joy is being a mom and grandmom.

Marjorie Woodall is the mother of two, stepmother of two, and grandmother of one darling baby. And even though she still tends to think she always knows best, she reluctantly admits that she continues to learn from her own mother even today.

Dallas Woodburn is a writer, editor, teacher, and literacy advocate living in the San Francisco Bay Area. To date, she has been a proud contributor to more than two-dozen titles in the *Chicken Soup for the Soul* series. She regularly blogs about simple, joyful, healthy living at DaybyDayMasterpiece.com.

Rebecca Yauger is the web manager for American Christian Fiction Writers. She worked in radio and TV before starting her writing career. She scribbles away on various projects and blogs at TalkingAmongFriends.com. She and her husband live near Dallas and have two grown children and one grandchild.

Hannah Yoder lives on a small farm in southern Ohio. She particularly enjoys training horses, especially ex-racehorses. She appreciates fine literature and would love to join the ranks of classic authors.

Amelia Zahm lives in rural northeastern Oregon and spends her time in the mountains, valleys, and canyons of Wallowa County, either on foot or on horseback. Her work has been published at The Manifest-Station, *Oregon East*, and Jenny. She holds an MFA in Creative Nonfiction from Eastern Oregon University.

Sheri Zeck enjoys writing creative nonfiction stories that encourage, inspire, and entertain others. She lives in Illinois with her husband and three daughters. Sheri's stories have appeared in *Guideposts*, *Angels on Earth*, *Farm and Ranch Living* and numerous *Chicken Soup for the Soul* books. Learn more at sherizeck.com.

BEST MOM EVER!

Meet Amy Newmark

~⌒⊃⊂⌒~

Thank You

~⌒⊃⊂⌒~

About Chicken Soup
for the Soul

Meet Amy Newmark

Amy Newmark is the bestselling author, editor-in-chief, and publisher of the *Chicken Soup for the Soul* book series. Since 2008, she has published 136 new books, most of them national bestsellers in the U.S. and Canada, more than doubling the number of Chicken Soup for the Soul titles in print today. She is also the author of *Simply Happy*, a crash course in Chicken Soup for the Soul advice and wisdom that is filled with easy-to-implement, practical tips for having a better life.

Amy is credited with revitalizing the Chicken Soup for the Soul brand, which has been a publishing industry phenomenon since the first book came out in 1993. By compiling inspirational and aspirational true stories curated from ordinary people who have had extraordinary experiences, Amy has kept the twenty-three-year-old Chicken Soup for the Soul brand fresh and relevant.

Amy graduated *magna cum laude* from Harvard University where she majored in Portuguese and minored in French. She then embarked on a three-decade career as a Wall Street analyst, a hedge fund manager, and a corporate executive in the technology field. She is a Chartered Financial Analyst.

Her return to literary pursuits was inevitable, as her honors thesis in college involved traveling throughout Brazil's impoverished northeast region, collecting stories from regular people. She is delighted to have come full circle in her writing career — from collecting stories "from the people" in Brazil as a twenty-year-old to, three decades later, collecting stories "from the people" for Chicken Soup for the Soul.

When Amy and her husband Bill, the CEO of Chicken Soup for the Soul, are not working, they are visiting their four grown children.

Follow Amy on Twitter @amynewmark. Listen to her free daily podcast, The Chicken Soup for the Soul Podcast, at www.chickensoup. podbean.com, or find it on iTunes, the Podcasts app on iPhone, or on your favorite podcast app on other devices.

Thank You

We are grateful to all our story contributors and fans, who shared thousands of stories about their mothers, grandmothers, stepmothers, mothers-in-law, and honorary mothers. Ronelle Frankel, Mary Fisher, Barbara LoMonaco, Kristiana Pastir, and D'ette Corona read all the stories that were submitted and narrowed down the list to a few hundred finalists. There were so many fabulous stories that it was impossible for editor-in-chief Amy Newmark to pare down the list to only 101 stories. She actually chose a couple of hundred stories and put together our Mother's Day book for 2018 at the same time as this one!

Associate Publisher D'ette Corona continued to be Amy's right-hand woman in creating the final manuscript and working with all our wonderful writers. Barbara LoMonaco and Kristiana Pastir, along with outside proofreader Elaine Kimbler, jumped in at the end to proof, proof, proof. And yes, there will always be typos anyway, so feel free to let us know about them at webmaster@chickensoupforthesoul.com and we will correct them in future printings.

The whole publishing team deserves a hand, including Senior Director of Marketing Maureen Peltier, Senior Director of Production Victor Cataldo, and graphic designer Daniel Zaccari, who turned our manuscript into this beautiful book.

Sharing Happiness, Inspiration, and Hope

Real people sharing real stories, every day, all over the world. In 2007, *USA Today* named *Chicken Soup for the Soul* one of the five most memorable books in the last quarter-century. With over 100 million books sold to date in the U.S. and Canada alone, more than 200 titles in print, and translations into more than forty languages, "chicken soup for the soul" is one of the world's best-known phrases.

Today, twenty-four years after we first began sharing happiness, inspiration and hope through our books, we continue to delight our readers with new titles, but have also evolved beyond the bookstore with super premium pet food, television shows, podcasts, positive journalism from aplus.com, and licensed products, all revolving around true stories, as we continue "changing the world one story at a time®." Thanks for reading!

Share with Us

We all have had Chicken Soup for the Soul moments in our lives. If you would like to share your story or poem with millions of people around the world, go to chickensoup.com and click on "Submit Your Story." You may be able to help another reader and become a published author at the same time. Some of our past contributors have launched writing and speaking careers from the publication of their stories in our books!

We only accept story submissions via our website. They are no longer accepted via mail or fax.

To contact us regarding other matters, please send us an e-mail through webmaster@chickensoupforthesoul.com, or fax or write us at:

Chicken Soup for the Soul
P.O. Box 700
Cos Cob, CT 06807-0700
Fax: 203-861-7194

One more note from your friends at Chicken Soup for the Soul: Occasionally, we receive an unsolicited book manuscript from one of our readers, and we would like to respectfully inform you that we do not accept unsolicited manuscripts and we must discard the ones that appear.

Chicken Soup for the **Soul**.

Thanks to My Mom

101 Stories of Gratitude, Love, and Lessons

Amy Newmark and Jo Dee Messina

A mother's job is never done, but in *Chicken Soup for the Soul: Thanks to My Mom*, she gets the praise she deserves! Children of all ages share their words of thanks in these 101 stories of love, learning, and gratitude to the woman they couldn't have done without!

978-1-61159-945-9

With heartwarming stories by mothers and their children of gratefulness, love, inspiration and even amusement, this book does what we so often fail to do — say "I Love You, Mom!"

978-1-61159-962-6

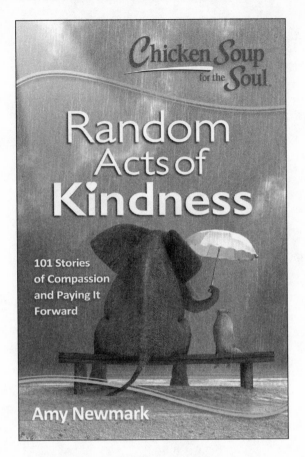

Chicken Soup for the Soul

Random Acts of Kindness

101 Stories of Compassion and Paying It Forward

Amy Newmark

This book shines a bright light on the widespread goodwill in our world as everyday heroes demonstrate acts of kindness, compassion and commitment to others. These stories will uplift you, inspire you, and brighten your day.

978-1-61159-961-9

More happiness and

A fast-paced and funny deep dive into simple ways to create a happy, confident, and positive life. Amy Newmark distills advice and wisdom from her life and more than 20,000 Chicken Soup for the Soul stories into this crash course in how to be happy.

978-1-61159-949-7

great advice for you

Changing lives one story at a time®
www.chickensoup.com